A POPULAR DICTIONARY OF

Judaism

A POPULAR DICTIONARY OF

Judaism

Lavinia and Dan Cohn-Sherbok

NTC Publishing Group
NTC/Contemporary Publishing Company

Library of Congress Cataloging-in-Publication Data

Cohn-Sherbok, Lavinia.
    A popular dictionary of Judaism / Lavinia and Dan
Cohn-Sherbok.
        p.   cm.
    Previously published: Richmond, Surrey : Curzon Press, 1995.
    ISBN 0-8442-0423-4 (paper)
    1. Judaism—Dictionaries.   I. Cohn-Sherbok, Dan.   II. Title.
BM50.C53   1997
296'.03—dc21
                                                            97-21950
                                                                CIP
                                                                r97

Cover design by Kim Bartko
Cover photograph by Sharon Hoogstraten

This edition first published in 1997 by NTC Publishing Group
An imprint of NTC/Contemporary Publishing Company
4255 West Touhy Avenue, Lincolnwood (Chicago), Illinois 60646-1975 U.S.A.
Manufactured in the United States of America
International Standard Book Number: 0-8442-0423-4

15   14   13   12   11   10   9   8   7   6   5   4   3   2   1

For Rabbi Brian Fox A.M.

JUDAISM – AN HISTORICAL INTRODUCTION

The history of the Jewish people began in the fertile lowlands alongside the Tigris and Euphrates rivers. It was here in Mesopotamia that successive empires of the ancient world flourished and decayed before the Jews emerged as a separate people. The culture of these civilizations had a profound impact on the Hebrew religion: ancient Near Eastern myths and traditions were filtered and refashioned to serve the needs of the faith of the Jewish nation. The Hebrew Scriptures are thus an amalgam of elements from neighbouring peoples, and modern archaeology provides a vast array of literary documents preserved on stone and clay tablets which shed light on this development. These sources give an account of the rise and fall of states and empires and the spread of religious ideas, and although only referring to Israel indirectly they help to clarify the intellectual and religious milieu in which the Bible was formed.

Scholars generally consider that the Jews emerged as a separate people between the nineteenth and sixteenth centuries BCE. Some writers maintain that the patriarchs (Abraham, Isaac and Jacob) were real persons – chiefs or founders of tribal units; others argue that the names of the patriarchs refer not to individuals but to families, clans or tribes. In either case, these ancestors of the Jewish nation appear to have been part of a wave of north-western Semitic-speaking peoples who moved into Canaan in the second millennium BCE. They and their descendants were semi-nomadic groups with small bands of sheep and goats coming from the desert in search of pasture and intermingling with the local inhabitants. It has been suggested that these immigrants and sojourners were part of a larger social stratum living on the fringes of settled society referred to in Near Eastern sources as *Habiru* – a term which resembles the Biblical word 'Hebrew'. The patriarchal clans may have been part of this *Habiru* element in ancient Canaan.

The Israelites believed they had at some stage endured slavery in Egypt and had conquered Canaan, the Promised Land. After a long period of tribal unity, the nation divided into two kingdoms. This separation was a reflection of an ideological division which had existed for much longer. The northern tribes led by Ephraim and the southern tribes led by Judah had only been united by their allegiance to David. But when Solomon and his son Rehoboam violated many of the ancient traditions, the northern tribes revolted. The reason they gave for this rebellion was the injustice of the kings, but in fact they sought to recapture the simpler ways of earlier generations. Then there had been no monarch, and leadership was exercised on the basis of charisma. What the north looked for was allegiance and loyalty to the King of Kings who they believed had brought them from Egyptian bondage into the Promised Land in the early days of their history. It was against this background that the pre-exilic prophets endeavoured to bring the nation back to the true worship of God. Righteousness, they declared, is the standard by which all people are to be judged.

Prophecy was not a phenomenon unique to the Israelites. There are records of prophets of other Near Eastern religions such as that of the Phoenician Baal. Like them, the official Israelite cult employed prophets, or prophetic bands known as sons of the prophets, to predict the outcome of battles and to serve near the shrines. Scholars have not determined the exact relationship between these official prophets and the solitary prophets whose words are recorded in the Scriptures. It used to be thought that the Biblical prophets were separate from and indeed stood against the cult prophets. Now it is recognized that there was probably a closer connection between the two groups. In any case, throughout the pre-exilic period the Biblical prophets provided a commentary on the historical events of their day, and continually reminded the kings that they were only rulers under God.

During the first millennium BCE the Jews watched their country emerge as a powerful state only to see it sink into spiritual and moral decay. The ten northern Tribes disappeared from history when they were conquered by the Assyrians in 721BCE. Then in 586, the Southern Kingdom was conquered by the Babylonians. Initially the Jews despaired of their fate – the Temple lay in ruins and Jerusalem was demolished. This must be God's punishment for their iniquity which the prophets had predicted. Yet despite defeat and exile, the nation rose anew phoenix-like from the ashes of the old kingdoms. In the years of exile which followed, the Jewish people continued their religious traditions and communal life. Though they had lost their independence, their devotion to God and His law sustained them through suffering and hardship and inspired them to new heights of creativity. In Babylonia they flourished, keeping their religion alive in the synagogues. These institutions were founded so that Jews could meet together for worship and study; no sacrifices were offered since that was the prerogative of the Jerusalem Temple. When in 538BCE King Cyrus of Persia permitted the Jews to return to their former home, the nation underwent a transformation. The temple in Jerusalem was rebuilt and religious reforms were enacted. This return to the land of their fathers led to national restoration and a renaissance of Jewish life which was to last until the first century CE.

The period following Herod's death in 4BCE was a time of intense anti-Roman feeling among the Jewish population in Judaea as well as in the diaspora. Eventually such hostility led to war only to be followed by defeat and the destruction, once again, of the Jerusalem Temple. In 70CE, thousands of Jews were deported. Such devastation, however, did not quell the Jewish hope of ridding the Holy Land of its oppressors. In the second century a messianic rebellion led by Simon Bar Kokhba was crushed by Roman forces, who killed multitudes of Jews and decimated Judaea. Yet despite this defeat, the Scribes and Pharisees carried on the Jewish tradition through teaching and study. Initially, the rabbinic academy at Javneh (Jamnia) near Jerusalem was the focus of Jewish learning. In time this centre of rabbinic scholarship was replaced by the great Babylonian academies of Sura and Pumpedita. In these schools sages and scholars expounded the Oral Law, and there in the fifth century CE they codified the *Babylonian Talmud* which was to become with the Hebrew Bible the central religious text of Jewish life for all time.

According to Pharisaic tradition both the written Torah and its interpretation (oral Torah) were given by God to Moses on Mt. Sinai. This belief implies that God is the direct source of all laws recorded in the Pentateuch and is also indirectly responsible for the authoritative legal judgements of the rabbis, and serves as the justification for the rabbinic exposition of Scriptural ordinances. Alongside this exegesis of the Jewish law, scholars also produced interpretations of Scripture in which new meanings of the text were expounded in rabbinic commentaries and in the *Talmud*. Within the texts is found a wealth of theological speculation about such topics as the nature of God, divine justice, the coming of the Messiah and the hereafter. In addition, ethical considerations were of considerable importance in the discussions of these teachers of the faith. Also in these sources and in short treatises the rabbis recounted their mystical reflections about God and His creation. Early rabbinic Judaism thus covered a wide variety of areas all embraced by the holy word revealed on Mt. Sinai, and this literature served as the foundation of later Judaism as it developed through the centuries.

By the sixth century the Jews had become largely a diaspora people. Despite the loss of a homeland, they were unified by a common heritage: law, liturgy and shared traditions bound together the scattered communities stretching from Spain to Persia and Poland to Africa. Though subcultures did form during the Middle Ages which could have divided the Jewish world, Jews remained united in their hope for messianic redemption, the restoration of the Holy Land, and an ingathering of the exiles. Living amongst Christians and Muslims, the Jews were reduced to a minority group and their marginal status resulted in repeated persecution. Though there were times of toleration and creative anxiety, the threats of exile and death were always present in the Jewish consciousness during this period.

During the early Middle Ages philosophical speculation became a central preoccupation of Jewish thinkers. The beginnings of this philosophical development took place in ninth-century Babylonia during the height of the Abbasid caliphate when rabbinic Judaism was challenged by Karaite scholars who criticized the anthropomorphic views of God in Talmudic sources. Added to this internal threat was the Islamic contention that Muhammad's revelation in the *Koran* superseded the Jewish faith. In addition Zoroastrians and Manichaeans attacked monotheism as a viable religious system. Finally some gentile philosophers argued that the Greek scientific and philosophical world view could account for the origin of the cosmos without reference to an external Deity. In combating these challenges, Jewish writers were influenced by the teachings of Muslim schools of the eighth to the eleventh centuries. These Islamic scholars maintained that rational argument was vital in matters of religious belief and that Greek philosophy could serve as the handmaiden of religious faith. In their attempt to defend Judaism from internal and external assault, rabbinic authorities frequently adopted this point of view as an important line of defence and as time passed also employed other aspects of Graeco-Arabic thought in their expositions of the Jewish faith.

Contemporaneous with the development of Jewish philosophy and theology, Jewish thinkers during the Middle Ages elaborated a complex system of mystical thought. Drawing on the traditions of early rabbinic Judaism, these thinkers expanded and elaborated many of the mystical doctrines found in the Commentaries and in Talmudic literature as well as in mystical tracts such as the *Sefer Yetsirah*. In their writings these mystics saw themselves as the transmitters of a secret tradition which describes a supernatural world to which all human beings are linked. One strand of this heritage focused on the nature of the spiritual world and its relationship with the terrestrial plane; the other more practical side attempted to utilize energies from the spiritual world to bring about miracle-working effects. According to these mystics, all of creation is in a struggle for redemption and liberation from evil, and their goal was to restore world harmony so that universal salvation would be attained through the coming of the Messiah and the establishment of the Kingdom of God.

In the centuries following the medieval period, the majority of Jews lived in Eastern Europe and in the lands of the Ottoman empire. Throughout this period most Jewish centres continued as autonomous communities regulated by traditional law. In the sphere of law, the development of legal codes standardized religious observance and mystical study enriched Jewish theological speculation. Yet despite these developments the Jewish population endured pogroms and massacres. Such suffering engendered messianic longing which culminated in the appearance of a messianic pretender, Shabbatai Zevi, who eventually converted to Islam to the dismay of most of his followers. This early modern period of Jewish life bridged the gap between the world of medieval Jewry and the later modern age when traditional Judaism underwent a major transformation in the light of emancipation, secularism and scientific advance.

By the middle of the eighteenth century, the Jewish community had suffered numerous waves of persecution and was deeply dispirited by the conversion of Shabbatai Zevi. In this environment the Hasidic movement – grounded in joyful mysticism – sought to revitalize Jewish life. Though Hasidism appealed to a large number of Jews, the spirit of humanism transformed Jewish existence. The French Revolution followed by the Napoleonic period radically changed the status of the Jewish masses, enabling them to enter into European life and culture. The spirit of emancipation unleashed by these events swept across Europe and freed Jews from their traditional lifestyle. These changes affected the structure of community organisation and raised important questions about the nature of Jewish life and existence in modern society.

At the end of the eighteenth century, the Enlightenment had brought about major changes in Jewish life. No longer were Jews insulated from non-Jewish currents of culture and thought, and this transformation of Jewish existence led many Jews to seek a modernization of Jewish worship. The earliest reformers engaged in liturgical revision but quickly the spirit of reform spread to other areas of Jewish life; eventually modernists convened a succession of rabbinical conferences in order to formulate a common policy. Such a radical approach to the Jewish tradition provoked a hostile response from a number of leading Orthodox rabbis, a reaction which stimulated the creation of the neo-Orthodox movement. Such opposition however did not stem the tide – the development of the Scientific Study of Judaism and the positive historical school inspired many reformers who were sympathetic to modern culture and learning.

By the second half of the nineteenth century Jewish existence had been transformed by the forces of emancipation. Some reformers believed that in such enlightened conditions anti-Jewish sentiment would disappear. Yet in the last decades of the century hostility towards the Jewish community intensified, resulting in the emergence of Jewish longing for a homeland. The foundation of the Zionist movement gave voice to such nationalistic aspirations and paved the way for the creation of the state of Israel in the next century. For many Jews America was also seen as a refuge from persecution, and at the end of the nineteenth century there was a mass migration of European Jews to the New World which brought about a resurgence of Jewish life and thought.

Despite this resurgence of nationalism, the Jewish people were faced with the emergence of violent anti-Semitism in the form of the Nazi Party. After the conquest of Poland in 1939, the Nazis occupied Denmark and Norway, the Netherlands, Belgium and France. In the spring of 1941, Hitler strengthened the Italian forces and extended their control over the Balkans and North Africa. In June of the same year Germany launched an attack on Russia, and by the end of the year most of the Ukraine had been captured. In December 1941 Germany and Italy declared war against the United States, and in the following year the invasion of Russia was recommenced. Throughout the war Hitler attempted to realize his plan of completely eliminating the Jews. When Hitler was defeated in 1945 probably six million Jews had been murdered.

After 2000 years of exile, the creation of a Jewish homeland in 1948 has provided renewed hope for the Jewish people in a post-Holocaust world. Since the Holocaust, the world's major Jewish communities are in Israel, the United States and the British Commonwealth. Within the communities, the Orthodox, the Reform and the completely secular maintain an uneasy relationship. Working to support the State of Israel and to combat Anti-Semitism has provided foci for communal activity. Nonetheless the temptations of assimilation and the material comforts of the twentieth century world have proved too seductive for many. If Judaism is to continue into the twenty-first century, this fragmentation and secularization must be confronted and reversed. What is at stake is no less than the survival of the Jewish heritage.

Dating Throughout this book the abbreviations BC (before Christ) and AD (Anno Domini, In the year of Our Lord) have been replaced with the more widely accepted BCE (Before Common Era) and CE (Common Era).

Asterisks (*) These are used in entries to refer to other relevant terms which the reader might find it useful to consult.

AARON   (C. 13th Century BCE) Brother of *Moses. After contributing to the liberation of the *Israelites from Egypt, he became *priest of the *sanctuary. All Israelite priests were said to be descended from him and he was remembered as a lover of peace among the people. Rabbi *Hillel advised his disciples to be followers of Aaron, 'loving and pursuing peace, loving your neighbours and drawing them to *Torah'. (See *Exodus 1–10, 28–29, 32, *AARONIDES).

AARONIDES   Hereditary *priests, descended from *Aaron the brother of *Moses. The descendants of Aaron 'shall attend to your *priesthood for all that concerns the *altar and that which is in the veil'. (*Numbers 18: 7). A distinction is made in the Scriptures between the Aaronides and the *Levites even though it is sometimes implied that all the Levites are priests. Some scholars believe that the Aaronides were Egyptian in origin because many Egyptian names can be found among their records. (See *KOHEN, *LEVITE, *PRIEST).

ABADDON   A place of destruction. Abaddon is mentioned in the *Wisdom books of the *Bible and in the *Talmud. It is an alternative name for *Gehenna.

ABLUTION   Ritual washing. Ablution is practised to restore a state of ritual *purity. It can involve total immersion either in the sea or in a ritual bath and this is undergone by *proselytes to *Judaism and by married *women seven days after their menstrual periods. The *priests of the *Temple in *Jerusalem also used to immerse themselves before taking part in the ritual. Today hands are ritually washed on various occasions, particularly before and after meals. A summary of the laws of ablution can be found in Joseph *Caro's *Shulhan Aruk. (See *MIKVEH, *NIDDAH, *PROSELYTE, *PURITY).

ABORTION   The termination of a pregnancy. Jewish law permits abortion if the life of the mother is threatened by the continuance of the pregnancy. Some authorities accept abortion for social as well as health reasons and it is generally agreed that an earlier abortion is more acceptable than a late one. The *Sages taught that the foetus attains full human status only when it has emerged from the womb.

ABRAHAM   Father of the Jewish people. The Book of *Genesis describes how Abraham was promised that he would be the *patriarch

1

of a great nation and his descendants would be as numerous as the stars of the heaven and the sand on the sea-shore. As a result of the *covenant with *God, the practice of *circumcision was introduced. Abraham had two sons, Ishmael who became the ancestor of the Arabs and *Isaac, from whom the *Jews are descended (See *Genesis* 12–22). In the *aggadah, Abraham is perceived as an ideal figure. He is the first *proselyte to *Judaism, a man who perfectly kept the *Oral Law even before it was given and a *prophet of God who received every *blessing.

ABRAHAM, APOCALYPSE OF   A *pseudepigraphic book. Possibly influenced by *IV *Ezra*, it dates from the 2nd Century CE and tells how *Abraham visits the seven heavens. During the course of the narrative, there is an attempted calculation of the date of the end of the world. (See *APOCALYPSE, *PSEUDEPIGRAPHA*).

ABRAHAM, TESTAMENT OF   A *pseudepigraphic book. Of unknown date and origin, it contains an account of the death of *Abraham. Many other testaments of Biblical figures survive also based on *aggadic legend. (See *PSEUDEPIGRAPHA*).

ABRAHAMITES   A Christian sect influenced by *Judaism. The Abrahamites practised *circumcision, kept Saturday as the *Sabbath, avoided pork and rejected the doctrine of the Trinity. They lived in Bohemia (Czechoslovakia) in the 18th Century. Although their leader Jan Pita was executed in 1748, the sect survived until the 1780s.

ACADEMY   See *BET HA-MIDRASH, *JABNEH, *PUMBEDITA, *RABBINICAL COLLEGE, *YESHIVAH*

ACCIDENT   Biblical laws of liability for accidents can be found in *Exodus* 21: 28–36 and 22: 4–8. The *rabbis classified four types of injury: i) that caused in the course of normal activity, ii) that caused by a stationary thing, iii) that caused on the private property of the injured and iv) consequential damage.

ADAM   (Hebrew, 'Man') The first human being. According to *Genesis* 1–2, Adam was created on the final day of *Creation. He was made in the image of *God from the dust of the earth. He and his wife *Eve had power over all living things, but as a result of

disobedience were evicted from the *Garden of Eden and condemned
to work for a living. In the *Midrash Adam is described as radiant like
the sun and in mediaeval philosophy, he was seen as the prototype
man. (See *ADAM KADMON).

ADAM, BOOK OF *Pseudepigraphic books. The *Book of the Life
of Adam and Eve* (2nd Century CE), the Syriac *Cave of Treasures* and
the Ethiopic *Book of Adam and Eve* are Christian versions of *aggadic
legends. They may have been influenced by *apocalyptic texts such
as the *Books of Jubilees* and *Enoch. (See *APOCALYPSE,
*PSEUDEPIGRAPHA).

ADAM KADMON (Hebrew. 'The primordial man'.) Adam
Kadmon first appeared in 13th Century texts. He was the perfect
prototype man created by *God. The *Kabbalists took up the concept
using it to describe the divine symbolism of the human body. Later
Adam Kadmon came to be identified with the *messiah and was
contrasted with the Devil *Adam Beliyya'al' (Hebrew. 'The evil
man'.) (See *KABBALAH).

ADLOYADA (Hebrew. 'Until one no longer knows'). *Purim celebration. The *rabbis taught that one should rejoice on Purim 'until one
no longer knows' the difference between 'Blessed be Mordecai' and
'Cursed be Haman'. In *Israel, Adloyada involves carnival pro-
cessions. (See *ESTHER, BOOK OF, *PURIM).

ADDITIONAL SERVICE See *MUSAF.

ADON OLAM (Hebrew, 'Lord of the World'). A hymn praising
the greatness of *God. It has been part of the *liturgy since the 14th
Century and is of unknown authorship. It is now normally placed at
the end of the *Musaf service.

ADONAI (Hebrew. 'My Lord') Title for *God. When the *tetragrammaton (JHWH) appears in the Biblical text, it is usual to read it
out loud either as Adonai or as *HaShem ('The Name'). (See
*NAMES OF GOD, *TETRAGRAMMATON).

ADOPTION The assumption of a parental relationship with an
individual who is not one's biological offspring. Jewish law provides

3

for adoption; a guardian may be appointed to supervise the welfare and property of the child. If the child is not of Jewish parentage, various provisions are laid down for his or her incorporation into the Jewish people.

ADULTERY   Sexual relationship between a betrothed or married woman and a man who is not her husband. Jewish law does not regard a sexual relationship between a married man and an unmarried woman as technically adulterous. Traditionally death was the punishment for adultery, but the adulterer seems to have been able to pay compensation to the husband instead. The children of adulterous relationships suffer a particular legal handicap in Jewish Law. (See *MAMZER).

AFIKOMEN   (Hebrew. 'Dessert'). A piece of *mazzah (unleavened bread) which is set aside during the *Passover meal and eaten at the end. It is the custom among *Ashkenazi Jews for the children to hide the afikomen during the course of the meal and only return it after a forfeit has been paid. (See *PESAH, *SEDER).

AFTERLIFE   The Jewish belief in life after *death has changed through the ages. In Biblical times, the dead were thought to live in *Sheol, a shadowy place beneath the earth. In the time of the Second *Temple, the *Pharisees taught that at some time in the future the dead would be *resurrected. The righteous would live in *God's presence for ever while the wicked would be punished. The mediaeval philosopher *Maimonides maintained that belief in the resurrection of the dead was a fundamental *principle of the Jewish faith. Today the bodily resurrection of the dead remains a belief for the *Orthodox even though most now reject the notion of eternal punishment. *Progressive Jews are more likely to prefer the doctrine of the immortality of the *Soul. (See *HEAVEN, *RESURRECTION OF THE DEAD, *SHEOL).

AFTERNOON SERVICE   See *MINHAH.

AGGADAH   (Hebrew. 'Narrative'). Teaching which is not legally binding. The aggadah developed in Palestine during the time of the Second *Temple until approximately 500 CE. It includes legends, history, prayers, jokes, ethical saws and stories. Sermons on Biblical texts and the discourses of eminent *sages have been preserved and provide an invaluable source for historical knowledge of Jewish thought and feeling over a long period. It was always accepted that aggadah did not have the same authority as *halakhah (the body of law), but was nonetheless preserved and enjoyed. (See *MIDRASH, *TALMUD).

AGGADAT BERESHIT (Hebrew. 'Narrative on 'In the Beginning' (Genesis)'). An *aggadic commentary on the Book of *Genesis dating from c. 10th Century CE. Explanations of verses from *Genesis are alternated with interpretations of verses from the *Psalms or *Prophets on similar themes.

AGUNAH (Hebrew. 'Tied Woman'). A woman who has been deserted by her husband or whose husband has disappeared without trace. If a married woman has neither a certificate of divorce (see *get) nor definite proof of her husband's death according to Jewish law she cannot remarry for fear of contracting an *adulterous relationship. Although various solutions have been suggested to the problem of the agunah, none have proved completely satisfactory. The prohibition against remarriage does not apply to deserted husbands because in certain circumstances, men are allowed to contract a second marriage. *Progressive Jews have abolished the category of agunah on the grounds that it is inhumane and discriminatory against women. (See *ADULTERY, *MAMZER).

AHRONIM (Hebrew 'Later Ones'). The name given to medieval and later rabbinic authorities. Their views are frequently contrasted with those of their predecessors, the *Rishonim.

AHIKAR, BOOK OF A book of folk-lore written in *Aramaic. It tells the story of Ahikar (who is also mentioned in the Book of *Tobit) and his advice to his adopted son Nadan. The book probably dates from the 7th Century BCE and several versions have survived.

AKDAMUT MILLIN (Hebrew. 'Introduction'). A poem written in *Aramaic by Rabbi Meir b. Isaac Nehorai praising *God as Creator and Lawgiver of the Universe. It is included in the *Ashkenazi service on the Festival of *Shavuot.

AKEDA (Hebrew. 'Binding'). The attempted *sacrifice by the *patriarch *Abraham of his son *Isaac (see *Genesis 22). The story

5

should probably be understood in the context of the ancient practice of child *sacrifice although in the Jewish tradition it is regarded as a supreme example of obedience to *God. The *Jerusalem *Temple was built over the supposed site of the Akeda. The incident has been the inspiration for moralists, philosophers, preachers and artists through the ages. (See *ABRAHAM).

AKIVA (c. 50–135 CE) *Sage and martyr. Akiva was the most prominent *rabbi of his day and was the teacher of many famous scholars, who, according to R. *Johanan all taught to the view of Akiva. He supported Simeon bar Kokhba in his *messianic revolt against the Romans and was ultimately flayed alive by the occupying army. Traditionally he is believed to have systematized the *Midrash.

ALENU (Hebrew. 'It is our duty'). Prayer proclaiming the greatness of *God. It is recited at the end of services in the *synagogue and was censored in the Middle Ages by Christians as being by implication insulting to Jesus. It is traditionally ascribed to *Rav.

AL HET (Hebrew. 'For the sin'). Prayer of confession recited on *Yom Kippur. It consists of an alphabetical list of sins and every section concludes with the petition 'And for all these *God of *forgiveness, forgive us, pardon us, grant us *atonement'.

ALIYAH (Hebrew. 'Going up')
i)   Emigration from other lands to *Israel with the intention of becoming a permanent citizen.
ii)   The going up of a member of the congregation to the *bimah of the *synagogue to say a *blessing or to read from the *Torah or *Haftarah.

ALLEGORY   A tale in which abstract ideas are expressed as concrete symbols. Allegories were used by the Biblical *prophets – such as *Ezekiel's characterisation of the Kings of *Israel as shepherds (Ch. 34: 2–16) and *Hosea's depiction of Israel's relationship with *God as that of an *adulterous wife with a faithful husband (Ch.3). Other texts, such as the *Song of Songs have often been interpreted allegorically. Allegory is also used by the *Talmudic *sages and the *Kabbalists.

6

ALMEMAR Dais in the *synagogue from which the *Torah is read and the service conducted. It is usually known as the *bimah among the *Ashkenazim and the tebah by the *Sephardim. (See *BIMAH*, *SYNAGOGUE*).

ALPHABET The *Hebrew alphabet is composed of twenty-two consonants. Symbols for vowel signs were not devised until the 7th Century CE and *Torah scrolls are written without them. Each letter has a numerical value and thus the value of Hebrew words can be calculated, compared and given significance. The Hebrew alphabet is used not only for Hebrew, but also for *Aramaic, *Ladino and *Yiddish.

ALTAR A table on which offerings are made to *God. There was an altar in the *tabernacle in both the courtyard and tent, and altars for the various types of *sacrifice in the *Temple in *Jerusalem. The *prophet *Ezekiel describes an altar in his vision of the new Temple (Ch. 43: 13–17). With the destruction of the Temple by the Romans in 70 CE, the household table took the place of the altar in Judaism. There are no altars in *synagogues.

AMEN (Hebrew, 'So be it'). The response to prayer. By saying 'Amen', the congregation and the individual gives assent to the prayer. The practice goes back to the days of the Second *Temple when it was said in response to the songs chanted by the *Levites. Usually the person reciting the prayer does not say Amen, but the *sages taught that *God nods Amen to the *blessings offered by his worshippers.

AM HA-AREZ (Hebrew. 'People of the Land'). A pejorative term for the ignorant. Although in Biblical *Hebrew, the Am ha-Arez simply referred to the local inhabitants, the term increasingly was used in contrast to those learned in *Torah. The *sages taught, for example, that 'a scholar though he be a *mamzar takes precedence over a *High Priest if he be an Am ha-Arez'.

AMIDAH (Hebrew. 'Standing'). A prayer consisting of eighteen *blessings which is recited at each of the three daily *synagogue services. The Amidah, which is also known as the *Shemoneh-Esreh ('Eighteen') or Ha-*Tefillah ('The Prayer') is said standing. *God is blessed as the 'shield of *Abraham', as 'the reviver of the dead', as the 'Holy God', as 'the giver of knowledge', as a 'delighter in

7

*repentance', as 'gracious and forgiving', as 'redeemer of *Israel', as 'the healer', as 'the blesser of the years', as 'the gatherer of *exiles', as 'the lover of righteousness', as 'the breaker of enemies', as 'the supporter of the righteous', as 'the rebuilder of *Jerusalem', as 'the hearer of *prayer', as 'the returner to *Zion', 'whose name is good' and as the one who 'blesses his people Israel with peace'. All eighteen blessings are recited on weekdays, but only the first and last three on *Sabbaths and *festivals. The *sages taught that the prayer should be said with the same reverence 'as if God's presence was opposite'.

AMORAIM (Aramaic 'Spokesmen'). The *sages who explained and interpreted the *Mishnah* in Palestine and Babylon between 200 and 500 CE. Their discussions are recorded in the Palestinian and Babylonian *Talmuds. Those in Palestine who had been ordained by the *nasi and the *Sanhedrin were given the title of *Rabbi while the Babylonian sages who were not ordained were known as *Rav. The amoraim were the successors of the *tannaim whose debates and opinions are collected in the *Mishnah. The *halakhic decisions of both the tannaim and the amoraim are considered to be binding and both groups contributed to the *aggadic tradition. At least two thousand individual amoraim have been identified although there is some confusion over names. Besides teaching their students, the amoraim also filled positions of leadership in their communities (See, *TALMUD).

AMOS, BOOK OF Biblical book of *prophecy dating from the 8th Century BCE. The prophet himself was a herdsman from Tekoa. He condemned the nations of the earth as well as the people of *Israel and *Judah for their wickedness. In particular he was appalled by social injustice, by those who 'sell the righteous for silver and the needy for a pair of shoes'. (Ch. 2: 6) Although he predicted coming disaster because the nation was more interested in religious observance than in justice and righteousness, he looked forward to future comfort and reconciliation. (See *PROPHECY).

AMULET An object which has magical protective qualities. Charms of magic triangles, stars of *David, hands or *kabbalistic letters were worn in the Middle Ages to ward off evil spirits. The philosopher *Maimonides wrote of the folly of believing in amulets, but the practice was accepted by many early authorities (See also *MAGIC).

ANAN BEN DAVID (8th Century CE). The supposed founder of *Karaism. According to legend, when Anan failed to be appointed *exilarch of Babylon, he broke away from Judaism. He taught his followers to reject the *Oral Law and rely on the written scriptures alone. Certainly his *Sefer ha-Mitzvot* ('Book of Precepts') became an important text in the later Karaite movement. (See *KARAISM*).

ANGEL Divine messenger. Angels appear in various Biblical stories (e.g. at *Abraham's *sacrifice of Isaac, to *Jacob in a dream and to *Balaam's donkey). They are mentioned in the *prophetic books, in the *Apocrypha*, the *Midrash, the *Talmud* and in the traditional liturgy. They were also included in the *kabbalistic world view. Many authorities today however regard them as symbolic figures who have no literal existence.

ANI MAAMIN (Hebrew. 'I believe'). A short creed based on *Maimonides thirteen *principles of the Jewish faith. It is of unknown authorship and dates back to c. 15th Century.

ANIMALS Cruelty to animals is expressly forbidden in the Hebrew scriptures (See *Deuteronomy* 22: 4). Although animals may be slaughtered for food, this must be carried out in a humane fashion (see SHEHITA). The *sages taught that before the flood, human beings were vegetarian (see *Genesis* 2: 9) and they maintained that this would be the case again in the *messianic age.

ANOINTING Pouring oil on an individual to indicate his status. In Biblical times, kings were anointed and this was connected with the giving of God's spirit (see *I *Samuel* 16: 13). *Priests were also anointed to symbolise their separation from the secular world (see *Exodus* 40: 9–13). Although the practice seems to have died out in c. 7th Century BCE, the term 'mashi'ah' – literally 'the anointed one' – came to mean the promised future king.

ANTHROPOMORPHISM The attribution of human characteristics to *God. God is frequently described anthropomorphically in the *Bible and *Talmud* (e.g. 'And they heard the voice of the Lord God walking in the garden in the cool of the day'. (see *Genesis* 3: 8).) Nonetheless it was always understood that God was not another human being and that therefore this language must be understood metaphorically. (See *Numbers* 23: 19). (See *GOD*).

ANTI-SEMITISM   Hostility against the *Jews. Although the term 'anti-Semitism' is of 19th Century origin, dislike and persecution of the Jewish people goes back to ancient times. The New Testament has a strong anti-Semitic bias and, as the humanist Erasmus remarked in the 16th Century, 'if it is incumbent upon a good Christian to hate the Jews, then we are all good Christians'. Jews fared rather better in Muslim lands although they did not generally achieve full civil rights. The *Zionist movement grew out of the conviction that Jews would always be the victims of anti-Semitism and that the creation of a Jewish homeland was the only solution. The State of *Israel was eventually declared after the devastation of the *holocaust, but because of Arab-Israeli conflict, Muslim anti-Semitism is particularly virulent today. (See *HOLOCAUST*, *ZIONISM*).

ANUSIM   (Hebrew. 'Compelled ones'). *Jews who were forced to convert to another religion. Instances of forced conversion have occurred throughout Christian and Muslim history (see *MARRANOS*). Frequently the Anusim tried to preserve their old Jewish customs in secret and to teach them to their children.

APIKOROS   A heretic. *Maimonides described an apikoros as a man who rejects God's foreknowledge, *prophecy and *revelation. The term first occurs in the *Mishnah* and is nowadays used to describe any type of heretic.

APOCALYPSE   (Greek. 'Revelation'). Revelations of the end of time and the last judgement. Apocalyptic literature deals with such subjects as *heaven, the future of this world, the activities of *angels and the *soul's future existence. Most Jewish apocalyptic writing was produced between the 2nd Century BCE and the 2nd Century CE and there are several examples in the *Apocrypha*.

APOCRYPHA   A collection of books largely preserved by the Church and incorporated into the Christian *Canon of Scripture. The

10

Apocrypha includes *Esdras*, *Tobit*, *Judith*, additions to *Esther*, the *Wisdom of Solomon*, *Ecclesiasticus*, *Baruch*, the *Song of the Three Holy Children*, *Susanna*, *Bel and the Dragon*, the *Prayer of Manasseh* and *I and II *Maccabees*. There are many other books of the same period in existence known as the *Pseudepigrapha which tend to be *apocalyptic in character. The *Apocrypha* was known as the 'Seferim hizonim' (extraneous books) by the *rabbis.

APOLOGETICS Literature defending the Jewish religion. In the past Jewish apologetic was produced against Paganism, Christianity and Islam, but today is more likely to be written against secular materialism, to combat *anti-Semitism and to defend the State of Israel.

APOSTASY Rejection of Judaism for another faith. Once Christianity became the dominant religion of the Roman Empire, many *Jews were baptized either from fear or from genuine conviction. The Jewish community maintained the distinction between those who became Christians for material advantage and those who were compelled to convert (see *ANUSIM*, *MARRANO*). In modern times, Jews were more likely to convert to gain acceptability in mainstream *gentile society (see *ASSIMILATION*). According to Jewish Law, an apostate is still counted among the Jewish community – he can, for example, contract a Jewish *marriage. However under the *Law of Return, apostate Jews may not become citizens of the state of *Israel.

ARAMAIC a language written in the *Hebrew script and much spoken in the Ancient World. Several of the *Dead Sea Scrolls were written in Aramaic and it is the language of the *Talmud*. It still survives today in isolated areas of Iraq.

ARBAAH TURIM (Aram. 'Four Rows'). The *Code of Jewish Law compiled by Jacob ben Asher in the 14th Century.

ARBA KOSOT (Hebrew. 'Four Cups'). The four cups of wine which are drunk during the course of the *Passover *Seder. The *sages taught that even the poorest person should obey this custom, which is based on the four ways *God was said to have delivered the Israelites from the Land of Egypt. (See *PESAH*, *SEDER*).

ARISTEAS, LETTER OF   A literary work describing the translation of the *Bible* into Greek. The composition dates c. later 2nd Century BCE and is in the form of a letter. It claims that the translation was made by seventy-two scholars over the course of seventy-two days. (See *SEPTUAGINT*).

ARK   (See *ARON KODESH*).

ARK OF THE COVENANT   Container for the Tablets of the Law (see *TEN COMMANDMENTS*). The Ark of the Covenant is described in *Exodus* 25: 10–22. During the wilderness period, it was kept in the *Tabernacle and after King *Solomon built the *Temple in *Jerusalem, it was kept in the *Holy of Holies. It was a gold box with two large *cherubim forming the foundation of the mercy seat from which *God communed with the Children of *Israel. The Ark of the Covenant was lost in the destruction of the Temple in 586 BCE.

ARON KODESH   (Hebrew. 'Holy Ark'). The alcove in the *synagogue in which the *Torah scrolls are kept. It is built in the wall facing *Jerusalem and is the focal point of the building. The congregation usually stands when the Ark doors are open and an eternal light (see *NER TAMID*) is kept burning before it. Among the *Sephardim, the Aron Kodesh is called the 'heikhal'. (See *SYNAGOGUE*).

ARTICLES OF FAITH   (See *IKKARIM*)

ASCETICISM   *Judaism is not normally regarded as an ascetic religion. Although *fasting is practised on *Yom Kippur and a few other days every year, the *sages taught that privation as such was not demanded by *God. Righteousness and justice are more important than mechanical religious observance (see *AMOS*). Within the community in the past, such groups as the *Essenes and *Nazarites followed an ascetic lifestyle, but in general most Jews have followed the advice of *Maimonides, steering a middle course between deprivation and self-indulgence. *Celibacy in particular has never been encouraged.

ASHAMNU   (Hebrew. 'We have sinned'). The opening of the penitential liturgy. The Ashamnu prayer is said on *Yom Kippur and on the *Fast of the *New Moon. It goes back to the days of the

*Temple when it was recited by the *High Priest once a year on the Day of *Atonement. (See *YOM KIPPUR).

ASHKENAZIM *Jews who settled in Northern France, Germany, Poland and Eastern Europe and their descendants in *Israel, the United States and the British Commonwealth. The Ashkenazim are contrasted with the *Sephardim who had their origins in Spain and North Africa. The community was aware of the distinction as early as the 11th Century. Separate customs, pronunciations, liturgies and terminology developed although communication was always maintained between the great rabbinic centres of Germany and Spain. *Yiddish was the everyday language of the Ashkenazim before World War II and they were estimated to comprise ninety per cent of World Jewry. Their numbers were decimated in the *holocaust and their main centres are now Israel and the United States.

ASHREI (Hebrew. 'Happy are they'.) The Ashrei is a *synagogue reading used three times in the daily services. It is composed of *Psalms 84:5, 144:15, and 115:18. The *sages taught that anyone who recited the Ashrei three times a day was assured of a place in the *World to Come – hence its repetition.

ASMODEUS An evil spirit. Asmodeus appears in the *Apocryphal book of *Tobit. Although he is described in later literature as the king of demons, in Jewish folk-lore he is mischievous and lively, a figure of fun and often a friend to people.

ASSIMILATION The loss of Jewish identity in mainstream *gentile culture. Since Jews have been scattered over the world with no homeland of their own (see *GALUT) assimilation has always been seen as a serious threat to the integrity of the community. Particularly since the 18th Century when many civil disabilities were removed from the *Jews, assimilation was frequently seen as a means of social advancement and acceptance (see *APOSTASY). The process of assimilation leads to secularism and greater opportunity for *intermarriage. In order to counteract the trend, the religious establishment has provided serious programmes of Jewish education and this has resulted in the community becoming more polarised between the fully observant and the totally assimilated (See also *ZIONISM).

13

ATARAH   Silver crown used as a *Torah ornament. (See *KETER).

ATONEMENT   Reconciliation with *God. The relationship between *God and human beings is damaged by *sin and, according to the Hebrew Scriptures, could be restored by *sacrifice (see *Leviticus 5). Because sacrifice was only permitted in the *Jerusalem *Temple, after the Temple's destruction in 70 CE, atonement for sin could only be effected by *prayer, *charity and *fasting. (See *FASTING, *SACRIFICE, *YOM KIPPUR).

AUSCHWITZ   The largest concentration camp. The Nazis founded the Auschwitz camp in 1940 and more than a million *Jews were exterminated there by gassing, shooting, overwork and starvation. Because of its size, it has come to symbolize all the horrors of the *holocaust.

AV 9   See *TISHAH B'AV.

AV 15   See TU B'AV.

AV BET DIN   (Hebrew. 'Father of the House of Judgment'). The chairman of the rabbinical court. In the *gaonic period, 'Av *Bet Din' was the title given to the *Gaon's assistant. From the 14th Century, it was employed for the local *rabbi particularly if he was head of a *yeshivah. Today it is exclusively used for the president of rabbinical courts. (See *BET DIN).

AV HA-RAHAMIM   (Hebrew. 'Father of mercies'). A prayer for Jewish *martyrs. It is recited during the *Sabbath morning service and dates from the 13th Century CE. The merits of those who died for the Jewish faith (see *KIDDUSH HA-SHEM) are extolled.

AVELEI ZION   (Hebrew. 'Mourners of *Zion'). *Jews dedicated to mourning the destruction of the *Jerusalem *Temple. Groups of Avelei Zion existed in Italy, Germany and the Yemen as well as in Palestine in the early Middle Ages. The groups lived *ascetic lives and were dependant on the *charity of *pilgrims.

AVINU MALKENU   (Hebrew. 'Our Father, Our King'). Poetic prayer recited on the *Ten Days of Penitence. It is based on Rabbi

14

*Akiva's prayer 'Our Father, our King, we have no king but you; Our Father, our King, for your sake have compassion on us'. The number and order of verses depend on local *custom.

AVODAH (Hebrew. 'Service') A description of the ritual performed in the *Temple in *Jerusalem on the *Day of Atonement (see *YOM KIPPUR). The Avodah is recited today as part of the Yom Kippur *musaf service and seems to have been based on *Leviticus 16.

AVODAH ZARAH (Hebrew. *'Idolatrous worship'). A tractate of the *Mishnah, *Tosefta and *Talmud. 'Avodah Zarah' is concerned with the laws of idolaters and idolatry. It is part of the order of Nezikim ('Torts').

AVOT (Hebrew. 'Fathers'). A section of the *Mishnah. Avot (or Pirke Avot ('Sayings of the Fathers')) is an anthology of the sayings of the *sages going back in an unbroken chain from the *Tannaim to *Moses. The work is the best known of all rabbinical compositions and is frequently studied in the *synagogue on the *Sabbath. The full text is frequently printed in the traditional *Prayer Book. In the Mishnah, it is located at the end of *Nezikim ('Torts'). (See *TANNAIM).

AZAZEL Place to which the *scapegoat was sent on the *Day of Atonement. Two goats were chosen and after one was *sacrificed, the other was let loose in the wilderness, symbolically carrying away the nation's *sins. The *Avodah describes this ritual. Azazel may refer to a particular place or possibly to a supernatural power. (See *SCAPE-GOAT, *YOM KIPPUR).

AZEI HAYYIM (Hebrew. 'Trees of life'). Staves on which the *Torah *Scroll is rolled.

BAAL An agricultural god of the ancient *Canaanites. The Israelites seem to have been very attracted to the worship of Baal and this was roundly condemned by the Biblical *prophets. Nonetheless many of Baal's qualities were ascribed to the Hebrew *God and almost certainly some aspects of Baal worship were incorporated into the *Temple liturgy. (See *CANAANITES).

BAAL SHEM (Hebrew. 'Master of God's name'). Title given to

15

those who possess special knowledge of *God particularly in *Hasidic circles. Legends of the Baal Shem concerning *miraculous healings and *exorcisms were circulated round Eastern European communities from the 17th Century on. (See *HASIDISM).

BAAL SHEM TOV See *ISRAEL BEN ELIEZER.

BAAL TESHUVAH See *TESHUVAH.

BABYLONIAN TALMUD See *TALMUD.

BADGE, JEWISH Distinctive emblem which *Jews were compelled to wear. From the 7th Century CE, Muslim rulers insisted Jews wear special clothing and the same provision was made by the Christian Church in the 13th Century. Sometimes the badge was circular and in medieval England it represented the tablets of the Law. The Nazis revived the Jewish badge legislation, forcing Jews to wear a yellow *Star of *David during the *holocaust period.

BAHIR, SEFER HA- (Hebrew. 'Book of Bahir') *Kabbalistic work. The *Book of Bahir* dates back to the late 12th Century and is an anthology of statements attributed to the *sages of the *tannaitic and *amoraic periods. It is the earliest work to discuss the *sefirot (the divine emanations of *God). Scripture is interpreted to reflect not the world of creation, but the divine world which is the arena for the activity of the sefirot. Later *mystics believed the *Sefer ha-Bahir* was an authoritative volume, but some authorities in the community rejected it as heretical. (See *KABBALAH).

BALAAM A figure in the *Book of *Numbers*. Balaam was instructed by Balak, King of Moab, to curse *Israel, but after he and his donkey had had a vision of an *angel, he defied the King and blessed them instead. (*Numbers 22–24*). the oracles are of an early date and were clearly influential on the prophecies of *ezekiel. some commentators regard balaam as a great *prophet while others see him as a proud and haughty figure.

BALFOUR DECLARATION A declaration of sympathy with *Zionism made by the British in 1917. The British were keen that Russian *Jews should put pressure on the Russian government to stay in World War I and also to detach Palestine from the Turkish Empire. The declaration was approved by the allies in 1920 at the San Remo Conference. (See *ZIONISM*).

BAN See *HEREM*.

BAPTISM, FORCED See *ANUSIM*.

BARAITA (Aramaic. 'Outside') A tradition of the *tannaim which has been preserved outside the *Mishnah*. Baraitot were given the name of particular *amoraim. The best known collection of the Baraitot is the *Tosefta* which was intended as a companion volume to the *Mishnah*. (See *MISHNAH*, *TOSEFTA*).

BARCELONA, DISPUTATION OF A debate between Christians and Jews held in 1263 in Barcelona between Pablo Christianus and *Nahmanides.

BAREKHU (Hebrew. 'Bless') The invitation to prayer in the *Synagogue. The phrase 'Barekhu et-*Adonai ha-Mevorakh' ('Bless the Lord who is to be blessed') functions as the introduction to both morning and evening prayer and before the *Torah reading. The congregation responds 'Blessed is the Lord who is to be blessed for ever and ever'.

BAR KOKHBA, SIMEON (d. 135 CE) Jewish rebel against the Roman Empire. The name Bar Kokhba means 'Son of a Star' and was believed to fulfil the prophecy 'A star shall come forth from *Jacob' (*Numbers* 24:17). The Bar Kokhba revolt lasted from 132–135 CE and was supported by R. *Akiva, the most eminent authority of the time. Bar Kokhba succeeded in capturing *Jerusalem and establishing an administration, but was killed by the Romans at the siege of Bethar. Traditionally Bethar fell on *Av 9. Bar Kokhba's supporters were decimated and nationalist hopes died with Simeon. (See *AKIVA*, *MESSIAH*).

BAR MITZVAH (Hebrew. 'Son of the Commandment') Status and ceremony of religious maturity. Traditionally it was taught that a boy had achieved adulthood at the age of thirteen and, to mark the occasion, the boy is called up to read the *Torah portion and *haftarah in the *synagogue morning service. Nowadays it is frequently the excuse for a large and lavish party. Although girls are considered to be religiously mature at the age of twelve, there is no real equivalent ceremony except among the non-*Orthodox movements. Among *Progressive Jews, the additional or alternative ceremony of Confirmation takes place when the student graduates from religion school at the age of sixteen.

BARUCH, APOCALYPSE OF   *Apocalyptic work ascribed to *Jeremiah's *scribe, Baruch. It contains Baruch's visions including his journey through the heavens. It survives in Syriac, Greek and Ethiopic versions. (See *APOCALYPSE, *PSEUDEPIGRAPHA).

BARUCH, BOOK OF   *Apocryphal work. The *Book of Baruch* contains a hymn to the law and lamentations for the destruction of *Jerusalem. It is set in the period after 586 BCE when Baruch reads his book to the *exiles who confess their sins and send money to *Jerusalem. Baruch himself appears in the *Book of *Jeremiah* as the *prophet's *scribe. (See *EXILE, *APOCRYPHA, *JEREMIAH).

BARUKH HA-SHEM   (Hebrew. 'Blessed be the Name') The first words of an ancient doxology. It is regularly recited after the first verse of the *Shema and, in *Orthodox circles, is said in a whisper 'Blessed be the name of the glory of his kingdom for ever and ever' (See *SHEMA).

BAT KOL   (Hebrew. 'Daughter of a voice'). A voice from *heaven. The *sages taught that the bat kol was frequently heard among the ancient Israelites. After *prophecy ceased, it became the only unequivocal means of communication between *God and his people. It was sometimes heard in dreams and at the death of martyrs for the faith.

BEARD   According to *Leviticus* 19:27, it is forbidden to cut the corners of the beard and the *sages of the talmudic period taught that the beard was the ornament of the face. Although *shaving is traditionally forbidden among the *orthodox, beards may be clipped with scissors or cut with a double edged electric shaver.

BEL AND THE DRAGON   A book of the *Apocrypha*. The book consists of two stories about the *prophet *Daniel and was probably written in Babylon in the 4th Century BCE. The *Septuagint* version appears to have been translated from the *Aramaic. (See *APOCRYPHA*).

BENEDICTIONS   Blessings. The practice of making Benedictions can be found in the Scriptures (eg. *I Samuel* 25:32). They follow particular formulae. At the beginning of a prayer, it is customary to say 'Barukh attah *Adonai, Eloheinu, Melekh ha-Olam' (Blessed art thou O Lord, our God, King of the Universe'). Before fulfilling a commandment 'asher kiddishanu b'mitzvotav vitzivanu' (who has sanctified us with your commandments and commanded us to . . .) is added. The *Amidah which is recited at all three daily services consists of eighteen benedictions. It is specified in the *Talmud* that every *Jew should pronounce one hundred blessings every day.

BENE ISRAEL   (Hebrew. 'Sons of *Israel') An Indian Jewish community. The Bene Israel claim that their community goes back to the days of the *Maccabbes. They seem to have lived in complete isolation from world Jewry for many centuries and they only made contact with the *Jews of Cochin in the 18th Century. There are many theories as to their origins; they have retained the practice of *circumcision and some *dietary laws; they keep the *Sabbath and say the *Shema. By 1969 the majority of the community had emigrated to *Israel although there was initial hesitation about their religious status.

BENSH   (Yiddish. 'Bless') A blessing. The term is used by *Ashkenazi *Jews to describe the act of making a *benediction, saying grace after meals or blessing a child. (See *BENEDICTIONS*).

BEN SIRA, WISDOM OF   See *ECCLESIASTICUS*.

BERAITOT   Passages paralleling passages in the *Mishnah* found in the *Tosefta*.

BERAKHOT   (Hebrew. 'Blessings') The first tractate of the *Talmud*. Berakhot discusses the laws concerning prayers and *benedictions including those of the *Shema and *Amidah. The *gemara of the Babylonian *Talmud* enlarges on the laws of the *Mishnah* and adds extra *aggadic material. The tractate is placed at the beginning of

Zeraim ('seeds') the first order, which is primarily concerned with agriculture. (See also *MISHNAH, *TALMUD).

BERESHIT See *GENESIS.

BERIT (Hebrew. 'Covenant') Agreement between individuals, nations or parties. The relationship between *God and the *Jews as presented in the Scriptures is essentially covenantal. It was ratified by an external sign – a rainbow in the case of *Noah (*Genesis 9:12), *circumcision for *Abraham (*Gen. 17:10) and the *Sabbath with the children of *Israel (*Exodus 31:13). Provided one party to the covenant fulfilled his side of the bargain, then the other party would also keep the agreement. As well as the above, the *Bible records a covenant with the descendants of *Aaron (*Numbers 25:12) and with the house of King *David (*II *Samuel 25:5). Because the Israelites seemed incapable of walking in God's ways and keeping his covenant, the *prophets looked forward to the days of a 'new covenant' when God would write the law within his peoples' hearts and they would all intuitively know him (*Jeremiah 31:31).

BET DIN (Hebrew. 'House of Judgment') A court of law. *Ezra the *scribe was believed to be the founder of the bet din, the lower court. The supreme court was the *Sanhedrin in *Jerusalem. A bet din is presided over by the *Av Bet Din (Father of the Court) and two other *rabbis who are learned in the law. Today it is concerned with such religious matters as the granting of *divorces and the supervision of *kashrut. In the Middle Ages, the jurisdiction of the Bet Din was far more extensive and every *diaspora community supported one. The great mass of *responsa literature grew out of the activities of these battei din. In *Israel today the bet din has jurisdiction over such matters as personal status while the Bet Mishpat ('House of Judgment') deals with secular cases. (See also *SANHEDRIN).

BET *HILLEL AND BET *SHAMMAI Schools of interpreting the *Oral Law. Both schools were active in the first and second centuries CE. Bet Hillel was generally considered to be more lenient and ultimately gained ascendancy in most areas. According to the *Talmud, a *bat kol declared that the law was in accord with the word of Bet Hillel. Many of the controversies and discussions of the two schools are recorded in the *Mishnah and *Baraita.

BET HA-MIDRASH (Hebrew. 'House of Study') Community centres for study. The institution of the bet ha-midrash goes back to the 2nd Century BCE. Although the bet ha-midrash is often merged with the *synagogue, a distinction has been maintained between the function of study and that of prayer. It is a source of merit to study in the bet ha-midrash and he who does so will be found worthy to study in the bet ha-midrash of the *world to come. (See also *SYNAGOGUE).

BETROTHAL See *MARRIAGE, *SHIDDUKHIN.

BIBLE See *TANAKH.

BIBLE, TRANSLATIONS OF The *Aramaic *Targum was the earliest translation of the Hebrew scriptures. The *Greek *Septuagint was produced in the 3rd Century BCE. The *Peshitta*, the Syriac version, dates from the 2nd Century CE and St. Jerome's Latin *Vulgate* appeared in the 4th Century. *Saadyah Gaon translated the Bible into Arabic in the 10th Century and a *Yiddish edition was produced in the 15th Century.

BIKKUR HOLIM (Hebrew. 'Visiting the sick') Organisation for sick visiting.

BIMAH (Hebrew 'Elevated place'). The platform in the synagogue from which the *Torah *Scroll is read. Traditionally it is placed in the centre of the building, but it is generally situated directly in front of the *Ark in *Progressive congregations. As well as readings, the *shofar is blown and sermons are preached from the bimah. The bimah is also known as the 'almemar' and, among the *Sephardim, as the 'tebah'. (See *SYNAGOGUE).

BIRKAT HA-MAZON (Hebrew. 'Blessing of the Meal') Grace after meals. The birkat ha-mazon consists of four *benedictions which are said at any meal at which bread is eaten. First *God is praised for giving the food, then thanked for his blessings, then asked for mercy and then thanked for his goodness. If bread is not eaten a shorter grace is recited. (See *BENEDICTIONS).

BIRKAT HA-MINIM (Hebrew. 'Blessing concerning heretics')

21

The twelfth *benediction of the *Amidah. The blessing dates back to the time of the Second *Temple and has been used against *Sadducees, collaborators, persecutors, *heretics and Judaeo-Christian sects. As a result of this benediction, *Jews have been accused of working against Christianity in their prayers, but the original intention was against Jewish heretics. (See *AMIDAH, *BENEDICTIONS).

BIRKAT HA-TORAH   (Hebrew. 'Blessing of the Law') The *benediction which is said before reading the *Torah. It should be said both publicly in the *synagogue and privately at home. (See *BENEDICTIONS).

BIRTH CONTROL   According to the *Midrash, the practice of contraception goes back to the evil days before the great flood. It is connected with the sin of *Onan who spilled his seed upon ground in preference to raising up children in his brother's name (*Genesis 38:1–9). Although birth control may be practised to protect the life and health of the mother, only female methods are permitted to avoid the sin of Onan. (See also *ABORTION).

BITTER HERBS   See *MAROR.

BLACK JEWS   Afro-Americans who have formed Jewish congregations. These congregations are generally centred round individual charismatic figures. Services are influenced by *Kabbalistic and rabbinic sources as well as the Christian Pentecostal tradition. There is little connection with the mainstream Jewish community and these groups are not recognised as Jews by the Israeli government under the *Law of Return. (See also *FALASHAS).

BLASPHEMY   Speaking scornfully of *God. Although the penalty for blasphemy is death (See *Leviticus 24:10–23) the *sages defined the offence in such a way that it was almost impossible to commit. (See also *CAPITAL PUNISHMENT).

BLESSING   See *BENEDICTION.

BLOOD   The Ancient Israelites believed the blood contained the life of an animal (see *LEVITICUS 17:11). Consequently it was forbidden to eat the blood and elaborate rules were devised to cleanse meat (see *KASHRUT). Also the Israelites were commanded to drain the blood of a *sacrifice because it was thought that expiation for *sin was made by the blood of the victim (See *SACRIFICE).

BLOOD LIBEL   The accusation that *Jews murder Christian children to obtain blood for their *Passover celebrations. Rumours of the blood libel go back to the 2nd Century BCE and the first definite case was in Norwich England in 1144 when the Jews were charged with torturing a child before the Christian festival of Easter. Although the community has consistently and vehemently denied the charge, the accusation was repeated in many places in Europe right up until the Second World War. (See *ANTI-SEMITISM).

B'NAI BRITH   (Hebrew. 'Sons of the Covenant') Oldest Jewish charitable organization. The B'nai Brith was founded in New York in 1843 and has a total membership of more than half a million individuals. It is organised into local chapters which take on particular charitable projects. (See *TZEDAKAH).

BOETHUSIANS   A sect of the Second *Temple period. The Boethusians were probably founded by the *High Priest Simon Boethus. They seem to have been similar to the *Sadducees in that they commanded the support of many of the *priests and did not believe in the *resurrection of the dead. Unlike the Sadducees however, they supported the established government. They may be identical with the Herodians mentioned in the New Testament.

BOOK OF LIFE   A book in which *God inscribes the names of the righteous. According to the *Talmud, on *Rosh Ha-Shanah the Book of Life is open for the righteous, the Book of Death for the wicked and an intermediate book which is only closed on *Yom Kippur. Thus during the *Ten Days of Repentance between Rosh Ha-Shanah and Yom Kippur, extra *benedictions are said during the *Amidah for inscription in the Book of Life.

BOOK OF THE COVENANT   The laws of *Exodus, Chapters 20; 23–23; 33. These laws are thought to date from before the days of the monarchy and include cultic legislation, the laws of *slavery, *capital offences, theft, *idolatry, *charity, social organization and the religious *calendar.

23

BRASLAV HASIDIM Followers of *Nahman of Braslav (1772–1811). One of the largest *hasidic groups, Braslav hasidim emphasize simple faith and prayer centred round the *zaddik. (See *NAHMAN OF BRASLAV and *HASIDISM).

BREASTPLATE Metal plate hung over the *Torah Scrolls in *Ashkenazi *synagogues. A breastplate was worn by the *High Priest in the days of the *Temple. It contained twelve stones for the *twelve tribes of *Israel and the Torah breastplate is frequently decorated in the same way.

BRIDGEGROOM OF THE LAW The reader who is called up to read the last portion of the *Pentateuch on the festival of *Simhat Torah. The reader who comes after and begins again at *Genesis is known as 'the bridgroom of the beginning'. In many communities, it is customary for the bridegrooms to host a party after the service. (See *SIMHAT TORAH).

BRIS (Hebrew abbreviation for BRIT MILAH 'Covenant of Circum- cision') The removal of the foreskin of the penis. Circumcision of male children takes place on the eighth day after birth. The child is held on the lap of the *sandak and a qualified *mohel carries out the operation. The child is given his Hebrew name and *benedictions over wine are pronounced. The ceremony is a sign of the *covenant between *God and his people and, traditionally goes back to the days of the patriarch *Abraham (*Genesis 17). Male *proselytes to Judaism are also expected to undergo circumcision.

BUBER, MARTIN (1878–1965) Theologian. Buber's work on *Hasidism and his I and Thou were highly influential on both Jewish and Christian theologians of his time. He collaborated with Franz *Rosenzweig in translating the *Bible into German.

BURIAL In Biblical times, the dead were buried in family graves and were said to 'sleep with their fathers'. Traditionally the dead are not buried on the *Sabbath or *Yom Kippur. Men are wrapped in their *tallis although coffins came into use in the Middle Ages. The corpse is escorted to the grave and the *Kaddish prayer is recited. Graves are marked with the headstones although the *Sephardim lay their gravestones flat while *Ashkenazim set them upright. (See *FUNERAL CUSTOMS).

BURNT OFFERING See *SACRIFICE*.

CAIN The eldest son of *Adam. According to *Genesis* 4. *God rejected his grain offering while accepting the animal offering of his brother Abel. Cain murdered Abel and was compelled to wander the earth as a fugitive and vagabond.

CAIRO GENIZAH See *GENIZAH*.

CALENDAR The Jewish calendar is calculated according to lunar months. The months are Nisan, Iyyar, Sivan, Tammuz, Av, Elul, Tishri, Heshvan, Kislev, Tevet, Shevat and Adar and in leap years two months of Adar are celebrated. The calendar is calculated from the supposed *creation of the world in 3760 BCE. Because the year 5000 began on 1st September in 1239, the current year can be calculated by deducting 1240 from the secular year and adding 5000 (eg. (1994 − 1240 = 754) + 5000 = 5754). For dates between September and December an additional year is added (eg. August 1994 = 5754; October 1994 = 5755). Rather than using the convention of BC and AD, *Jews tend to use BCE (Before Common Era) and CE (Common Era).

CALF, GOLDEN Image constructed by *Aaron when *Moses was receiving the law on Mount *Sinai (*Exodus* 32). In fury, Moses ordered the idol to be destroyed, burnt and ground to dust. (See *IDOLATRY*).

CANAAN The land promised by *God to the Israelites (see *Exodus* 6:4). Canaan can refer to an extensive area comprising the whole of Palestine and Syria or to a strip along the shore of the Mediterranean Sea. Before it was conquered by the Israelites (see Book of *Judges*), it seems to have been divided into self-governing city states. (See *CANAANITES*, *PHILISTINES*, *PROMISED LAND*).

CANAANITES The inhabitants of the Land of *Canaan. Traditionally they were thought to be descended from Ham, the son of *Noah. They worshipped the god *Baal and his consort Ashtoreth and with their agricultural sites were perceived to be a real spiritual danger to the Israelites. The *Jews were forbidden from mixing with them or intermarrying with them. Ultimately they were associated with or destroyed by the *Philistines, Aramaeans and Israelites.

25

CANDELABRUM See *MENORAH*.

CANDLES Candles are frequently used in Jewish worship. On *Sabbaths and *Festivals they are lit by the mother of the household to symbolise peace and joy and the appropriate *benediction is said. This tradition goes back to the time of the second *Temple and is one of the most universally practised customs in the world-wide Jewish community. The end of the *Sabbath is also marked by lighting a plaited candle (see *HAVDALAH) and extinguishing it in a cup of wine. Candles are lit and placed by the head of a dead person; they are used during the week of mourning (see *FUNERAL CUSTOMS, *SHIVA) and lit on the anniversary of deaths (see *YAHRZEIT). Candles are lit for every day of the Festival of Lights (see *HANUKKAH) and a light burns in front of the *Ark in the *Synagogue (see *NER TAMID). Candlesticks and *menorot are cherished objects in house and synagogue and are frequently of great artistic merit.

CANON OF SCRIPTURE The Hebrew Scriptures are divided into three sections, the *Torah (Pentateuch), *Neviim (Prophets) and *Ketuvim (Writings) (see *TANAKH). The Torah is traditionally believed to have been written in entirety by *Moses (see *DOCU-MENTARY HYPOTHESIS) and contains *Genesis, *Exodus, *Leviticus, *Numbers and *Deuteronomy. The prophetic books include *Joshua, *Judges, I and II *Samuel, I and II *Kings, (the former prophets) and *Isaiah, *Jeremiah, *Ezekiel, *Hosea, *Joel, *Amos, *Obadiah, *Jonah, *Micah, *Nahum, *Habakkuk, *Zephaniah, *Haggai, *Zechariah and *Malachi (the latter prophets). The Ketuvim consists of *Psalms, *Proverbs, *Job, the *Song of Songs, *Ruth, *Lamentations, *Ecclesiastes, *Esther, *Daniel, *Ezra, *Nehemiah, and I and II *Chronicles. Various books are also cited in the Bible (e.g. the Book of *Jashar) which have been lost. Those that are included in the Canon probably reached their present form between the 9th and the 2nd Century BCE. With the exception of parts of Daniel, Ezra and Jeremiah, they are all written in Hebrew. The *Apocrypha was not considered to be part of the Canon of Scripture by the *Sages.

CANTILLATION Chanting of scripture or liturgical texts in the *synagogue service. A system of accents is used to aid cantillation; they indicate punctuation and stress and show the rise and fall of the chant. The chanting is led by the cantor (*hazzan).

CANTOR See *HAZZAN.

CAPITAL PUNISHMENT According to scripture, the death penalty was invoked for murder, *blasphemy, *adultery, various sexual crimes, *idolatry, desecration of the *Sabbath, witchcraft, kidnapping and dishonouring parents. Two witnesses must testify to the crime and the perpetrator must previously have been warned. The sentence could be carried out by stoning, burning or hanging. *Talmudic law mentions strangulation and slaying by the sword. In fact capital punishment was rarely imposed; several *sages advocated its abolition and, from early times, for some crimes, compensation could be paid instead. In the *diaspora, Jews were subject to the same laws and punishments as were current in their adopted countries.

CAPPEL See *YARMULKE.

CARO, JOSEPH See *SHULHAN ARUKH.

CELIBACY See *ASCETICISM.

CEREMONIAL OBJECTS Objects which are used in Jewish ritual in the *synagogue include *Torah scrolls, *breastplates, Torah cases and covers, pointers (*yadim), crowns and *vimpels. Also eternal lights (*ner tamid), candelabra (*menorot) and the *Ark furnishings. Every Jewish home has *Sabbath candlesticks, a *kiddush cup, *mezuzot on the doors, *Passover *seder plates, a *havadalah spice box and a *Hanukkah menorah. Associated with life-cycle events are the *Chair of Elijah, the *wedding ring, the wedding canopy (*huppah) and the memorial candle (*Yahrzeit). Many of these objects are the product of exquisite workmanship and are passed down through families.

CHAIR OF ELIJAH The chair on which the child is placed before being taken on the lap of the *sandak for circumcision. It is normally placed on the right of the sandak and it is symbolically set aside for the *prophet *Elijah. (See *BRIS *ELIJAH).

CHANUKAH See *HANUKKAH.

CHARIOT See *MERKAVAH.

CHAROSET   See *HAROSET.

CHARITY   See *ZEDAKAH.

CHASTITY   See *SEXUAL MORALITY.

CHERUB   Supernatural creature. Cherubim were set to guard the gates of the *Garden of Eden (*Genesis 3:24) and formed the *mercy seat on the *Ark of the covenant (*Exodus 25:18–20). *Ezekiel in a vision describes four cherubim around the throne of God (*Ezekiel 1). They were winged creatures and in post-Biblical literature were identified with *angels.

CHIEF RABBI   *Diaspora communities have frequently appointed Chief Rabbis who have acted as the central established authority. In England the Chief Rabbi is appointed by the *United Synagogue (*Orthodox) but is widely seen as the foremost representative of British Jewry. Israel has both a *Serphadi and an *Ashkenazi Chief Rabbi, but there is no such figure in the United States.

CHOLENT   See *HOLENT.

CHOSEN PEOPLE   The conviction that the *Jews are the Chosen People of *God is traditionally based on God's promise to the patriarch *Abraham (see *Genesis 15). The covenantal relationship was renewed on Mount *Sinai (*Exodus 20) although it was made clear that the election depended on observance of the *Torah (*Deuteronomy 7:6). *Israel is described as a holy nation, a nation of *priests (Exodus 19:6), but the *prophets emphasized that destruction would follow if the people lost sight of righteousness and justice (see *Amos). *Hosea described the relationship as that of a loving, patient husband with an erring, unfaithful wife. The *sages of the *Mishnah and *Talmud emphasized that Chosenness did not imply superiority; the role of the Jewish people is to bring the nations of the world to the knowledge of God and such a task has involved hardship and suffering. (See *BERIT, *SUFFERING SERVANT).

CHRONICLES   Two books in the *Hagiography section of the *Bible. They contain genealogical lists of the Israelites from the time of *Adam to the accession of King *David. The reigns of Kings David and *Solomon are described in detail followed by a history of the kingdom of *Judah until its destruction by the Babylonians in 586 BCE. The *Chronicles* are thought to have been composed in *priestly circles in the late 6th/early 5th century BCE. They cover much of the same ground as the *Books of *Samuel and *Kings*, but from a different perspective.

CHUPPAH   See *HUPPAH.

CIRCUMCISION   See *BRIS.

CITIES OF REFUGE   Cities nominated in *Numbers* 35:13 as places where those who had committed accidental manslaughter could flee. There they were protected from vengeance. Six cities were named although it is questionable whether they were so used. (See also *SANCTUARY*).

CLOTHING   See *BADGE, JEWISH, *GARTEL, *HASIDIM, *SHATNES, *SHEITEL, *STREIMEL, *TALLIS, *YARMULKE, *ZITZIT.

CODES OF LAW   Compilations of Jewish law were made in the time of the *gaonim. The *Halakot Pesukot* and *Halakot Gedolot* were collected in the 8th Century and were arranged in the order of the *talmudic tractates. The Code of Isaac Alfasi (11th/12th Century) was a synopsis of talmudic law which was still applicable to the life of the community. *Maimonides' *Mishneh Torah* (12th Century) included all talmudic law. Jacob ben Asher's *Arbaah Turim* (14th Century) was the basis of the *Shulhan Arukh* of Joseph Caro. Moses Isserles added addenda (Mappah) to the *Shulhan Arukh* to reflect current *Ashkenazi practice. Later *posekim (authorities) have given *responsa and interpreted the law according to the needs of their own community and thus contributed to its codification.

COHEN   See *KOHEN.

COMING OF AGE   See *BAR MITZVAH.

COMMANDMENTS   See *HALAKHAH, *MITZVAH, *TEN COMMANDMENTS.

CONFESSION   *Sin must be confronted and confessed before it can be forgiven. In the days of the *Temple, sin offerings accompanied by *prayer were an important part of the sacrificial ritual. In the *synagogue liturgy, confession of sin is regularly made and is the central theme for the Day of Atonement (*Yom Kippur). A special confession (viddui) is prescribed when facing *death.

CONFESSION OF FAITH   The declaration that the Lord *God is One is the major confession of the Jewish faith. It should be said on rising in the morning, on going to bed at night and ideally at the moment of *death. (See *SHEMA).

CONFIRMATION   See *BAR MITZVAH.

CONSERVATIVE JUDAISM   A religious movement within *Judaism which arose in the mid-nineteenth century. As against the *Orthodox, adherents of Conservative Judaism accept that some elements of the *halakhah should be modified, but, unlike the *Reform, they believe in the validity of the traditional forms and precepts. The movement supports its own *rabbinical seminary (the Jewish Theological Seminary of America) a rabbinical association (the Rabbinical Assembly of America) and congregational organisation (the United Synagogue of America).

CONSISTORY   Organization of Jewish congregations in France, originally set up by the Emperor Napoleon in 1808. Each local consistory sends delegates to the Central Consistory in Paris. The Central Consistory maintains the *Chief Rabbinate and the *rabbinical seminary.

CONVERSION FROM JUDAISM   See *ANUSIM, *APOSTASY, *MARRANO.

CONVERSION TO JUDAISM   See *PROSELYTE.

CONTRACEPTION   See *BIRTH CONTROL.

COPPER SCROLL   One of the *Dead Sea Scrolls. The Copper Scroll was discovered in 1952 and includes an inventory of the treasures of the *Qumran community and directions for finding them.

CORPORAL PUNISHMENT According to the *Book of *Deuteronomy* (Ch 28:58–9) forty lashes was the maximum that could be inflicted for a single offence. Although corporal punishment was thus recognised in Jewish law, the *sages decreed that, except for the case of disobedience, it could only be administered in Palestine. *Maimonides specified 207 cases for which corporal punishment was appropriate.

COSMOGENY See *CREATION*.

COURSES, PRIESTLY The rota in which the *priests participated in the conduct of the *Temple ritual. They were divided into twenty-seven groups and each group conducted the sacrificial *liturgy for two weeks every year. (See *KOHEN*, *LEVITE*, *PRIEST*).

COURT JEWS Individual *Jews who served as agents of European rulers particularly from the 16th to 18th Centuries. Court Jews enjoyed special privileges and were frequently able to obtain civil rights for their fellow Jews. With their international connections, such Jews were useful to absolutist rulers and many became extremely rich and influential.

COURTS See *BET DIN*, *SANHEDRIN*.

COVENANT See *BERIT*.

CREATION According to Jewish belief, *God is the creator of the universe. There are two creation stories in the *Book of *Genesis*. In Ch. 1:1–24, God created everything in six days and rested on the seventh. In Ch. 2:4–24, the first man *Adam is formed out of dust of the earth and Eve created from his rib. In the *Wisdom literature, wisdom is seen as God's agent in creation. There was considerable speculation about creation among the *sages and *mystics (see *KABBALAH*). Other thinkers, influenced by *Hellenistic philosophers, tried to reconcile the Biblical account with the doctrine of creatio ex nihilo ('creation out of nothing') (see *PHILO*). Among modern *Jews the literal account of creation has largely been rejected and most theologians make some attempt to harmonise the Biblical insights with the theory of evolution.

CREATION, BOOK OF   See *SEFER YETZIRAH*.

CREED   A declaration of belief. the *Pentateuch* contains no formal list of the central principles of the Jewish faith even though the *Shema, 'Hear, O Israel, the Lord our God, the Lord is One' (*Deuteronomy* 6:4) is the essential tenet of Judaism. Subsequently there were several attempts to present the beliefs of Judaism in credal form. In the 12th Century, *Maimonides formulated thirteen *principles of the Jewish faith although other scholars such as Hasdai Crescas and Joseph Albo proposed other alternatives. In modern times, Maimonides' principles have been generally accepted by the *Orthodox, but not by the *Progressive movements. Judaism, in any case, does not depend on correct belief among its adherents – Jewishness is a matter of physical descent and only in a small minority of cases the result of *conversion from conviction.

CRYPTO-JEWS   *Jews who inwardly remained faithful to Judaism while outwardly practising another faith. Examples of such Crypto-Jews include those who were forcibly convicted by the Visigoths in Spain in the 7th Century, the Neofiti in Southern Italy from the 13th–16th Centuries, the *Marranos of Spain and Portugal (14th/15th Century) and the Jedid al-Islam in Persia in the 19th Century.

CUP OF ELIJAH   Cup of wine placed on the table at the *Passover *seder. It is not drunk and is saved for the prophet *Elijah who will return to earth to herald the *messiah in the Passover season.

CURSING   A supernatural appeal to bring harm on a group or a person. The Hebrew Scriptures forbid cursing *God, one's parents and those in authority and any curse involving *God's name is abominated. Nonetheless the *Talmudic sages believed in the efficacy of cursing and allowed it in certain cases if it were done for religious reasons.

CUSTOM   See *MINHAG*.

DAILY PRAYER   In the days of the *Jerusalem *Temple, daily *sacrifices were offered. After its destruction in 70 CE, sacrifice ceased. Fixed morning (*Shaharit) and afternoon (*Minhah) services in the *synagogue were established by the *sages to correspond with the morning and afternoon sacrifices and the evening service (*Maariv) was a substitute for the nightly burning of fats. Ideally a *minyan (quorum of ten adult men) is present at each of these services since, without it, certain parts of the liturgy cannot be recited. On weekday mornings, a *tallis (prayer shawl) is worn and *tefillin (phylacteries) are laid (See *SHAHARIT, *MINHAH, *MAARIV).

DANGER TO LIFE   The *Talmud contains many prohibitions in order to prevent danger to life. The duty of preserving life (and even health) takes precedence over keeping any of the *Commandments with the exception of *idolatry, sexual immorality and murder. This concern for avoiding danger goes back to the Biblical injunction, 'Take good heed to your souls'. (*Deuteronomy 4:9).

DANIEL, BOOK OF   Biblical book among the *Hagiography. It contains the story of the *Jew Daniel who is in exile in Babylon; his upbringing, his miraculous escapes from persecution and his visions of the rise and fall of empires are described. The book is exceptional in that much of it is written in *Aramaic and it probably should be dated in the 4th Century BCE. Daniel is also the hero of the *apocryphal books of *Susanna and the Elders and *Bel and the Dragon.

DARSHAN   (Hebrew. 'Expounder'). Title given to a preacher. A darshan would expound on both the *aggadic and the *halakhic meaning of a text. By the Middle Ages, a darshan was a professional preacher and frequently had an official position within the community. A *maggid, on the other hand, could be an itinerant preacher, but the term was often used as an alternative to darshan.

DAVEN   *Ashkenazi term meaning to pray.

DAVID   (11th –10th Century BCE) King of *Judah and *Israel. David's adventures are described in the Biblical Books of *Samuel and *Chronicles. While King *Saul was still alive he emerged as a great military hero, having been *anointed by the *prophet *Samuel. He succeeded in uniting the *twelve tribes after Saul's death and was king of both Israelite kingdoms. He dominated the surrounding people, made his capital in *Jerusalem and attained riches and power. Despite various crises within his family circle, he succeeded in handing on the crown of the united kingdom to his son *Solomon. In

33

later centuries, David's reign was regarded as a golden era and it was believed that the future *messiah would be of the Davidic line. He was also credited with composing many of the Biblical *psalms.

DAVID, CITY OF   See *JERUSALEM.

DAVID, STAR OF/SHIELD OF   See *MAGEN DAVID.

DAY OF ATONEMENT   See *YOM KIPPUR.

DAY OF JUDGMENT   The day when *God will judge all humanity according to their deeds. Although belief in reward and punishment is one of *Maimonides' Thirteen *Principles of the Jewish Faith, there was no agreement as to the exact course of events. *Saadiah Gaon (9th/10th Century CE), for example, argued that after death the *souls of the wicked and the souls of the righteous were kept separately. After the coming of the *messiah, the dead would all be *resurrected and after all the bodies and souls were reunited, the day of judgment would take place. The victims would enjoy God's presence in the world-to-come while the wicked would endure torment. Maimonides himself taught that the wicked would simply be extinguished. In the liturgy for *Rosh Hashanah, the *New Year is regarded as a day of judgement and the *Book of Life in which the names of the righteous are inscribed, is finally closed on *Yom Kippur. (See *BOOK OF LIFE).

DAY OF THE LORD   A day described by the Biblical *prophets. On the Day of the Lord, *God will punish the wicked and justice will ultimately triumph. The prophets used the Day of the Lord as a warning to the people; the impression was given that it would happen in the near future so that now was the time to turn away from evil ways. The prophet *Malachi promises that *Elijah will return to earth before the great and terrible day of the Lord (Ch. 3:4) and this is the origin of the belief that Elijah will be the herald of God's *messiah.

DAYS OF AWE   See *YAMIM NORAIM.

DAYYAN   The title conferred on the judges in a *bet din. The chairman is known as the Av Bet Din (Father of the Court) while the other two rabbinical judges are known as dayyanim.

DAYYENU   (Hebrew. 'It would have satisfied us'). Chorus of a *Passover hymn of praise. The song goes through the fifteen stages of the Jews' liberation from Egyptian slavery and as each one is recited, the chorus 'Dayyenu' is chanted.

DEAD, PRAYERS FOR THE   See *KADDISH.

DEAD SEA SCROLLS   Collection of ancient scrolls found in caves near the Dead Sea between 1947–1956. Dated between 150 BCE and 68 CE and written in *Hebrew or *Aramaic, the scrolls probably originated in a monastic community, traces of which have been found in *Qumran. Among the scrolls are copies of *Biblical, *Apocryphal and *Pseudepigraphical books as well as new material such as the *Manual of Discipline, the *Temple Scroll, the *War Scroll and the *Copper Scroll. It is generally believed that the monastic community was made up of *Essenes as described by the historian *Josephus and the scrolls thus reflect Essene theology. They have not all yet been deciphered and published and they are housed in the Shrine of the Book in *Jerusalem. (See *COPPER SCROLL, *ESSENES, *MANUAL OF DISCIPLINE, *QUMRAN, *WAR SCROLL).

DEATH   Belief in the *resurrection of the dead was not a feature of Biblical Judaism. The dead were said to dwell in a shadowy place beneath the earth known as *Sheol. In the period of the Second *Temple, the concept of the resurrection of the body, the *day of Judgement and reward and punishment in the world to come became important features of the teaching of the *Pharisees. The *Sadducees rejected the doctrines on the grounds that they were not in Scripture. Belief in the resurrection of the dead was one of *Maimonides' *Principles of the Faith and is still maintained by the *Orthodox. (See also *FUNERAL CUSTOMS).

DEATH ANNIVERSARY   See *YAHRZEIT.

DEATH PENALTY   See *CAPITAL PUNISHMENT.

DEBORAH   (c. 12th Century BCE) One of the Israelite leaders whose exploits are described in the Book of *Judges. She promoted the war of liberation from the oppression of Jabin King of *Canaan and was the author of the Song of Deborah (Ch. 5) which describes the battle and subsequent victory. The song is thought to be one of the oldest passages in Scripture. (See also *JUDGES).

DECALOGUE   See *TEN COMMANDMENTS.

DEMONOLOGY   The study of demons. Various demonic beings are mentioned in the *Bible and in the *kabbalistic literature *angels and demons inhabit two different spheres. Demons were also common in folk tales and legends. Although there was considerable scholarly disapproval, ordinary people used charms, *amulets and magic spells to protect themselves from demons.

DERASH   (Hebrew. 'Enquiry, exposition') See *MIDRASH.

DEREKH ERETZ   (Hebrew. 'Way of the Land'). Behaviour that was in accord with civilized etiquette and politeness. In rabbinic writings the notion refers to correct conduct in everyday life and is regarded as essential to a well-ordered society.

DESECRATION OF THE HOST   The defilement of the consecrated wafer used in the Christian Eucharist. During the Middle Ages, the *Jews were frequently accused of stealing and torturing the wafer as the Body of Christ. This charge was the pretext of numerous massacres in the 13th–15th Centuries although it was consistently and vehemently denied by the Jewish community. (See also *ANTI-SEMITISM, *BLOOD LIBEL).

DEUTERO-ISAIAH   See *ISAIAH.

DEUTERONOMIC HISTORIAN   The editor and redactor of the *Books of *Samuel* and *Kings*. The Deuteronomic historian is so called because he was influenced by the ideas of the *Book of *Deuteronomy* including the conviction that the one true *Sanctuary is in *Jerusalem and that the kings of *Israel and *Judah were judged by their faithfulness to the *covenant. The books relate the history of the Israelites from the end of the period of the *Judges to the destruction of Jerusalem by the Babylonians in 586 BCE. The editor was probably writing in the late 6th Century and was attempting to understand the cataclysmic events of his country's history.

DEUTERONOMY   The fifth book of the *Pentateuch. *Deuteronomy* contains *Moses' review of events after the *Torah had been given on Mount *Sinai. This is followed by an ethical exhortation and a summary of Jewish law. Moses then makes his final speeches to the Israelites including his blessing and an account of his death is given. It was probably a version of *Deuteronomy* that was found in the *Temple in the reign of King *Josiah in the 7th Century. This prompted a thorough-going reform of the cult and a centralization of worship in *Jerusalem. Although traditionally of Mosaic authorship, the book probably dates from the 7th Century when it was 'discovered' in the Temple.

DEVEKUT   (Hebrew. 'Cleaving (to *God)') The state of spiritual communion achieved by prayer and meditation. The expression is taken from the Biblical verse 'Love the Lord your God . . . and cleave unto him' (*Deuteronomy* 11:20). The idea of devekut is very important in *kabbalistic thought and is normally described as the highest step on the spiritual ladder in the human *soul's ascent to the divine.

DEVIL (Satan)   In the *Bible, the term Satan means an adversary and in the later books, Satan came to refer to a supernatural being who accused men in the heavenly assembly. This was Satan's role in the *Book of *Job. In the *Apocrypha and later Jewish literature, Satan becomes a more powerful figure who acts independently in tempting humanity to defy *God. In the *Testament of the Twelve Patriarchs* he is known as Behal and in the *Dead Sea Scrolls* as the *Angel of Darkness. Nonetheless *Judaism is not a *dualistic system. It is understood that ultimately God is the only god and is all-powerful. Yet before the days of the *messiah, the Devil is a powerful figure although most modern Jews prefer to speak of the forces of *evil rather than of a personal Satan. (See also *DEMONOLOGY*).

DEVOTION   See *KAVVANAH*.

DIASPORA   (Greek 'Dispersion') The dispersion of the Jewish people outside the land of *Israel after the *Exile in Babylon of the 6th Century BCE. Many *Jews settled in Babylon and did not return in the Persian period and from *Hellenistic times there were Jewish communities in most urban centres round the Mediterranean Sea. In the Middle Ages in Christian Europe, Jews were much persecuted (See *ANTI-SEMITISM*) and were frequently expelled. Many gravitated to Muslim countries, Eastern Europe and, eventually, to the United States, South America, Australia and South Africa. From the late 19th Century, many sought to return to Palestine (see *ZIONISM*) and the founding of the State of Israel has had a profound effect on Diaspora Jewry. With the destruction of the great Eastern European communities in the *holocaust, the focus of the Diaspora has become the United States and the countries of the British Commonwealth. (See also *GALUT*).

DIBBUK   Evil spirit which takes possession of an individual. Dibbuks were believed to cause madness, to speak through the mouth and to cleave to the human soul. They can be *exorcised by pronouncing and conjuring the *Name of *God. Such exorcism was practised in the circle of Isaac *Luria and various *hasidic *zaddikim. Among 20th Century Jews, such beliefs have largely disappeared. (See also *DEMONOLOGY*).

DIETARY LAWS   See *KASHRUT*.

DIN   (Hebrew. 'Judgment') A legal decision. The term is usually used in the context of a lawsuit or legal dispute.

DINA DE-MALKUTA DINA   (Aramaic. 'The Law of the land is the law'). The *halakhic rule that the Law of the land is legally binding on the Jewish community. This principle was laid down by the *sage Samuel in the 3rd Century in Babylon. It was realised that the survival of the Jewish people depended on reconciliation with the secular government.

DIN TORAH   (Hebrew. 'Judgment of the Law') A legal hearing conducted in accordance with the provisions of Jewish law.

DISCIPLINE, MANUAL OF   One of the *Dead Sea Scrolls. The *Manual of Discipline* enumerates the beliefs and organisation of the community that produced it. The customs described are similar, but not identical to those described by the historian *Josephus as being practised by the *Essenes. The Manual dates from the 1st Century BCE/CE and is our most valuable source of information about the *Qumran community. (See also *DEAD SEA SCROLLS).

DISPERSION See *DIASPORA.

DISPUTATIONS See *BARCELONA, DISPUTATION OF, *TORTOSA, DISPUTATION OF.

DIVORCE See *GET.

DOCUMENTARY HYPOTHESIS The suggestion that the *Pentateuch was composed from different documentary sources. Traditionally it was believed to have been composed in entirety by *Moses and this remains a cornerstone of *Orthodox belief. However the German Biblical scholar Wellhausen argued that different strands within the text can be discerned. He identified them as J (because *God is called *JHWH), E (God is *Elohim), D (the writer of *Deuteronomy) and P (the *Priestly source). Most *Progressive Jews have accepted Wellhausen's hypothesis at least in modified form.

DOME OF THE ROCK Mosque in the *Temple area in *Jerusalem. It is built on the site of Mount Moriah over the rock on which *Abraham nearly *sacrificed Isaac (see *AKEDA), on which King *Solomon built his Temple and from which the Muslim *prophet Mohammed ascended to *Heaven. *Orthodox Jews today do not walk over the Temple Mount for religious reasons and pray instead by the outer western well. (See *WAILING WALL).

DONMEH Judaeo–Muslim sect formed in the 17th Century. As followers of *Shabbetai Zevi, they also coverted to Islam, but continued to observe many Jewish customs. They also retained their belief that Shabbetai was the *messiah. In the course of time, the group formed several different sects mainly based in Salonica.

DOORPOST See *MEZUZAH.

DOWRY Property brought by a bride to her husband. By talmudic times the practice of giving a dowry was well-established. The wife was protected in that the dowry was specified in the marriage contract (see *KETUBAH) and had to be returned in the event of *divorce or the death of her husband.

DREAM In ancient times dreams were regarded as being of spiritual significance. The *Bible records the dreams of *Joseph and *Daniel as divine communications and both men had the ability to interpret. Different views are presented of dreams in the *Talmud and interest continued through the Middle Ages until modern times. The *Hasidim and *kabbalists were particularly interested in dreams and this has continued in a somewhat different form, in the work of the psychoanalysts.

DREIDEL (Yiddish. 'Spinning Top') A dreidel has Hebrew letters on each side which bear the initial letters of the Hebrew sentence, 'A great miracle happened here'. It is spun like a traditional spinning top in a game played at the *festival of *Hanukkah.

DRESS See references in *CLOTHING.

DREYFUS AFFAIR Dreyfus was a Jewish officer in the French army. In 1894 he was found guilty of treason and sentenced to life imprisonment. Although he was, after a lengthy campaign, exonerated, the case revealed the latent *anti-Semitism of 19th Century Europe. It deeply influenced the thinking of Theodor *Herzl and thus was an important contribution to the development of *Zionism. (See *ANTI-SEMITISM).

DRINK OFFERING Offering of wine which was added to all the animal *sacrifices in the *Temple. The quality of wine varied according to the animal being offered (*Numbers 15:5–9). (See *SACRIFICE).

DUALISM A philosophical or religious doctrine which posits two ultimate beings. The universe is perceived as a cosmic struggle between the forces of good and the forces of evil, or *God and the *Devil. Although this doctrine was found among the *gnostics and the Zoroastrians, it was condemned by the Jewish authorities on the grounds that God is the ultimate power. Nonetheless dualism can be found in some *kabbalistic texts. The term dualism is also used for the belief in a radical opposition between matter and spirit as is found in the writings of Greek philosophers. This idea was influential on *Philo and medieval Jewish philosophers.

DUKHAN The platform in the *Temple from which the *Levites sang and the *Priests recited the Priestly *Benediction. By extention, it was used to mean the platform in the *synagogue and the dais where teachers sat to instruct children. (See also *BIMAH).

DUTY Jewish law recognises different types of duty. A 'hovah' is an obligation, a *'mitzvah' is a commandment while 'reshut' is a commendable action. An alternative distinction has been made between the duties of the limbs (ceremonial and practical obligations) and the duties of the heart (spiritual obligations). All duties are ultimately grounded in the will of *God as revealed in the *Written and *Oral Law.

EARLOCKS See *PAIS.

EBIONITES Judeo-Christian sect of 2nd–4th Century Palestine. Although they believed Jesus to be the *Messiah, they observed the Law of *Moses. They also seem to have held all property in common.

ECCLESIASTES A book of the *Bible; one of the five *scrolls in the *Hagiographa. The author is described as 'Kohelet' (Hebrew. The preacher) and the book is a meditation on the meaning of life. Although the constant theme is 'vanity of vanities, all is vanity', the work ends on an optimistic note. It is read in the *synagogue on *Sukkot. Traditionally it was believed to have been written by King *Solomon, but was probably produced in the 6th/5th Century BCE.

ECCLESIASTICUS (*The Wisdom of Jesus Ben Sira*) A book of the *Apocrypha. It was written by Jesus ben Sira and translated into Greek by his grandson in the 2nd century BCE. It contains liturgical poems about the Biblical heroes as well as moral maxims and advice. (See also *WISDOM LITERATURE).

EDEN, GARDEN The place created by *God as the abode for the first human beings (see *ADAM). According to *GENESIS 2 the garden was full of beautiful plants which were good to eat, but Adam and Eve were expelled for disobeying God's command. In rabbinic

41

literature the Garden of Eden (Hebrew, 'Gan Eden') is the *Paradise where the righteous live after their deaths.

EDUCATION   The *Book of *Deuteronomy* (ch. 6:7) stipulates that the commandments of *God must be taught to children and by the era of the Second *Temple, an elaborate system of education had been set up for boys. Attached to *synagogues were elementary schools ('Bet Sefer', *'Heder') and community schools (*'Bet ha-Midrash'). In the *academies of Babylon and Palestine, famous *sages taught their students and *yeshivot were subsequently established throughout the Jewish world. The tradition of *Bar Mitzvah ensured that every Jewish boy could read the Hebrew text of the *Torah and the prestige of scholarship guaranteed the survival of Jewish learning. In modern times *rabbinical seminaries, teacher training colleges and *Orthodox and *Progressive day schools have been established. Although in the past, girls only received an elementary education and were largely taught domestic skills at home, in this century they have had similar opportunities to boys. (See also *BET HA-MIDRASH, *HEDER, *RABBINICAL SEMINARIES, *TALMUD TORAH, *YESHIVAH).

EHAD MI YODE'A   (Hebrew. 'Who knows one?') Progressive counting song. The poem is medieval in origin and is sung at the *Passover *seder in many communities.

EIGHTEEN BENEDICTIONS   See *AMIDAH.

EIN SOF   See *EN SOF.

EL   See *NAMES OF GOD.

ELDER   One of the members of the governing class of the community or nation. *Moses appointed seventy elders to help him rule over the *Israelites (*Numbers 11:16) and elders are mentioned as representatives and judges of the people until the time of the Second *Temple (eg. *Psalm 107:32) The title 'Zaken' (Elder) continued to be given to members of community councils in some areas in the Middle Ages.

ELDERS OF ZION, PROTOCOLS OF THE   A document which was supposed to prove the existence of a world Jewish conspiracy.

The *Protocols* was first published in Russia in the early 20th Century. From there it was introduced into Western Europe after World War I. It describes a conference at which the leaders of world Jewry made plans to overthrow Christian society and attain world domination. Although known to be a forgery, it played a part in *Anti-Semitic Nazi propaganda and has recently been circulated in Muslim countries. (See *ANTI-SEMITISM).

ELECTION   See *CHOSEN PEOPLE.

ELEPHANTINE   (Yeb) Ancient town on the West Bank of the River Nile. Between 590–333 BCE a Jewish garrison was stationed at Elephantine and a *temple was built there. Although the building was destroyed by an Egyptian riot, it was subsequently rebuilt. Papiri discovered near the site describe the rituals and customs of the community.

ELIJAH   Biblical (9th Century BCE) *prophet. According to I *Kings 17f, Elijah prophesied in the *Northern Kingdom in the reigns of King Ahab and Azariah. Ahab's wife Jezabel had encouraged the worship of *Baal and Asherah. Elijah declared that *God had sent a drought in punishment and subsequently staged a trial of strength between Baal and the God of *Israel. According to *II Kings 2*, Elijah never died, but was taken up to *Heaven in a fiery chariot. From this the belief arose that he would return to earth 'before the great and terrible *Day of the Lord' (*Malachi 4:5). The *sages taught that Elijah would be the herald of the *messiah. As he would return at *Passover time a place is laid for him at the *seder table and a cup of wine is reserved for him. Similarly a *chair for Elijah is placed at the *circumcision ceremony.

ELIJAH, APOCALYPSE OF   *Pseudepigraphical work. *The Apocalypse of Elijah* gives an account of the archangel *Michael showing *Elijah the future destruction of the Roman empire, the destruction of the wicked, the final judgement and the establishment of the heavenly *Jerusalem. It dates from the 1st century. (See *APOCALYPSE).

ELIJAH BEN SOLOMON ZALMAN   (1720–1797) (The Vilna Gaon). Lithuanian scholar and tireless opponent of *Hasidism. Elijah was regarded as the spiritual leader of the *Mitnaggedim and his reputation made Vilna an important centre of Jewish learning. He wrote Biblical commentaries, annotations on the *Midrash, *Talmud* and *Zohar* and in his *halakhic decisions, he based his rulings on the plain meanings of the text. Although he encouraged the study of natural science, he forbade philosophy and was adamantly opposed to the *Haskalah and its effects on the Jewish Community, (see also *HASIDISM, *HASKALAH, *MITNAGGEDIM).

ELISHA (9th century BCE) Biblical *prophet. Elisha was the disciple and successor of the prophet *Elijah and he prophesied in the *Northern Kingdom during the reign of Jehoram. He foretold Hazael's accession to the throne of Syria and, on his instructions, one of his followers anointed Jehu King of *Israel to depose the house of Ahab (see *II *Kings* 2–9).

EL MALE RAHAMIM (Hebrew. 'O God full of compassion'). Opening words of a *funeral prayer. It originated in the Middle Ages and was recited for the Jewish *martyrs of the Crusades. It is said at funeral services, on the anniversary of a death (*Yahrzeit), on visiting a grave and when called up to read from the *Torah scroll. In some communities it is also said on the Day of Atonement (*Yom Kippur).

ELOHIM (Hebrew 'God') One of the names of *God. It is the name used by the author of one of the sources of the *Pentateuch (See *DOCUMENTARY HYPOTHESIS). (See *NAMES OF GOD).

EMANATION A flow from a primary source. The *Kabbalists taught that the entire universe was derived from ten emanations (*sefirot) from the ultimate source (*En Sof). The idea was taken over from the Neo-Platonists by the Arab philosophers and was then adopted by Jewish *mystics. (See *KABBALAH).

EMANCIPATION The removal of social restrictions from Jews between 18th–20th Century. Once Christianity became the official religion of the Roman Empire, the Jewish community suffered various discriminations which were not lifted in Western Europe until the late 18th/19th century. In Eastern Europe emancipation came later and it was in pursuit of political and religious freedom that so many Jews emigrated to the United States in the late 19th/early 20th Century. (See also *HASKALAH).

ENGAGEMENT See *SHIDDUKHIN*.

EN (AYIN) HA-RA (Hebrew. 'The evil eye'). A glance which has evil consequences. Belief in the evil eye occurs in *rabbinic literature and *kabbalistic sources. Various remedies are suggested such as the weaving of *amulets, reading the Scriptures and reciting spells. These folk beliefs are now rare in the Jewish community (See also *DIBBUK, *MAGIC).

ENLIGHTENMENT See *HASKALAH

ENOCH, BOOK OF *Pseudepigraphical works i) One surviving *Book of Enoch* was translated from Greek to the Slavonic in the 10th/11th Century. It gave a description of Enoch's journey through the seven heavens, his return to earth and his second ascent. ii) A book dating from the Second Temple period. Of Ethiopian origin, it describes the visions of Enoch and reflects the *messianic yearnings of the period. Enoch himself appears in the *Book of *Genesis* as one who 'walked with God; then he was no more for God took him' (ch. 5:23). Because he did not die naturally, there was room for interpretation on the manner of his disappearance. The Slavonic and Ethiopian *Books of Enoch* are two of several existing apocalyptic works centred on him (See *APOCALYPSE).

EN SOF (Hebrew. 'The Infinite') *Kabbalistic name for the Infinite. The early kabbalists taught that the En Sof was total perfection, the ultimate singularity. It is beyond all human thought or understanding and from it emanate the ten *sefirot (emanations). Through *creation, reflection and devotion, the sefirot are revealed and union with En Sof achieved. (See *DEVEKUT, *SEFIROT, *KABBALAH).

EPHOD A garment worn by the *High Priest in the days of the First *Temple. The ephod was probably an embroidered or decorated tunic worn over the traditional blue robe. On top of it was tied the *breastplate and the *urim and thummim. The ephod, urim and thummim were used for divination purposes, but this practice died out by the Second Temple period.

EPHRAIM One of the sons of *Joseph. Joseph had no tribe named after him; instead his double share went to his two sons Ephraim and

Manasseh. The tribe of Ephraim became very prominent in the time of the *Judges and when the *Northern Kingdom rebelled against the *Davidic monarchy, the king chosen, Jeroboam I, was an Ephraimite. So powerful did the tribe become that the 8th Century *prophets frequently referred to the entire Northern Kingdom as Ephraim (eg. *Hosea 11:8). The area occupied by the Ephraimites subsequently became the territory of the *Samaritans (See *NORTHERN KINGDOM, *SAMARITANS, *TEN LOST TRIBES, *TRIBES, THE TWELVE).

EPICOROS   See *APIKOROS

EPITROPOS   (Greek 'Guardian') Talmudic term for one who cares for the property of minors, the physically handicapped, or mentally infirm.

EREZ ISRAEL   (Hebrew. 'The land of Israel'). The country promised by *God to the *patriarch *Abraham and his descendants. The scope of Erez Israel is laid down in the *Covenant (*Genesis 15:18–19) and alternative boundaries are given in *Numbers 34:2–12. Love for Erez Israel has been a characteristic of the Jewish community from the first and it is expressed in the *Bible, *Talmud, liturgy, law and folk legends. (See also *CANAAN, *PROMISED LAND, *ZIONISM).

ERUV   (Hebrew. 'Missing') A symbolic act which facilitates the performance of otherwise forbidden acts on the *Sabbath and *festivals. By amalgamating ('missing') individual homes, it is permissable to carry burdens (such as small children) within the area of the eruv and walking further than the traditional Sabbath day's journey from home (since the entire area within the eruv counts as home). Eruvim have been set up in many cities in *Israel and the United States.

ESCHATOLOGY   Beliefs about the last things and the end of days. The Biblical *prophets spoke of coming disasters which were the consequence of the Israelites neglecting their moral obligations. They also looked forward to a golden age after the catastrophe when *Israel's relationship with God would be restored. In the time of the Second *Temple, extensive apocalyptic beliefs were circulated; *prophecy would return to the land; the coming disasters were a sign

46

of the advent of the *messiah; the *exiles would return to *Jerusalem; the dead would be resurrected; the kingdoms of this world would be overthrown; *God would judge all the people; the righteous would dwell with him in the *World to Come while the wicked would be cast out to eternal punishment. At various times in Jewish history, it has been believed that these events were imminent (see *SHABBETAI ZVI). Today the *Orthodox still look for the coming of the messiah and anticipate the final resurrection of the dead. Adherents of the *progressive movements tend to be less definite in their expectations. (See also *APOCALYPSE, *DAY OF JUDGMENT, *INGATHERING, *MESSIAH, *RESURRECTION).

ESDRAS   Two books of the *Apocrypha. The books are known as III and IV Esdras since *Ezra and *Nehemiah are also known as I and II Esdras. Supposedly written by Ezra the *Scribe, III Esdras covers the history of *Israel from the days of King *Josiah to the reading of the Law to the returned *exiles by Ezra himself. IV Esdras is also known as the Apocalypse of Ezra and examines the problem of suffering, the future of the Jewish people and the coming of the *messiah. Both books date from early in the Second *Temple period. (See also *APOCALYPSE, *EZRA).

ESHET HAYIL   (Hebrew 'A woman of valour') The phrase occurs in *Proverbs 31 as part of a passage praising worthy women. The whole passage is often recited by the householder before *Kiddush on Friday evenings. The *Sabbath *candles are lit and before the meal the wife is praised and the children blessed. (See also *SABBATH).

ESSENES   A 1st century ascetic sect. The Essenes are described by Pliny and *Josephus. They lived in closed communities which particularly emphasized the importance of ritual *purity. It seems probable that it was a group of Essenes who lived at *Qumran and who were responsible for the *Dead Sea Scrolls. Among the Scrolls, the *Manual of Discipline describes the customs and religious practices of the sect and other scrolls reveal their particular *apocalyptic beliefs. The sect seems to have evolved in the 1st Century BCE and they appear to have been completely destroyed in the Jewish War of 66–70 CE.

ESTHER, BOOK OF   A Biblical book from the *Hagiographa section. The *Book of Esther* tells the story of how a Jewish woman, Esther, became the wife of King Ahasuerus of Persia. Encouraged by her uncle Mordecai, she was able to foil the plans of the wicked grand vizier Haman who wished to destroy the Jewish community. An addition to the book is found in the *Apocrypha. These verses were part of the *Septuagint*, but cannot be found in the Hebrew text as it survives. The *Book of Esther* was composed c. 350 BCE and reflects the conditions of the Jews in the Persian empire. It is known as 'megillah' (Scroll) (see *SCROLLS, FIVE*) and is read in entirety in the *synagogue on the *festival of *Purim. This is a particularly happy occasion when the *rabbis instructed that one should rejoice 'until one no longer knows' (*adloyada) 'the difference between Blessed be Mordecai and Cursed be Haman'. (See also *PURIM*).

ESTHER, FAST OF   *Fast on Adar 13, the day before the *festival of *Purim. (See *FASTS*).

ESTHER, FEAST OF   See *PURIM*.

ETERNAL LIGHT   See *NER TAMID*.

ETHICAL LITERATURE   See *MUSAR*.

ETHIOPIAN JEWS   See *FALASHAS*.

ETROG   (Hebrew 'Citron') A fruit used in the ritual of the *festival of *Sukkot. During the services the etrog is held while the *lulav ('four species') is waved. During the Second *Temple period the etrog was a popular symbol for graves, coins and *synagogue art. The etrog was often kept in a beautiful silver container. (See *SUKKOT*).

ETZ HAYYIM   (Hebrew 'Tree of life'). A metaphorical expression for Jewish law – 'it is the tree of life to which we cling'. The phrase is derived from *Proverbs* 3:18 and it is also used for the wooden staves round which the *Torah *Scroll is wound. (See *SCROLLS*).

EUTHANASIA   Mercy killing. Judaism teaches that life is a blessing from *God and hastening death is the equivalent of bloodshed. The *Shulhan Arukh* teaches that a dying person has the same rights as a living person and 'it is forbidden to cause him to die quickly'. However with the advent of modern technology, some authorities permit the cessation of artificial means of prolonging life when there is no possibility of recovery. Among *progressive Jews there is some discussion of the ethics of voluntary euthanasia, but in general the traditional view is accepted.

EVE   The first woman. According to *Genesis 1:27, both male and female were created in the image of *God. In *Genesis 2:22, Eve was formed from the rib of *Adam; in the *Garden of Eden she was seduced by the serpent to be disobedient to God and persuaded Adam to follow her example. In consequence they were expelled from the Garden and Eve was condemned to labour in child-birth and to be subservient to her husband. Her name means the mother of all living things. (See *Genesis 2–4). (See also *ADAM, *LILITH).

EVENING SERVICE   See *MAARIV.

EVIL EYE   See *EN HA-RA.

EXCOMMUNICATION   See *HEREM.

EXECUTION   See *CAPITAL PUNISHMENT.

EXEGESIS   See *MIDRASH.

EXILARCH   Head of the Babylonian Jewish community from 1st–13th Century CE. The office of Exilarch was hereditary and the holders were believed to be descendants of the House of King *David. His position was recognised by the ruler of Babylon and he organised the collection of taxes from the community. He also appointed judges and was responsible for the administration of justice for his people. There was a close relationship between the exilarch and the head of the *Babylonian *academies, the *geonim, and there were also frequent conflicts.

EXILE   See *GALUT.

EXILE, BABYLONIAN   Exile of the *Jews in the land of Babylon in the 6th Century BCE. After the fall of *Jerusalem in 586 BCE, the inhabitants of *Judah and their king were taken captive to Babylon. They were not permitted to return until the Babylonians had been conquered by the Persians in c. 538. Nonetheless, encouraged by the *prophets and sustained by the new institution of the *synagogue, the community remained faithful to the beliefs of their ancestors ('By the waters of Babylon I sat and wept and thought of *Zion' *Psalm 137). After the return to the land, many Jews, who had prospered, remained behind and by the 1st Century BCE, there were Jewish communities in most urban areas around the Mediterranean coast. (See also *DIASPORA).

EXILES, INGATHERING OF   During the Babylonian *Exile, the *prophet *Ezekiel predicted the return of the *Jews to the *Promised Land. Not only would the inhabitants of *Judah return, but also the members of the *Ten Lost *Tribes would be gathered in, and the full twelve *tribes would be restored. Even after the rebuilding of *Jerusalem after the Babylonian exile, this belief persisted and was an important feature of *rabbinic *eschatology. It is prayed for in the liturgy and it will occur in the days of the *messiah. Since the founding of the State of *Israel in 1948, the ingathering of the exiles (Hebrew 'kibbutz galuyyot') has come to mean the immigration of *diaspora Jews to Israel. (See also *ESCHATOLOGY).

EXODUS, BOOK OF   The Second Book of the *Bible, part of the *Pentateuch. The Book of Exodus describes the enslavement of the Israelites by the Egyptians, the early life of *Moses, the ten plagues, and the departure of the Israelite slaves from Egypt (the exodus). This is followed by the drowning of the Egyptians at the Red Sea, the wandering in the wilderness and the revelation at *Sinai. Details of the *covenant between *God and *Israel are given, followed by the episode of the Golden *Calf. The Book is traditionally believed to have been written by Moses. (For an alternative view see *DOCUMENTARY HYPOTHESIS).

EXORCISM   The driving out of evil spirits by *prayers or magical formulae. Exorcism was practised as part of Jewish folk religion and in particular by the *kabbalists and *hasidim who believed individuals could be possessed by the *souls of the dead.

EXPULSION   Throughout their history, Jews have been expelled from their homes in the *diaspora. In 139 BCE, they were driven out of Rome; in Christian Europe they were expelled from England in 1290, France in 1306, 1322 and 1394, Germany in 1348, Andalusia in 1484, Spain in 1492, Portugal in 1497, Navarre in 1498, Provence in 1512, Naples in 1541 and the Papal States in 1569. The Russian community was expelled from Little Russia in 1727, 1739 and 1742 and in the 19th Century they were restricted to the Pale of Settlement. Initially the German Nazis were keen to encourage Jews to emigrate and only after the boarders were closed did the *Final Solution take place. (See *HOLOCAUST).

EZEKIEL, BOOK OF Biblical book of a 6th Century BCE *prophet. Ezekiel prophesied among the Babylonian *exiles from 592–570 BCE and consoled those in captivity after the destruction of *Jerusalem. The *Book of Ezekiel* is the third book of the major prophets and contains a description of the divine chariot (*'merkavah') which was the basis of later *mystical speculations. It also includes prophecies of destruction written before the fall of Jerusalem. This is followed by predictions of disaster for the *gentiles, words of consolation for the *Jews and visions of the restored *Temple.

EZRA, BOOK OF A Biblical book describing the activities of a *scribe of the 5th Century BCE. Ezra served as a scribe in the Persian government and was given permission to lead the Jewish exiles (see *EXILE, BABYLONIAN) back to *Jerusalem. With *Nehemiah, he persuaded the people to keep the *Torah and in particular to observe the *Sabbath and avoid *intermarriage. The *Book of Ezra* is part of the *Hagiographa and describes the return from Babylon from the time of *Zerubbabel to the time of Ezra. The story is continued in the *Book of *Nehemiah*.

EZRA, APOCALYPSE OF See *ESDRAS

EZRAT NASHIM (Hebrew 'Court of Women') Court in the *Temple of *Jerusalem beyond which women could not go. Further inside was the Court of Israelites, the Court of *Priests and the *Holy of Holies. Later Ezrat Nashim came to refer to the section of the *synagogue in which the women sit (See *MEHIZAH, *WOMEN).

FABLE See *MASHAL.

FAITH Judaism distinguishes between faith meaning 'believing in' (Hebrew 'Emunah') and faith meaning 'trusting in' ('Bittahon'). The Scriptures take it for granted that *God exists; emunah was used for believing in the fulfilment of His promises. In the Middle Ages, it was used for believing in such statements as *Maimonides' Thirteen *Principles. At the same time, it was always understood that the Jewish religion was based not on cognitive belief, but on a unique personal relationship which involved trust and obedience.

FAITH, CONFESSION See *CONFESSION OF FAITH, *SHEMA.

FAITH, THIRTEEN PRINCIPLES OF See *MAIMONIDES, *THIRTEEN PRINCIPLES OF FAITH.

FALASHAS Members of the ancient Jewish community of Ethiopia. The Falashas claim to be descended from the notables of *Jerusalem who accompanied Menelik, the son of King *Solomon and the Queen of Sheba, back to his own country. Their form of Judaism is based on the *Bible, *Apocrypha and other post-Biblical books. They are not familiar with the deliberations of the *sages in the *Talmud. Rumours of a community of Black Jews were current among world Jewry for many centuries and the Falashas were subsequently recognised as members of the House of *Israel. In the mid 1980s, many Falashas were air-lifted to Israel and there is now a substantial community there. (See *BLACK JEWS, *INGATHERING).

FALL *Adam and *Eve's disobedience in the Book of *Genesis. In consequence of the Fall, the first human beings were expelled from the *Garden of Eden; Adam was condemned to earn his own living and Eve to suffer pain in childbirth and be subservient to her husband. The *sages taught that death was the result of the Fall, but Judaism, unlike Christianity, does not teach a doctrine of original sin.

FALSE WITNESS The *Ten Commandments forbid the bearing of false witness (see *Exodus 20). This includes perjury, slander, defamation and lying. In the law courts (see *BET DIN) the accused can only be convicted on the testimony of a pair of witnesses – a single hostile report is not enough.

FASTS See *FASTING, *ESTHER, FAST OF, *FIRST-BORN, FAST OF, *TISHAH B'AV, *YOM KIPPUR.

FASTING Abstention from taking food. Individuals may fast as a sign of *repentance or *mourning. Through fasting, atonement can be made for *sin. The whole community observes specific fast days (see *FASTS). The two major fasts, *Tishah B'Av and *Yom Kippur last from sunset to sunset and involve abstention from food, drink, sexual intercourse and wearing leather. The other fasts last from sunrise to sunset and only involve avoiding food and drink.

FATHERS, MERITS OF The belief that through the worthy deeds of one's ancestors, *blessings may be secured. In particular the merits of the *patriarchs, *Abraham, *Isaac and *Jacob are thought to secure benefits for the Jewish people.

FATHERS, SAYINGS OF See *AVOT.

FEAR OF GOD The fear of *God is traditionally regarded as the start of religious consciousness. The BOOK OF *PROVERBS states that 'the fear of the Lord is the beginning of *wisdom' (Ch. 10:10). (See *WISDOM LITERATURE).

FEMINISM Many leading 20th Century feminists have been of Jewish origin and the feminist movement has brought marked changes in the Jewish community. Traditionally within Judaism the sphere of *women and men have been very different, but since the 1970s in the *Progressive movements, women have served congregations as ordained *rabbis; they have trained as *cantors and educationalists and have played an increasingly prominent role in communal life. These changes have been resisted as contrary to the *halakhah by the *Orthodox establishment and there little has changed. (See also *ABORTION, *BIRTH CONTROL, *KETUBAH, *MARRIAGE, *WOMEN).

FENCE AROUND THE LAW *Rabbinic rulings designed to safeguard traditional practice. According to the *Mishnah, one of the three guiding precepts of the men of the *Great Synagogue was to make a fence around the law. Thus they produced regulations that were more stringent than the original commandments to ensure that the original commandments were fully kept.

FESTIVALS   Days of rejoicing in the *Calendar. All work is forbidden on the Biblical festivals (which include the first and last days of festal seasons). In the *diaspora, the *Orthodox celebrate most festivals on two consecutive days while they are kept for one day in *Israel and by *Progressive Jews. The later post-Biblical festivals do not involve abstention from work. (See *HANUKKAH. *HIGH HOLY DAYS, *LAG B'OMER, *PESAH, *PILGRIM FESTIVALS, *PURIM, *ROSH HASHANAH, *SABBATH, *SHAVUOT, *SUKKOT, *TU B'AV, *TU BI-SHEVAT, *YOM ATZMAUT, *YOM TOV).

FIFTEENTH OF AV   See *TU B'AV.

FIFTEENTH OF SHEVAT   See *TU-BI SHEVAT.

FINAL SOLUTION   The genocide practised by the Nazis against the Jews in World War II. The final solution was decided at a secret meeting by the Nazi leaders and resulted in the setting up of such extermination camps as *Auschwitz and Treblinka. (See *HOLOCAUST).

FINES   In the Scriptures, fines are imposed for ravishing a virgin (50 shekels), seducing a virgin (50 shekels), falsely accusing one's wife of not being a virgin at *marriage (100 shekels) and one's ox killing a slave (30 shekels). Later fines were imposed by the rabbinical courts (see *BET DIN) for a variety of community offences. From early times, *capital punishment for many offences was transmuted into a fine.

FIRST-BORN   Jewish law recognises the special status of the first-born male. He is entitled to a double portion of the inheritance (*Deut 21:15) and traditionally is dedicated to *God. (See *PIDYON HA-BEN).

FIRST-BORN, FAST OF   A *fast-day celebrated by the *first-born on the day before *Passover (Nisan 14). The fast day is to express gratitude to *God for sparing the first-born of the Israelites in the tenth plague of Egypt (see *Exodus 12). This custom has largely been forgotten.

FIRST-BORN, REDEMPTION OF   See *PIDYON HA-BEN.

FIRST FRUITS   The portion of the harvest dedicated to *God. According to *Deuteronomy 26:1–11, every Israelite must give the first fruits of his crop to the *priests of the *Temple. Traditionally on the second day of *Passover (Nisan 16) a sheaf of barley was offered. *Shavuot was also known as the festival of the first fruits (Hag ha-Bikkurim) and this *pilgrim festival was the time for making the offering. Although the practice ended with the destruction of the Temple in 70CE, first fruit celebrations are still held today in the State of *Israel.

FISH   According to Jewish Law, the only fish which may be eaten must have both fins and scales. As creeping things are also forbidden, in practice no shell fish of any sort is permissible. See *KASHRUT.

FIVE SCROLLS   See *SCROLLS.

FLOOD   The flood is described in *Genesis 6–9. Apparently so evil were human beings that *God decided to destroy them in a great deluge. Only *Noah, his immediate family and a male and female of each species were allowed to survive. After the waters have gone down, God sent a rainbow as a token of his promise that never again would he try to destroy the earth. Great flood legends can be found in other cultures and the Biblical version is not dissimilar to the Babylonian epic of Gilgamesh. It is unique however in its emphasis on the ethical obligations of humanity.

FOOD   See *KASHRUT.

FORGIVENESS   The Ancient Israelites believed that by making *sacrifice, God's forgiveness could be obtained. However the Biblical *prophets constantly emphasized that it was necessary to make full restitution for wrongdoing; there must be full *repentance and this repentance must be accompanied by a complete change of heart (eg. *Jeremiah 4). Nonetheless the Israelites could feel confident of God's forgiveness because God is a loving God and he longs to have a fatherly relationship with his people (eg. *Hosea 11). After the destruction of the *Temple in *Jerusalem in 70CE, there were no more sacrifices. Instead God's forgiveness could be found through *prayer and *fasting. Yet it was still necessary to receive forgiveness from the injured party as well as from God which is why it is customary to ask forgiveness from those who have been wronged before the Day of Atonement. (See *YOM KIPPUR*).

FOUR CAPTIVES   A mediaeval legend. Four *rabbis were captured by Muslim pirates and ransomed by various Jewish communities. The legend arose in Spain and may have some basis in fact.

FOUR QUESTIONS   Questions asked as part of the *Passover liturgy. During the course of the *seder meal, the youngest competent person present asks why the *festival night is different from every other night. This gives the opening for the officiant to explain all the Passover traditions. (See *PESAH*, *SEDER*).

FOUR SPECIES   Four types of plant which are used for the *Sukkot liturgy. According to the *Book of *Leviticus* 23:40, the fruit of goodly trees, palm branches, leafy boughs and willows should be used. The leafy boughs are understood to be myrtles and the fruit is the *etrog. The three branches are bound together and known as the *lulav and held in one hand while the etrog is held in the other. There is no general agreement as to the symbolic meaning of the species. (See *SUKKOT*).

FRANK, JACOB   (1726–1791) Sect founder. Jacob Frank believed himself to be the *messiah and the successor to *Shabbetai Zevi. After his *excommunication by the *rabbis of Poland, Frank and his followers renounced the *Talmud* and were formally baptized as Christians. It became clear however that they regarded Frank rather than Jesus as the messiah and for a time Frank was imprisoned by the Church authorities. Initially adherents of the Frankist sect only married within their community, but by the mid-19th Century intermarriage became more common. The Frankists themselves were frequently accused of immorality. Many of their descendants became prominent among the Polish nobility.

FREE WILL   The belief that each individual can make free moral choices. According to *Deuteronomy* 30:19, *Moses told the Israelites, 'I have set before you life and death, blessing and curse; therefore choose life.' Later the *prophets emphasized the importance of *repentance – a concept that presupposes free will. The belief in free will became a central principle of rabbinic Judaism and philosophers such as *Maimonides tried to reconcile this with the belief in *God's omniscience. In the 20th Century, the insights of modern psychology have proved to be more of a threat to the notion of human freedom, but most Jewish thinkers still maintain that moral responsibility is an inherent part of the created order.

FRINGES   See *ZITZIT.

FROMM   (Yiddish) Term meaning 'strict in religious observance'.

FUNDAMENTALISM   Originally a term used by Christians to mean the belief in the inerrancy of Scripture. *Orthodox *Jews are accused by *Progressive Jews of fundamentalism because they believe that the *Written and *Oral Law were given directly by *God to *Moses on Mount *Sinai and must be obeyed in entirety. Because of this conviction, the findings of modern *Biblical scholars are condemned out of hand (see *DOCUMENTARY HYPOTHESIS). Orthodox Jews, on the other hand, point to the way *Torah has been adapted to the circumstances of modern life and would only acknowledge such sects as the *Karaites to be fundamentalist.

FUNERAL CUSTOMS   The dead are normally buried (see *BURIAL) although cremation is accepted by *Progressive Jews. The corpse is washed and men are buried in their prayer shawls (see *TALLIT). The *Psalms are recited at home and the body is escorted to the cemetery. Before the funeral, the mourners tear a portion of their garments as a sign of mourning (see *KERIAH). In the cemetery, it is usual to halt three times to recite Psalm 91 and after the grave is filled the mourners throw grass and dust behind them. Hands are washed before leaving the cemetery and *Kaddish is recited. Different communities have different funeral customs and orders of service. (See also *BURIAL, *DEATH, *MOURNING).

GABBAI   ('Collector') Officer of the community. Originally a gabbai collected dues or charitable contributions, but the term came to mean any official of the community.

GABRIEL   Archangel. The *angel Gabriel is mentioned in the Hebrew Scriptures in the *Book of *Daniel. The *sages described him as one of the highest angels in the heavenly host. (See *ANGEL).

GALUT (Hebrew. 'Exile') The state of exile from the *Promised Land. The term Galut implies degradation and alienation and is an expression at the despair of the Jews in the face of persecution and expulsion in the *Diaspora. Only by returning to *Zion, could the Israelite people be restored. By extension, the *Kabbalists explained the evil in the world as a consequence of the 'galut of the Divine Presence.' (See also *DIASPORA).

GAMBLING Gambling is forbidden in Jewish law. A distinction is made between those who gamble for fun and those who make a profession of it. So untrustworthy are the latter, that they are not even allowed to act as witnesses in a *bet din.

GAON Title of the head of the great Babylonian *Academies of *Sura and *Pumbedita between the 6th and 11th Centuries CE. At this period the geonim were regarded as the highest religious authorities in Judaism. They were chosen by the hereditary *exilarchs and their responsibilities included interpreting *Talmudic Law, responding to *halakhic questions from the *diaspora communities (see *RESPONSA) and presiding over the supreme court (*bet din). They were maintained by voluntary contributions and local taxes and were expected to maintain a large establishment. After the 9th Century their influence declined and the title was used by the head of the academy in *Israel in the 10th Century and also in Egypt, Damascus and Baghdad in the 12th and 13th Centuries. Famous geonim include Yehudai Gaon, *Saadiah Gaon, Sherira Gaon and Samuel ben Hophni. (See also *PUMBEDITA, *SURA, *YESHIVAH).

GAPAT Acronym for the *Tosafot printed in the *Talmud.

GARDEN OF EDEN See *EDEN.

GARTEL (Yiddish. 'Girdle') Belt worn by the *hasidim. The gartel is worn for prayer in order to fulfil the commandment to divide the upper from the lower body. It is also intended as a reminder of the necessity of girding one's loins in the service of *God.

GEDALIAH, FAST OF *Fast commemorating the death of Gedaliah, the governor of *Judah. He was assassinated in 586BCE thus ending any hope of independence from Babylonian rule. The fast is kept on Tishri 3.

GEHENNA   A valley in *Israel near *Jerusalem. Traditionally it was a place where children were *sacrificed to the pagan god Moloch and, by association, it became the name for *Hell, a place of flames, torment, cruelty and torture. (See *HELL).

GEIGER, ABRAHAM   (1810–1874). Leader of *Reform Judaism. Geiger was the governor of the first meeting of Reform *rabbis in Germany. He himself was rabbi of the Berlin Reform Congregation and director of the Hochschule für die Wissenschaft des Judentums. (See *REFORM JUDAISM).

GEMARA   (Aramaic. 'Completion') The recorded discussions of the *amoraim on the *MISHNAH. The gemara on a topic is printed in the *Talmud surrounding the particular Mishnah passage. (See *TALMUD).

GEMATRIA   (Greek. 'Geometry') The science of interpreting a sacred text according to the numerical value of the letters of the words. There are different systems of gematria and it was much used in the Middle Ages and later by the *kabbalists and followers of *Shabbetai Zevi. It goes back to the 2nd Century CE when Rabbi Judah argued that *Jeremiah* 9:10 ('No one passes through. . .and the beasts are fled') implies that *Judah was deserted for fifty-two years. This is because the numerical value of the Hebrew word for beasts is fifty-two. Gematria was always much criticized and its use has largely died out except in *hasidic circles. (See also *KABBALAH).

GEMILUT HASIDIM   (Hebrew. 'The giving of kindness') Concern for other human beings. Gemilut hasidim is an essentially Jewish virtue and one of the fundamental characteristics of the ethics of Judaism. The *sages taught that the whole religion rests on three pillars, *Torah, *Temple Service and Gemilut Hasidim.

GENESIS   The first book of the *Bible. The *Book of Genesis* tells of the *creation of the universe, the story of the first human beings (see *ADAM and *EVE), the history of the great *flood, the exploits of the patriarchs *Abraham, *Isaac and *Jacob and the story of *Joseph. It ends with the Israelites settling in the land of Egypt. *Genesis* is known as 'Bereshit' ('In the beginning') and is traditionally believed to have been written by *Moses (see *DOCUMENTARY HYPOTHESIS). The essential theme of the book is the development of the *covenantal relationship of *God first with humanity in general (as represented by Adam and *Noah) and later with the *Jews in particular (through their forefather Abraham.) *God's saving plan in history is being unfolded and the chronology is highly schematised (ten generations from Adam to Noah and from Noah to Abraham). *Genesis* is the first book of the *Pentateuch and, with the other four books, is read from every week in the *synagogue. (See *PENTATEUCH, *TORAH, READING FROM*).

GENIZAH (Hebrew. 'Storing') A place for storing old sacred books. It is forbidden by Jewish Law to destroy anything which contains the *Name of *God. Consequently it was the practice to store damaged or obsolete books in small rooms attached to the *synagogue. Many very ancient texts in this way have been preserved and, in some cases (as in Cairo) rediscovered.

GENTILE See *GOYIM*.

GEONIM See *GAON*.

GER (Hebrew. 'Stranger') See *PROSELYTE*.

GERIZIM Mountain in *Israel overlooking the modern town of Nablus. Gerizim is the most sacred place for the *Samaritans. Since they were excluded from participating in the building of the *Temple in *Jerusalem in the time of *Nehemiah, they built their own temple on Mount Gerizim. To this day, the Samaritan community holds their various *festivals there and on their festival of *Passover, they actually stay on the mountain (See also *SAMARITANS*).

GER TOSHAV (Hebrew. 'Righteous stranger') Traditionally a ger toshav is one who keeps the laws given to *Noah after the *flood. He must eschew *idolatry, murder, incest and sexual immorality and eating what has been strangled. Such a person will have a share in the World to Come and thus the *Jews feel no obligation to convert other nations to *Judaism. (See also *PROSELYTE*).

GERSONIDES See *LEVI BEN GERSHON*.

GEROUSIA (Greek 'Old people') Council of elders. The historian

*Josephus dates the gerousia to Biblical times and during the Hellenistic period, it served as a legislative and judicial body. It was probably the forerunner of the Great *Sanhedrin of *Jerusalem.

GET (Hebrew. 'Divorce') Divorce is permitted in Jewish law. It is known as a 'Sefer Keritut' in the *Book of Deuteronomy* (Ch. 24:3) and consists of a document written by the husband and handed to the wife in the presence of witnesses. This document is essential if the woman wants to remarry. The *sages disagreed as to reasonable grounds for divorce and today the practice is that a religious divorce is not granted until the secular legal formalities are completed. In the State of *Israel a get is the only form of divorce. Since it is the husband who gives the wife a divorce, serious hardship can result if the husband refuses to do so. There have been some attempts in modern times to remedy this injustice. Most *Progressive movements do not issue gittin and do not require them for remarriage. (See also *MAMZER*).

GEULLAH (Hebrew. 'Redemption) The title given to several prayers. The section between the *Shema and *Amidah in the morning service is known as Geullah as is the seventh *benediction of the Amidah and the benediction recited after the Great *Hallel in the *Passover *seder.

GEZERAH (Hebrew. 'Decree') Traditionally a Gezerah is a *rabbinic prohibition. By extension it came to mean an anti-Jewish decree, an evil decree or a program.

GHETTO A Jewish residential district. The first enclosed ghetto was that of Venice (1516) and several other cities of Christian Europe restricted the living quarters of the Jewish population. Nonetheless because of *Sabbath regulations (see *ERUV*) Jews often voluntarily chose to live in specific areas (eg. Brooklyn in New York, Golders Green in London). By extension the term ghetto came to be used of any area predominantly occupied by ethnic minorities. Compulsory Jewish ghettos were revived by Hitler and the Nazis; they were used as a means of herding the Jews together before transporting them to the death camps. (See *HOLOCAUST*).

GIDEON One of the *Judges in the *Bible. Gideon's exploits are described in the *Book of Judges* Chs. 6–8. Despite his military success against the Midianites, he refused to be made King of the Israelites declaring, "The Lord will rule over you."

GILGUL (Hebrew. 'The transmigration of souls.') Belief in the transmigration of souls has never been an essential part of the Jewish faith. However it was taught by *Anan ben David, the founder of *Karaism and it was held by some *Kabbalistic authorities. *Levirate marriage was understood as proof of gilgul and it solved the problem of the innocent suffering. Through gilgul it was believed that the *soul was purified and although some scholars maintained that the soul could only be reborn three times, others argued for an infinite number of times in many different forms. (See also *DEATH, *RESURRECTION).

GLEANINGS Remnants of the crop left after harvesting. According to Jewish law, the corners of fields should not be harvested so the gleanings are left for the poor (see *Leviticus 19:9, 23:2). These regulations are discussed further in tractate Peah in the *Talmud.

GNOSTICISM A mode of thinking that flourished in the *Hellenistic period. Gnosticism is characterized by the belief that through special, sometimes esoteric, knowledge, selected human beings can be released from the bondage of their physical lives. Although gnosticism was regarded as a heresy (see *MINIM) by the *sages, gnostic ideas influenced such Jewish philosophers as *Philo.

GOD The supreme Being. *Judaism teaches that God is One; all forms of *idolatry are unequivocally condemned and so exalted is God that it is forbidden to try to contain him in any graven image or likeness. He is the *Creator of the Universe, all-powerful, all-knowing and all-good. Although he is King of all the nations, the *Jews are his special *chosen people. He has made a *covenant with them and they are obliged to keep his *Torah as expressed in the *Written and *Oral law. Ultimately they will be his agents for the *salvation of the whole world. The duty of all human beings is to love him. His name, the Tetragrammaton, is sacred and must not be uttered – euphemisms such as *Adonai ('The Lord') or *Hashem (the Name) must be used instead. Inevitably Jewish philosophers were influenced by the Hellenistic Christian, Muslim or secular ideas of their time (eg. see *PHILO, *MAIMONIDES, *ROSENZWEIG). The *Kabbalists taught a doctrine of emanations from the divine (see *SEFIROT*), arguing that nothing could be said about God himself (*En Sof). Although on occasion the Biblical writers describe Him *anthropomorphically, figurative images are also used such as father, shepherd, king, judge, healer or husband. These are all echoed in the prayers of the *liturgy. Among the very *Orthodox, it is customary to avoid even writing the word 'God' – 'G-d' is preferred.

GOD, NAMES OF   See *NAMES OF GOD*.

GOLDEN CALF   The image made by *Aaron in *Exodus* 32 to satisfy the Israelites' desire for a god. The people were disturbed by *Moses' long absence on Mount *Sinai, but when Moses returned he ordered the calf to be smashed. It was ground into powder and scattered into water, which the Israelites were compelled to drink. The *sages accounted for many subsequent evils by reference to the calf. (See *IDOLATRY*).

GOLEM   A legendary creature made through the power of the letters of the divine name (see *GEMATRIA, *TETRAGRAMMATON*). Golems appear in medieval folk legends. They became slaves of their creators and frequently caused chaos.

GOVERNMENT, PRAYER FOR   See *HA-NOTEN TESHUAH*.

GOYIM   (Yiddish. 'Gentiles') Non-Jews. Through the ages, Jewish attitudes have varied towards the goyim. Sometimes great friendship and sometimes great hostility has been shown. Gentiles are not expected to keep the *Torah. It is sufficient for them to keep the seven laws given to *Noah (see *NOACHIDE LAWS*) and a distinction was made between *idolators and those who believed in One God such as Christians and Muslims. Intercourse with the goyim was always problematic because of the laws of *Kashrut and since the time of *Ezra, *intermarriage has been strictly forbidden.

GRACE BEFORE MEALS   A *benediction said before eating. The blessing over bread (Blessed art thou Lord *God, King of the Universe, who brings forth bread from the earth) is based on *Psalm 104 and exempts the participants from other benedictions.

GRACE AFTER MEALS (Hebrew. *'Birkhat ha-Mazon') A
*benediction said after eating. Normally four blessings are said – for
providing food, for the good land, a request for mercy on the Jewish
people and thanks for God's goodness. The Birkhat ha-Mazon should
only be said at a meal in which bread has been served and is a central
rite in an *Orthodox home. If no bread has been eaten, other blessings
are said.

GREAT ASSEMBLY The supreme authority of the Jewish
religion during the Second *Temple period. Traditionally the Great
Assembly was made up of one hundred and twenty elders known as
'the men of the Great Assembly.' Much of the *liturgy goes back to
the discussions and formulations of this body. (See *Nehemiah 8–9).

GREAT HALLEL See *HALLEL HA-GADOL.

GREAT SANHEDRIN See *SANHEDRIN, GREAT.

GREAT SYNAGOGUE See *SYNAGOGUE, GREAT.

GREETINGS Common Hebrew greetings include *'Shalom'
('Peace') or 'Shalom aleikhem' ('Peace be with you'). On the
*Sabbath it is customary to say 'Shabbat shalom' ('Sabbath Peace')
or the *Yiddish 'Gut Shabbos'. On *festivals 'Hag Sameah' ('Good
festival') or the Yiddish 'Gut yomtov'. On the *New Year, *Jews
wish each other 'Le shanah tovah tikkatenu' ('May you be inscribed
for a good year.') (See *SHALOM).

GREGGER A rattle noisemaker. The gregger is sounded on the
*festival of *Purim so the name of Haman is blotted out while the
Book of *Esther is read. (See *ESTHER, BOOK OF, *PURIM).

GUILT OFFERING See *SACRIFICE.

HABAD A movement within *Hasidim. Habad Hasidim was
founded by *Shneur Zalman and based on the teachings of the *Baal
Shem Tov and Isaac *Luria. The Habad were the first hasidic group
to found their own *yeshivot and their doctrines are centred round the
ideas of knowledge, understanding and wisdom. (See also
*HASIDISM.)

HABAKKUK THE BOOK OF   A Biblical book among the canon
of *Minor Prophets. It was written in the 6th Century BCE after the
Babylonian conquest and the destruction of the *Temple. Its central
question is why do the wicked prosper. The three chapters of the book
contain five short oracles and a prayer which affirms the *prophet's
trust in *God.

HABIRU   An ethnic group mentioned in ancient middle eastern
sources. The *Tel el Amarna letters (15th/14th Century BCE) in particular portray them as bands of bandits who attack local townships.
The precise relationship, between the Habiru and the Hebrews is the
subject of much scholarly speculation.

HADASSAH   An American women's *Zionist organization.
Founded in the early 20th Century, Hadassah is dedicated to providing educational programmes and raising funds for specific projects
in *Israel. (See also *ZIONISM).

HAFTARAH   (Hebrew 'Conclusion') The second reading in the
*synagogue on *Sabbaths and *festivals. The haftarah reading is from
the *Biblical *prophets and is chosen for its connection with the
particular *Torah reading of the day. One *benediction is said before
and four afterwards and it is chanted according to particular rules of
*Cantillation. (See also *TORAH, READING OF).

HAGBAHAH   (Hebrew. 'Lifting') The ceremonial lifting of the
*Torah *scroll during the course of the *synagogue service. The
congregation stands and declares 'This is the Law which *Moses set
before the children of *Israel' (*Deuteronomy* 4:44). After it has been
lifted for all to see, it is rolled and bound ('Gelilah') and returned to
the *Ark. The *Sephardim lift the scroll before rather than after the
reading. (See *TORAH, READING OF).

HAGGADAH   (Hebrew. 'Telling') The order of service of the
*Passover meal. The original haggadah was laid down by the *sages
in the *Mishnah* and includes the *mazzah ritual, the *four questions,
tales of the *rabbis, *midrash on the *Exodus story, the significance
of the *Paschal lamb, the unleavened bread and the *bitter herbs, the
*hallel, *grace after the meal and *benedictions. Extra poetry and
songs have been added to the haggadah over the centuries. The oldest

preserved manuscript goes back to the 10th Century. Illustrated versions tend to be of the Spanish type (with full-page Biblical scenes), the *Ashkenazic (decorated in the margins round the liturgical text) or the Italian. The *progressive movement have produced their own haggadot with modified prayers and there is also a *Karaite version (See also *PASSOVER, *SEDER).

HAGGAI, THE BOOK OF   A *Biblical book among the canon of *Minor Prophets. Haggai himself is mentioned in the *Book of *Ezra* 5:1. His prophecies are mainly concerned with the rebuilding of the *Temple. His first oracles can be dated to the late 6th Century BCE. After the people had begun to rebuild, Haggai predicted that the second Temple would be even more splendid than the first and that the Israelites' leader, *Zerubbabel, would be the 'signet ring of the Lord'.

HAGIOGRAPHA   (Greek. 'Holy Writings') The third section of the *Bible (the first being *Law and *Prophets). It is known in Hebrew as *Ketuvim and includes *Psalms, *Proverbs, *Job, *Song of Songs, *Ruth, *Lamentations, *Ecclesiastes, *Esther, *Daniel, *Ezra, *Nehemiah and *I and II *Chronicles.

HAIR   See *PAIS.

HAKHAM   (Hebrew 'Wise') *Rabbinic title. Originally scholars who had not formally received *semikhah were known as hakham. It was also used as a title for the third in status after the *nasi and *av bet din. Among the *Sephardim, the title is used for the local rabbi.

HAKHEL   (Hebrew 'Assemble') The assembly of the seventh year. According to *Deuteronomy* 31:10, the Israelites were to assemble every seventh year to 'hear and learn to fear the Lord your *God.' Although the practice is mentioned in the *Mishnah, it was discontinued after the destruction of the *Temple.

HAKHNASAT KALLAH   (Hebrew. 'Bringing in the bride'). The practice of providing a *dowry for poor brides. During the Middle Ages, societies were set up to raise dowries known as Hakhnasat Kallah societies. (See also *DOWRY, *KETUBAH).

HAKHNASAT OREHIM (Hebrew. 'Entertaining travellers') The duty of hospitality. Hospitality is a central duty of *Judaism; it is mentioned in connection with such *Biblical figures as *Abraham, Laban and Jethro and is often described in later *rabbinic literature.

HAKKAFOT A ceremonial circuit. The *Mishnah* describes how the *Lulav was carried ceremoniously round the *Temple during the *festival of *Sukkot. Today the *Torah *scrolls are carried round the *synagogue on *Simhat Torah and, in some communities, brides encircle their husbands and mourners encircle the coffin at *funerals.

HALAKHAH (Hebrew. 'Way of going') A commandment or the whole body of Jewish law. It is a fundamental tenet of *Orthodoxy that the entire *halakhah goes back to *Moses who was given it by *God on Mount *Sinai. It is made up of the *Written Law as recorded in the *Pentateuch and the *Oral Law which includes later *responsa and established custom. In the days of the *Temple, the *Sadducees denied the authority of the Oral Law and this stand was also taken later by the *Karaites. However the *Oral Law was collected by *Judah ha-Nasi in the *Mishnah* and the discussions of the *amoraim are recorded in the *Talmud*. Subsequently it was *codified in such volumes as *Maimonides' *Mishneh Torah* and Karo's *Shulhan Arukh*. While the Orthodox accept the halakhah as totally binding, the *Progressive movements have adapted it to the exigences of modern life. This process has been unequivocally rejected by the Orthodox. (See also *CODES*, *MISHNAH*, *ORAL LAW*, *TALMUD*, *TORAH*, *WRITTEN LAW*).

HALIZAH Release for a childless widow from the duty of marrying her brother-in-law. (See *LEVIRATE MARRIAGE*).

HALLAH Originally a portion of dough set aside for the *priests of the *Temple as part of the grain *sacrifice (see *Numbers* 15:19–20). The *Orthodox still set aside a piece of hallah the size of an olive when making bread and subsequently burn it. More commonly hallah refers to the plaited load which is eaten on the *Sabbath.

HALLEL *Psalms 113–118. The Hallel is chanted on the *festivals of *Passover, *Sukkot and *Hanukkah. It is mentioned in

67

the *Talmud* as being incorporated into the *synagogue liturgy from an early period. At the *Passover *seder it is divided into two parts, one of which is said before and one after the meal.

HALLEL HA-GADOL (Hebrew. 'The Great Hallel') *Psalm 136. The Great Hallel is said on *Sabbaths and *festivals.

HALLELUJAH (Hebrew. 'Praise the Lord') An expression of praise which occurs frequently in the *Psalms.

HALUTZ (Hebrew. 'Pioneer') The Jewish settlers in Palestine before the foundation of the State of *Israel in 1948.

HAMESH MEGILLOT See *SCROLLS*.

HAMEZ (Hebrew. 'Leaven') Fermented dough. Hamez could not be used in the making of meal offerings for *Temple *sacrifices. It is also forbidden during the *Passover *festival. On the eve of the festival, it is customary to conduct a ceremonial search for leaven throughout the house. (See *PESAH*).

HANDS, LAYING ON From early times the laying on of hands was a symbol for the transfer of authority – thus *Moses laid hands on *Joshua in front of the whole congregation (see *Numbers* 27:18–23). This tradition has persisted and is part of the ceremony of ordination for *rabbis. (See *SEMIKHAH*).

HANDS, WASHING OF According to the *halakhah, hands must be ceremonially washed after rising from sleep, touching a corpse, urinating or defecating and before eating or praying. (See *ABLUTION*).

HA-NOTEN TESHVAH (Hebrew. 'Prayer for the government'). The *Mishnah* emphasizes the duty of prayers for the civil authorities and such prayers became a regular part of the *Synagogue liturgy in the 14th Century. Nowadays the prayer is generally recited after the reading of the *Torah scroll and, in *Orthodox services, is often the only part of the service in the vernacular.

HANUKKAH (Hebrew 'Dedication'). The winter *festival of lights. Hanukkah lasts for eight days beginning on Kislev 25. It commemorates the *Maccabee victory over the *Hellenists and the miraculous lasting of the holy oil for eight days rather than one. In fact the festival goes back earlier. In the days of the *Temple, torches and lamps were kindled in the Temple courts and water poured out so it reflected back the lights. Today it has become a major festival as a substitute for the Christian Christmas which occurs at much the same time. All observant households have a *menorah for eight candles and one is lit on the first day, two on the second and so on. Card playing and spinning the *dreidel are associated with the festival; it is forbidden to *fast and the *hallel is chanted in *synagogue. It is a particularly important holiday in *Israel as it symbolises the survival of the Jewish people against enormous odds.

HAROSET   Concoction eaten at the *Passover *seder. Haroset is made from *mazzah meal, fruit, wine and spices. It symbolises the mortar made by the Israelite slaves in Egypt and is eaten with mazzah and *bitter herbs. (See *PESAH).

HARVEST FESTIVAL   All three *pilgrim festivals were originally agricultural festivals. Passover (*Pesah) commemorates the start of the barley harvest and the first sheaf was offered in the *Temple. *Shavuot (the feast of Weeks) marks the conclusion of the grain harvest and *Sukkot (the feast of tabernacles) was also known as the feast of ingathering. Celebrations were held to give thanks that the harvest was brought in and this was an occasion of merrymaking (*Isaiah 16:10). (See *PESAH, *SHAVUOT, *SUKKOT, *TU B'AV).

HA-SHEM   (Hebrew. 'the Name') Ha-Shem is frequently used as a substitute for the name of God when the *tetragrammaton appears in the Hebrew text (See *ADONAI, *NAMES OF GOD, *TETRA-GRAMMATON).

HASHKAMAH   (Hebrew. 'Early rising') Early morning prayers said before the official morning service (see *SHAHARIT).

HASHKAVAH   (Hebrew. 'Lay to rest.') Memorial prayer. The hashkavah is the *Sephardi name for the memorial prayer which corresponds to the *Ashkenazi *Yikzor. (See *MEMORIAL PRAYERS).

HASHKIVENU (Hebrew. 'Cause us to lie down') Introductory word of the second *benediction after the *Shema at the *synagogue evening service (See *MAARIV). It is mentioned in the *Talmud and asks for *God's protection during the coming night.

HASIDEI ASHKENAZ (Hebrew. 'The pious ones of Germany') 12th and 13th Century movement among German Jewry. The movement was influenced by *merkabah mysticism. Its leaders included Samuel b. Kolonymus and the writings of Abraham ibn Ezra and *Saadiah Gaon were much read. Disciples of the movement displayed extraordinary religious fervour. The ultimate sign of love for *God was martyrdom for the faith (*kiddush ha-shem) and adherents of the Hasidei Ashkenaz showed great courage under persecution. The movement shows similarity to Christian pietism; it was influential on the whole of medieval Jewry including the communities of Spain, Poland and Lithuania.

HASIDEI UMMOT HA-OLAM (Hebrew. 'The pious ones of the world's nations') Righteous *gentiles. The hasidei ummot ha-olam are those who observe the seven commandments of *Noah (see *NOACHIDE LAWS) and who are therefore believed to have a place in the world to come. Since World War II, the term has increasingly been used for those non-Jews who helped individuals escape from the Nazi *holocaust. (See also *GER TOSHAV).

HASIDIM (Hebrew. 'the pious') Those who led pious lives. In the Talmudic period the hasidim ha-rishonim ('the just and pious men') were famous for their *ritual purity and scrupulousness in obeying the *mitzvot. The hasidim ve-anshei ma'aseh (the 'pious who were also men of action') were notable for their good deeds and miracle working. Although the hasidim were always admired, the *sages stressed that intelligence as well as piety were necessary to be pleasing to *God. (See also *HASIDISM)

HASIDIM, SEFER (Hebrew. 'Book of the Pious') A medieval moral guide. The *Sefer Hasidim* dates from the 13th Century. It was the chief ethical work of the *Hasidei Ashkenaz movement and is attributed to Rabbi Judah he-Hasid. (See *HASIDEI ASHKENAZ).

HASIDISM A religious movement which emerged in Eastern Europe in the late 18th Century. Hasidism was characterised by great enthusiasm, ecstasy and extraordinary personal devotion to the individual leader, the *zaddik. Such leaders included *Israel b. Eliezer (Baal Shem Tov), Dov Baer of Mezhirech and Jacob Joseph of Polonnoye. These formed circles of disciples round them and were the founders of dynasties of zaddikim. Although initially the *Orthodox disapproved of Hasidism as being influenced by *Shabbateanism and *Frankism (See *ELIJAH BEN SOLOMON ZALMAN), by the mid 19th Century, and in the face of the threat of the *Reform movement, it was accepted as a legitimate form of *Judaism. Their worship is notable for its burning enthusiasm and includes song and dance. Social life is centred round the court of the particular zaddik and Hasidic teaching is profoundly influenced by the *Kabbalistic ideas of Isaac *Luria. The Eastern European centres of Hasidism were destroyed in the *holocaust, but centres still flourish in the United Kingdom, United States and Israel. The most numerous hasidic sects are the *Liubavicher (*Habad), the *Satmar, *Braslav, the Klausenburg-Sandz, the Telem and the Skver. Hasidic men are readily recognisable by their distinctive dress (*gartel, Homberg hat, *streimel, dark suit, visible *zitzit) and the women always follow the laws of modesty (knee-covering skirt, long sleeves, high neck and the married women in *sheitels). Hasidism rejects modern forms of contraception so hasidic families tend to be large.

HASKALAH   The secular enlightenment of the 18th and 19th Centuries. Jewish followers of the haskalah were known as the *maskilim and they were bitterly opposed by the *Orthodox *mitnaggedim. Moses *Mendelssohn is regarded as the forerunner of the Haskalah and enlightenment was brought about by educated *Jews increasingly wanting to experience secular culture. The first school influenced by the Haskalah was the Berlin Freischule opened in 1778. The curriculum was taught in German rather than *Yiddish and included science, history, geography, French and mathematics. The maskilim were anxious to achieve emancipation from the civil disabilities imposed by the European governments against Jews and were extremely patriotic towards their host countries. The movement spread across Europe as far as Russia in the 19th Century. Increasingly Judaism came to be seen as a religious system rather than as a peoplehood and the community became more diverse. (See also *MASKILIM, *MENDELSSOHN, MOSES, *MITNAGGEDIM, *PROGRESSIVE JUDAISM, *REFORM JUDAISM).

71

HASKAMAH (Hebrew. 'Agreement') A formal rabbinic approval of a printed book. From the 16th Century, some communities insisted that books should only be published if they carried a haskamah. This was both a tool of censorship and a positive recommendation.

HASMONEANS *Talmudic title for the *Maccabees. The Hasmoneans led the rebellion against the Selucid kings in the 2nd Century BCE. Under the leadership of Mattathias and his sons *Judah, Simon and Jonathan, an independent Jewish kingdom was established until the Roman conquest in 67 BCE. (See *MACCABEES, BOOK OF).

HA-TIKVAH (Hebrew. 'Hope') The title of the national anthem of the State of *Israel. The verse was written by Naphtali Herz Imber in 1878 and the tune is based on a *Sephardi melody and Smetana's Vltava.

HAVDALAH (Hebrew. 'Distinction') Ceremony for the ending of the *Sabbath. *Benedictions are said over wine, a *candle and spices and a final blessing thanking *God for the distinction between the sacred and the profane. Different customs are practised in the different communities, but a plaited lighted candle is generally extinguished in the wine. The havdalah ceremony is said to date back to the days of the *Great Synagogue. (See *SABBATH).

HAVER (Hebrew. 'Member') A member of a group which observed certain *tithing laws in *Mishnaic and *Talmudic times. The regulations described in the *Talmud for becoming a haver are not dissimilar to the rules outlined in the *Qumran *Manual of Discipline. However many haverim seem to have lived normally in the community. In the time of the *geonim, a haver was simply a scholar.

HAVURAH A mutual benefit society. Originally a havurah was set up for a specific aim such as visiting the sick or burying the dead. Increasingly in the 20th Century, it has come to mean a small informal worship group. The havurah movement has been responsible for some highly innovative liturgy in recent years.

HAZZAN Cantor. In the *talmudic era, the hazzan was an officer of the local community who performed particular duties in the *synagogue. In the *gaonic era, a hazzan was the permanent representative of the congregation. Later the hazzan provided melodies for the *piyyutim when they became part of the liturgy and from this he developed the role of leading the chanting in the services. Today the hazzan is in charge of the synagogue music and leads the congregation in prayer. In recent years, the *Progressive movement has trained women as cantors, but among the *Orthodox only men are eligible. (See also *CANTILLATION).

HEAD, COVERING OF   See *SHEITEL, *YARMULKE.

HEAR O ISRAEL   See *SHEMA.

HEAVEN   The abode of *God. The *Bible indicates that Heaven is located in the upper part of the universe and the *sages taught that there were many heavens in which the various orders of *angels live. Reward and punishment are fundamental *principles of the Jewish faith and it is believed that the righteous will ascend to Heaven after *death. The term 'Heaven' is also frequently used as an alternative to *God (see *TETRAGRAMMATON) as in 'the fear of Heaven' and 'for the sake of Heaven'. (See also *EDEN, GARDEN OF, *PARADISE).

HEAVE OFFERING   See *SACRIFICE.

HEBREW   The language of the ancient Israelites. Hebrew is a Semitic language. Although it was superseded by *Aramaic by the *Jews in c.2nd Century BCE, it continued to be used for the liturgy and for *Scroll reading. *Yiddish became the vernacular language of the Eastern European Jews and *Ladino and Arabic for the *Sephardim, but nonetheless, Hebrew was chosen as the language of the Jewish State and is thus the official language of *Israel.

HEBREWS   The Jewish people, also known as Israelites. (See also *HABIRU).

HEDER   (Hebrew 'Room') An elementary school. Each community, however small, had at least one heder. Small boys and a few girls were taught literacy through the media of the *Prayerbook and *Pentateuch. The teacher was known as a *melamed and this was the first step in Jewish education and preparation for *yeshivah. Such schools were despised by the *maskilim as perpetuating Jewish isolation and ignorance of the *gentile world. Today the term heder is frequently used for a traditional religion school attached to a *synagogue which children attend in addition to their secular school.

HEFKER (Hebrew 'Ownerless') Property which has no apparent owner. This property is, according to Jewish law, exempt from the laws of *tithe. These regulations, which were complicated, have fallen into disuse since the law of the land supersedes Jewish law in this area.

HEIFFER, RED See *RED HEIFFER.

HEKDESH Property which is sacred to *God. Property conse-crated to the *Temple came under category of hekdesh, the laws concerning which were highly complex. The practice fell into disuse with the destruction of the Temple in 70CE although it was still possible to give away property to a charity or the *synagogue. Because of the charitable connection, the term hekdesh came to mean a shelter for the poor, sick or old.

HEKHALOT, BOOKS OF Collections of *midrash. The books are attributed to Ishmael ben Elisha (2nd Century CE) and contain mystical descriptions (see *MERKAVAH). Some of the more poetic passages have been incorporated into the *Ashkenazi literature.

HELL The place of torment for the wicked after death. (See also *GEHENNA, *HEAVEN).

HELLENISM The ideas associated with the ancient Greeks from the 4th Century BCE. Greek ideas spread through the Middle East after the conquests of Alexander the Great. Although the *sages did their best to counteract Hellenism, its influence is to be found in the *Talmud, rabbinic literature and the works of Jewish philosophers. (See also *DUALISM, *HANUKKAH, *PHILO).

HEREM (Hebrew 'Separated out.') A prohibition or ban. In Biblical times, spoils taken in war were herem – they could not be used or enjoyed. Later a herem was a ban placed on an individual. It was the ultimate sanction against an erring individual and involved total exclusion from the Jewish community for an indefinite period. It was often employed against *heretics who were thus completely cut off socially, financially and religiously. Among those who were subject to herem, were the philosopher Benedict *Spinoza and the disciples of Jacob *Frank and *Shabbetai Zevi. (See also *HERESY).

HERESY Belief in unorthodox religious ideas. While a heretic is still regarded as a *Jew, he was described as an *apikoros or *min. The traditional punishment was *herem which was justified on the grounds of maintaining unanimity within the community. Examples of movements which have been deemed heretical in the past include *Samaritanism, *Christianity, *Karaism, *Shabbataism, *Frankism, *Hasidism (for a short time) and all the *Progressive movements.

HERMANEUTICS The system of *biblical interpretation employed by the *sages and later authorities. It was believed that by following certain rules, a deeper meaning of the text could be discovered. The best-known systems of hermaneutics were devised by Rabbi *Hillel (seven rules), Rabbi *Ishmael (thirteen rules) and Rabbi Eliezer b. Yose ha-Gelili. Later it was usual among the *kabbalists to understand the sacred text in terms of sacred numbers and *gematria.

HEROD The name of several rulers of *Judea in the 1st Centuries BCE/CE. Herod I (73–4BCE) (the Great) was responsible for rebuilding the *Temple in *Jerusalem and constructing the fortress on *Masada.

HERZL, THEODOR (1860–1904) Founder of the World *Zionist Organisation. After attending the *Dreyfus trial, he became convinced that a Jewish homeland was the only solution to *anti-Semitism. He was the author of *Der Judenstaat* (The Jewish State) which went through many editions and he was chairman of the First Zionist Conference. After the foundation of the State of *Israel, his remains were brought to *Jerusalem and the anniversary of his death (Tammuz 20) is kept as a memorial day. (See also *ZIONISM).

HESSAH DAAT (Hebrew 'Removal of the Mind') Lack of attention when performing religious duties so that the action becomes invalid. The rituals which required complete concentration were separation of the *heave offering, keeping the laws of *ritual purity and preparing the ashes of the *red heiffer.

75

HEVRA KADDISHA (Aramaic. 'Holy brotherhood') A mutual benefit society. From the 17th Century the term was used exclusively for *burial societies. Because the dead cannot be buried for material gain, the duty of burial devolves on the community as a whole. Membership of the hevra kaddisha was a communal duty and regarded as a great honour. (See also *FUNERAL CUSTOMS).

HEXATEUCH The first six books of the Bible. The Hexateuch comprises *Genesis, *Exodus, *Leviticus, *Numbers, *Deuteronomy and *Joshua. (See also *DOCUMENTARY HYPOTHESIS, *PENTATEUCH).

HIGH HOLY DAYS The *festivals of *Rosh Hashanah (New Year) and *Yom Kippur (the Day of Atonement). The ten days between the two are often described as the High Holy Day period. (See *ROSH HASHANA, *YOM KIPPUR).

HIGH PLACES Shrine built on a hill in the Land of *Israel. Once the *Temple in *Jerusalem had been built, it was condemned as *idolatrous to worship at a high place. However once the *Northern Kingdom had separated from the *Southern, the *Northern Kings encouraged worship at the high places to prevent their people going down to Jerusalem.

HIGH PRIEST The Israelite Chief *Priest who served in the *Temple in *Jerusalem. According to *Leviticus, the High Priest must be a descendant of *Aaron, but as the office became increasingly political under the *Hasmonean kings, a Hasmonean High Priest was appointed. By Roman times, the office was constantly criticised by the *Pharisees as being the tool of the government. The High Priest wore the blue robe, the *ephod, the *breastplate and the *urim and thummim. He was the only person who entered the *Holy of Holies once a year on *Yom Kippur. After the destruction of the *Temple in 70CE the office lapsed. (See also *AARON, *AARONIDES, *KOHEN, *LEVITE, *PRIEST).

HILLEL (Early 1st Century CE) Sage of the Second *Temple period. Hillel was president of the *Sanhedrin and formulated the seven rules of *hermaneutics. He was the last of the pairs (*zugot) of scholars with *Shammai and his school (*Bet Hillel) was considered to be more lenient than that of *Bet Shammai. He was the author of the saying 'What is hateful to you, do not unto your neighbour; this is the entire *Torah, all the rest is commentary.' (See *BET HILLEL AND BET SHAMMAI).

HILLUL *HA-SHEM (Hebrew 'Profanation of the Name') An action that profanes the name of *God. Hillul ha-Shem is any action which brings disgrace to the Jewish community and sets a bad example. It is the converse of *Kiddush ha-Shem.

HINNOM, VALLEY OF See *GEHENNA.

HIRSCH, SAMSON RAPHAEL (1808–1888) Most prominent opponent of the *Reform movement in the 19th Century. An *Orthodox *rabbi, he defended traditional *Judaism through his writings and educational work. He founded several schools which were strictly Orthodox, but which also taught secular subjects and he served important congregations in Germany. Although initially he tried to maintain the unity of the Jewish establishment, he ultimately recognised that separation between the Orthodox and Reform was inevitable. (See also *ORTHODOX JUDAISM, *REFORM JUDAISM).

HOLENT *Ashkenazi *Sabbath dish. Holent is prepared the day before the Sabbath and cooked in a very slow oven overnight to avoid breaking the Sabbath Law against kindling a light on the Sabbath. It is generally made of beans. The *Sephardi equivalent is known as 'hamin'.

HOL HA-MOED (Hebrew 'Weekday of the *festival'). Name given for the intermediate days of *Passover and *Sukkot. The first and last days of both festivals are *holy days, but normal work may be done on the in-between days. Nonetheless *mourning is forbidden and no *marriages may be celebrated (See also *PESAH, *SUKKOT).

HOLINESS CODE The laws enumerated in *Leviticus 17–26. These laws relate to *sacrifice, *sexual conduct, the *priesthood, the *Holy Days, *Sabbatical years and various *benedictions and warnings. The Holiness Code is traditionally thought to have been written by *Moses although most scholars now date it to the First *Temple period. It parallels the codes in *Deuteronomy 12–28 and *Exodus 20–23.33.

HOLOCAUST (Hebrew 'Shoah'). The destruction of the European Jewish community between 1933–1945. The Nazi government of Germany was committed to *anti-Semitic policies. Until the declaration of war in 1939, Jews were systematically excluded from public office and the intellectual and cultural life of the time. After 1939 emigration was no longer possible. Jews were then herded into *ghettos and finally transported east and slaughtered in concentration camps (see *AUSCHWITZ). Six million Jews are estimated to have died in the holocaust. Nisan 27 is kept as the Holocaust Memorial Day and *Yahrzeit is observed for the unknown dead on Tevat 10. The holocaust finally destroyed the *shtetls and *yeshivot of Eastern European Jewry and persuaded the world community that the *Zionist hope of a Jewish homeland must become a reality. The state of *Israel was created in 1948. The holocaust has underlined the religious problem of reconciling human evil with the existence of a loving *God.

HOLY DAYS Five holy days besides the weekly *Sabbath are mentioned in the *Bible:- Passover (*Pesah), Weeks (*Shavuot) and Tabernacles (*Sukkot) – the three *pilgrim festivals – and the *High Holy Days – the New Year (*Rosh Hashanah) and the Day of Atonement (*Yom Kippur). As both Pesah and Sukkot are seasons only the first and last days of each period count as holy days, (for the intermediate days see *HOL HA-MOED). All work is forbidden on holy days and each *festival or *fast has its own particular customs. In the *diaspora among the *Orthodox, each holy day (except for Yom Kippur and the Sabbath) is celebrated for two days because of the doubt of the dating of each new month (See *SECOND DAY OF FESTIVALS). In *Israel and among the *Progressive only one day is observed. On the post biblical festivals such as *Hanukkah, *Purim, *Lag Ba'Omer and on fasts such as the Fast of *Gedaliah and *Tishah b'Av, work is permitted. (Also see entries under individual holy days).

HOLY OF HOLIES Inner shrine of the *Temple in *Jerusalem. The Holy of Holies was only entered by the *High Priest once a year on *Yom Kippur (the Day of Atonement). It had no windows and a raised floor so it was the highest spot in the Temple. Here the *Ark of the Covenant was kept and it was regarded as the most holy spot in the Jewish world. (See also *TEMPLE).

HOLY PLACES   Today, the principle holy places in the Jewish tradition are the *Wailing Wall in *Jerusalem (the last remnant of the *Temple of King *Herod) and the tombs of various Biblical and Talmudic figures. Increasingly with the destruction of Eastern European Jewry in the *Holocaust, the death camps such as *Auschwitz and the remains of Jewish quarters in towns which had important Jewish communities have become holy places. Among the *Hasidim, the court of the *zaddik is a place of *pilgrimage. (See *PILGRIMAGE).

HOLY SPIRIT   The spirit of *God. The *Hebrew term 'Ruah ha-Kodesh' is used to mean divine spirit in the *Bible (eg. *Psalm 51:13). The prophet *Joel predicted that in the final days, God would pour out his spirit on all flesh. The *sages referred to the Spirit as divine inspiration and whether or not a book had been inspired by the Holy Spirit was the criterion for incorporation into the *canon of scripture. Although it was believed that *prophecy had disappeared from *Israel in the period of the Second *Temple and that outpourings of the Spirit would be a characteristic of the *world to come, the *rabbis taught that communication with the Holy Spirit was possible after a long period of religious discipline.

HOME   The home is an important focus of Jewish life. The *mezuzah fixed to the doorposts is a reminder of the sacred nature of the home. The *Sabbath *candles are reminiscent of the *Temple and the dining table on which *kiddush and *havdalah are celebrated recalls the Temple's altars. In an *Orthodox home, *grace is said before and after meals, the *Sabbath is kept, the laws of *shatnes and *kashrut are observed and sexual relationships are regulated accordingly to the laws of *niddah. Both *Pesah and *Sukkot are essentially home *festivals with the *seder meal and the construction of the *sukkah. *Hanukkah candles are lit at home and *Purim is a time of home merrymaking. Birth and Death ceremonies such as circumcision (*Bris), the redemption of the first born (*Pidyon Ha-Ben) and mourning (sitting *shiva) are all conducted at home and the home is the fundamental place of education of children into the values and practices of *Judaism. The above reflects the ideal; inevitably the growth of secularism, increased *divorce and the breakdown of the nuclear family has threatened the primacy of the Jewish home as the bulwark against *assimilation.

HOMILECTICS The art of preaching. Traditionally sermons are based on Biblical verses which provide grounds for explaining or expounding particular ritual practices or ethical teaching. Generally the Biblical verse was part of the assigned *Torah or *haftarah reading for the week. (See also *DARSHAN, *MAGGID).

HOMOSEXUALITY Sexual relationships between people of the same gender. Such relationships are condemned unequivocally in the *Bible (eg. *Leviticus 18:22) and this stand was continued by the *sages. Homosexuality is perceived as debasing human life, as being contrary to the first Biblical command to be fruitful and multiply, as 'spilling the seed in vain' and as being threatening to the Jewish *home. The *Progressive movement has taken a more tolerant line and there are even a few 'Gay Congregations' in the United States.

HOSEA A *minor prophet of the Hebrew *Bible. The *Book of Hosea* was produced in the *Northern Kingdom in the 8th Century BCE and contains an account of the *prophet's marriage to an unfaithful woman and the birth of his three children. This relationship is understood as a symbol of *God's relationship with faithless *Israel (Chs 1–3). In Chs 4–14, which may well have a different author, the prophet condemns *idolatry and moral corruption. The book ends with a plea to turn back to God.

HOSHANAH RABBAH (Hebrew 'The Great Hosanna') The seventh day of the festival of *Sukkot. Traditionally Hoshanah Rabbah was regarded as the day when *God's decrees are finally sealed. In the *Temple, seven circuits (*Hakkafot) were made around the altar carrying the *lulav. Now the *bimah is circulated in the *synagogue and after the seventh circuit, willow branches are beaten on the ground. There is a widespread custom of sitting up the night before Hoshanah Rabbah to read through the whole *Pentateuch (See *SUKKOT).

HOSHANOT Prayers recited during the *synagogue Hoshanah Rabbah service. They consist of short lines, each of which begins and ends with the word 'Hoshana'. (See *HOSHANA RABBAH).

HOSPITALITY An essential duty. The *sages gave much advice on how to entertain guests and in the Middle Ages, *Hakhnasat

Orehim ('hospitality') societies were founded to look after Jewish travellers. (See *HAKHNASAT OREHIM).

HOST, DESECRATION OF   See *DESECRATION OF THE HOST

HOUSE OF WORSHIP   See   *BET HA-MIDRASH,   *HIGH PLACES, *SANCTUARY, *SYNAGOGUE, *TEMPLE.

HUKKAT HA-GOY   (Hebrew 'Custom of the *gentile') A custom forbidden because of its *idolatrous or heathen connotation. According to *Leviticus 20:23, *Jews may not 'walk in the custom of the nation'. As a result wearing particular kinds of clothing are forbidden as leading to lewdness and the *Orthodox have condemned the *Reform practice of organ music and mixed *synagogue choirs on the same basis.

HUMMASH   (Hebrew '*Pentateuch') The first five books of the *Bible. The Hummash is printed in separate editions to be used in *synagogues. (See *PENTATEUCH).

HUPPAH   (Hebrew 'Canopy'). The Jewish marriage canopy. *Weddings are conducted under the huppah which symbolises the marriage chamber. A huppah is open at the sides and can be anything from a simple *tallit held over the bridal party to an elaborate bower of flowers.

HYMN   *Liturgical song.

ICONOGRAPHY   Primarily the art of illustrated manuscripts. Following the commandments against making graven images, (see *TEN COMMANDMENTS), there is little iconography from Jews living in Muslim countries. No doubt influenced by their Christian neighbours, manuscripts from Europe are illustrated by *Biblical and *aggadic scenes and vary according to their community of origin. In particular illustrations can be found in *Haggadah, *Mahzor and *Siddur manuscripts. (See also *HAGGADAH).

IDOLATRY   The worship of idols. Idolatry is unequivocally forbidden in the *Torah (see *TEN COMMANDMENTS) and idolatry, together wrath, *murder and *incest are sins that should not be

81

committed even to save life. Idol worship, however, persisted in Ancient *Israel; the cults of *Baal and Asherah were condemned by the *prophets and the *Bible gives instances of child *sacrifice to Moloch (*II*Kings*), star worship (*Amos* 5:26) and sacred prostitution (*Ezekiel* 16:17). The reforms of King Hezekiah and *Josiah must be seen in this context. The *sages forbade any contact with idolaters; food may not be shared with idol worshippers and no houses in the land of *Israel may be leased or sold to an idolator.

IKKARIM   (Hebrew 'Articles') Articles of faith. Many authorities have formulated the articles of Jewish faith. *Philo spoke of eight essential principles, *Maimonides set out thirteen principles and Joseph Albo argued for three ikkarim (the existence of *God, the divine origin of *Torah and reward and punishment.) The tradition was continued into the modern period with such thinkers as Moses *Mendelssohn. Nonetheless every Jew is part of the *covenant of *Israel independent of his or her attachment to dogmas. The most important Jewish belief is that expressed in the *Shema ('Hear O Israel, the Lord our God, the Lord is One.')

ILLEGITIMACY   See *MAMZER*

IMITATION OF GOD   The obligation to imitate *God in his nature and actions. The *Book of *Genesis* teaches that humanity was made in the image of God and according to *Deuteronomy* 10:12, Man is commanded to 'walk in all his ways'. The *sages explained the Deuteronomic verse by declaring that human beings should imitate the attributes of God by such activities as visiting the sick and clothing the naked. *Maimonides lists the emulation of God in all his ways as one of the essential commandments.

IMMERSION   See *MIKVEH*.

INCENSE   The burning of incense accompanied the *sacrifices in the *Temple in ancient times and the *High Priest used to carry incense into the *Holy of Holies once a year on *Yom Kippur. *Exodus* 30:34–38 enumerates the ingredients of incense and there was an *altar of incense in the Temple Court. Although the use of incense is discussed in the *Talmud*, it ceased to be used in worship.

INCEST Sexual relationships between close relations. The prohibited relationships are listed in *Leviticus* 18:6–18 and the *Talmud* extended this catalogue. The product of an incestuous (as well as an *adulterous) relationship is a *mamzer. Incest, together with *idolatry and *murder, are the three crimes which must never be committed even to save life. (See also *MAMZER).

INCLINATION, EVIL See *YETZER HA-RA.

INCLINATION, GOOD See *YETZER HA-TOV.

INGATHERING OF THE EXILES The return of the *Jews to the land of *Israel. The ingathering of the exiles is mentioned by the *Biblical *Prophets (eg. *Jeremiah 23:3). The *sages taught that it would be a feature of the days of the *messiah and it is looked forward to in the tenth *benediction of the *Amidah – 'Blessed art thou O Lord who gatherest the dispersed of thy people Israel.' In modern times, since the foundation of the State of Israel, the ingathering has been understood as the immigration of the Jews of the *diaspora to become Israeli citizens. This is understood independently of the messianic age. (See also *DIASPORA, *GALUT).

INHERITANCE The laws of inheritance determined by the *sages are as follows:- i) Sons and their descendants (with the first-born receiving a double portion) ii) daughters and their descendants iii) the father iv) brothers and their descendants v) sisters and their descendants vi) father's father vii) paternal uncles and their descendants viii) paternal aunts and their descendants ix) paternal great-granddaughter etc. It was the case of Zelophehad in *Numbers 27:8.11 that determined a daughter's right of inheritance.

INITIATION See *BRIS, *MIKVEH, *PROSELYTES.

INTENT See *KAVVANAH.

INTERMARRIAGE *Marriage between a *Jew and a *gentile. Since the time of *Ezra, intermarriage has been deplored by the Jewish community as leading to *apostasy and *idolatry. It was rare before the 19th century, but with emancipation, equal access to the universities and the professions, it has become increasingly common.

No *Orthodox *rabbi will participate at an intermarriage, but particularly in the United States, some *progressive rabbis will do so to prevent the family being lost to *Judaism.

ISAAC   Son of the *patriarch *Abraham by his wife *Sarah. Isaac's birth was miraculous in that his mother was beyond childbearing age and, from birth, he was the heir to the *covenant rather than his elder brother Ishmael (who was the son of the concubine Hagar). Isaac was a nomadic herdsman who was rich in stock. The *sages taught that he was one of only three beings who was not subject to the *yetzer ha-ra (the evil inclination). (See also *AKEDA, *PATRIARCHS).

ISAIAH, THE BOOK OF   Prophetic book of the *Bible. It is generally agreed that the *Book of Isaiah* is the work of at least two different authors. The first Isaiah lived in the 8th Century BCE and is mentioned in II*Kings 19–20 and II*Chronicles 26 and 32. He is thought to have written Chapters 1–39 in which he protests against injustice. He rejected all alliances with neighbouring states and insisted that *God alone was the source of salvation. Even when disaster struck, he believed that a faithful *remnant would survive. Chs. 40–66 are the work of an unknown prophet writing during the time of *exile in Babylon and include the *Servant songs. It is possible that more than one writer contributed to Chs. 40–66 – hence the terms Deutero–Isaiah and Trito–Isaiah.

ISAIAH, ASCENSION OF   *Apocalyptic work. The *Ascension of Isaiah* is a Christian book showing how *Isaiah's death foreshadows the death of Jesus. It is built however round an original Jewish *Pseudepigraphic work *The Martyrdom of Isaiah*.

ISHMAEL BEN ELISHA   (early 2nd Century CE) *Sage. Ishmael was a spokesman for the *academy at *Javneh and was a frequent disputant with *Akiva. He was the author of the thirteen rules of *hermaneutics and the originator of many mystical sayings. (See *HERMANEUTICS).

ISRAEL   i)   Name bestowed on the *patriarch *Jacob after he wrestled with a stranger near the Ford of Jabbok (*Genesis 32:28–29) ii)   As 'Israelite', name bestowed on all the descendants of Jacob – thus on all the Jewish people particularly in *Biblical times.

iii)   The *Northern Kingdom of the Jews. The ten northern tribes rebelled against the Davidic monarchy in 930 BCE and set up their own kingdom known as Israel, *Samaria or sometimes *Ephraim. It was conquered by the Assyrians in 721 BCE and the tribes were scattered. (See *NORTHERN KINGDOM, *TEN LOST TRIBES)
iv)   The modern state founded in 1948. The state of Israel was the culmination of the *Zionist hope and was created by a resolution of the United Nations. Under the *Law of Return, it provides a homeland for any *diaspora Jew. (See also *EREZ ISRAEL, *HOLOCAUST, *ZIONISM).

ISRAEL BEN ELIEZER   (Besht, Baal Shem Tov) (1700–1760) Founder of *Hasidism. Israel ben Eliezer's life is the subject of many legends. As a teacher and leader, he travelled round the communities of Eastern Europe. His teachings were based on the *Kabbalah and the importance of individual *salvation. He stressed joy in prayer and worship and discouraged melancholy and *fasts. He encouraged study of the *Torah and used *gematria as a tool. He also was the originator of the doctrine of the *Zaddik. Israel himself left no writings, but his teachings were preserved by his disciples and, by the time of his death, his influence was felt throughout the Jewish world. (See *HASIDISM, *ZADDIK).

ISSERLES, MOSES BEN   (Rema) (c1530–1572) *Halakhist. Isserles was one of the great legal authorities of his day and was known as the '*Maimonides of Polish Jewry'. His supplement to Joseph Caro's *Shulhan Arukh made that work acceptable to *Ashkenazi Jewry and his rulings are regarded as binding.

ISSUR VE-HETTER   Legal rulings about forbidden food. In the Middle Ages, many books were written on the laws and customs (*see *MINHAGIM) of forbidden food. (See also *KASHRUT).

JABNEH   (Jamnia) (Javneh) Location of the reconstituted *Sanhedrin. After the fall of *Jerusalem in 70CE, the Sanhedrin was transferred to Jabneh under *Johanan ben Zakkai. It remained the centre of Jewish life under such *sages as *Akiva until the *Bar Kokhba Jewish revolt of 132CE.

JACOB   *Patriarch. Jacob was the son of *Isaac and the grandson of *Abraham. His exploits are described in *Genesis 25–36 and he was the father of twelve sons, the ancestors of the *twelve tribes of *Israel. In the rabbinic tradition, there was a strong tendency to interpret Jacob's conduct in a good light and in the *midrash he is therefore portrayed as a reasonably virtuous character (See also *ISRAEL, *PATRIARCHS).

JASHAR, BOOK OF   Ancient work. The *Book of Jashar* is now lost, but was mentioned in *Joshua* 10–13, II *Samuel* 1:18 and I *Kings* 8:53. Apparently it contained poems about events and characters in the period of the *Judges.

JEHOVAH   The English vocalized form of the *tetragrammaton. (See *TETRAGRAMMATON).

JEREMIAH, BOOK OF   A *Biblical book of *Prophecy. Jeremiah himself was of priestly descent. During his lifetime, King *Josiah reformed the cult, the Babylonians conquered Judah, the *Temple in *Jerusalem was destroyed and the people were taken to *exile in Babylon. The book includes the *Scribe *Baruch's scroll (Chs. 1–6), Jeremiah's sermon in the temple (Chs. 7–10) and various oracles, parables and accounts of incidents in the prophet's life. Chs. 30 and 31 are known as the 'Book of consolations' and are placed among the incidents. Jeremiah is thought to have died in Egypt having been persuaded to flee after the murder of *Gedaliah. The *Book of *Lamentations* is also traditionally ascribed to Jeremiah.

JEREMY, EPISTLE OF   *Pseudepigraphic book. The *Epistle of Jeremy* is supposed to be a letter from the prophet *Jeremiah to the Babylonian *exiles. In the Latin Vulgate, it is placed in the *Apocrypha attached (Ch. 6) to the *Book of *Baruch*.

JERUSALEM   (City of *David). The capital of the modern State of *Israel. After King *David had captured the fortress from the Jebusites (*II Samuel 5), he made it his capital. His son, King *Solomon, placed the *Temple there and it remained the capital of the *Southern Kingdom until its capture by the Babylonians in 586BCE. Through the period of the *exile, the Jewish people kept alive the hope of return and, in the Persian period the Temple was rebuilt and Jerusalem became again the centre of the cult. King *Herod greatly enlarged the Temple in the 1st Century BCE, but, apart from the

*Wailing Wall, it was almost entirely destroyed in the Jewish revolt of 70CE. After the *Bar Kokhba revolt of 132, the city was renamed Aeolia Capitolina and *Jews were forbidden to live there. In the Muslim period this ban was lifted and Jerusalem became a place of *pilgrimage for the Jews as well as for Christians and Muslims. The longing to return to the land of Israel and particularly to Jerusalem was expressed regularly in the *liturgy particularly at the *festival of *Passover – the *seder actually concludes with the words, 'Next year in Jerusalem.' The city was partitioned between Jew and Arab in 1948 when the State of Israel was created, but the Arab part (including the Wall) was captured in the Six Day War in 1967. The united city was then declared the Israeli capital. (See also *ZION).

JEW A member of the *Israelite people. A Jew is defined by the *Orthodox as one born from a Jewish mother or who has formally converted to *Judaism (see *PROSELYTE). By virtue of maternal descent, an individual is obliged to observe the *halakhah (commandments). An individual is still a full Jew even if not circumcised (see *BRIS) or has declared himself an *apostate. Conversion entails *circumcision for men and ritual *immersion in the *mikveh (ritual bath). The American *Reform movement recognises partrilineal as well as matrilineal descent in its understanding of who is a Jew and conversion requirements are more flexible. Consequently many members of the Reform Movement are not accepted as Jews by the *Orthodox even though such individuals are entitled to become citizens of the State of *Israel under the *Law of Return.

JEWISH WAR The rebellion against Roman rule in the 1st Century CE. The Jewish War was led by the *Zealots and described in detail by the historian *Josephus. It resulted in the siege of *Jerusalem and the almost complete destruction of the *Temple in 70CE. The centre of Jewish life moved to *Jabneh under *Johanan ben Zakkai, but the ancient institutions of *priesthood, *sacrifice and temple worship were completely lost. The Jewish war ended with the capture of *Masada. The Roman triumph is portrayed on the triumphal arch of Titus in Rome, which shows the sacred *menorah being removed from the Temple. (See *ZEALOTS).

JHWH See *TETRAGRAMMATON.

JOB, THE BOOK OF   A *biblical book in the *Ketuvim ('Writings') section. The *Book of Job* tells the story of how the upright Job was tested by *God by the destruction of his family and worldly goods. Job refuses to accept that these disasters are the result of his *sin and ultimately God speaks to him and everything is restored. The date, authorship and precise meaning of the book are the subject of much scholarly discussion. In general, the *sages compared Job with *Abraham as being the subject of a divine trial. (See also *AKEDA*).

JOEL, THE BOOK OF   A Biblical *prophetic book. The *Book of Joel* describes a terrible plague of locusts and the people are urged to entreat *God's mercy. This is followed by lengthy prophecy of the 'great and terrible *Day of the Lord' from which only a small *remnant would be saved and the *Holy Spirit would be poured out on all flesh. The book falls into two clear parts and it is possible that each part had a different author. In any case its date is uncertain.

JOHANAN BEN ZAKKAI   (1st Century CE). *Sage. During the *Jewish War, Johanan ben Zakkai, the leading authority of his day, managed to leave the besieged city of *Jerusalem to join the existing *academy in *Jabneh. Under his leadership, the *bet din at Jabneh attained the status of *Sanhedrin. Although he himself was never declared *nasi, his successor, Rabban Gamaliel was so styled. As a result of his efforts, the institutions of *Judaism managed to survive the catastrophic loss of the *Temple. Johanan's own ordinances were issued 'in remembrance of the Temple' and he is remembered as the first sage to engage in *kabbalah (Jewish mysticism).

JONAH, BOOK OF   A prophetic book of the *Bible. The *Book of Jonah* is largely an account of the story of Jonah who fled to Tarshish rather than preach *God's wrath to the wicked people of Nineveh. After a storm and being swallowed by a great fish, Jonah did go to Nineveh, but, because the people repented, God did not execute his vengeance. The book is referred to in the *Book of *Tobit* so it must have been composed before the 4th Century BCE.

JOSEPH   The son of the *patriarch *Jacob by his favourite wife Rachel. The lengthy story of Joseph is narrated in the *Book of *Genesis* Chs. 37–47. Joseph himself did not have one of the *twelve tribes named after him. Instead his descendants belonged to the two tribes named for his sons *Ephraim and Manasseh so in a real sense, although not the *firstborn, Joseph inherited a double portion.

JOSEPHUS (1st Century CE) Historian. Although initially Josephus fought for the rebels in the *Jewish War, he surrendered to the Romans in 67CE and accompanied them to the siege of *Jerusalem. His two major works, *The Antiquities* and the *Jewish War* are our major source of knowledge of the Jewish history of the Second *Temple period.

JOSHUA, BOOK OF The final book of the *Hexateuch. The *Book of Joshua* describes the conquest and the settlement of the land of *Canaan after the *exodus from Egypt and before the period of the *Judges. Joshua himself took over the leadership of the people after the death of *Moses and organised the takeover and appointment of the land between the *twelve tribes. Traditionally the book was believed to have been written by Joshua himself, but this is now not accepted by scholars. (See *DOCUMENTARY HYPOTHESIS).

JOSIAH (640–609BCE). King of the *Southern Kingdom. According to the author of *II *Kings*, Josiah was responsible for a thoroughgoing reformation of the cult resulting from the discovery of a version of the *Book of *Deuteronomy* in the *Temple. In the late 7th Century BCE, Assyria was the dominant power in the Middle East and it is probable that Josiah's rejection of any form of *idolatry was a gesture of independence and an exploitation of Assyrian weakness. The provincial *High Places were destroyed and the people publicly agreed to keep the Law of *God. Josiah is commended warmly in the Biblical account of these events (*II Kings* 22 and 23). (See *DEUTERONOMIC HISTORIAN).

JOSIPPON History of the Second *Temple period. *Josippon* was written in the 10th Century CE and was frequently quoted in mediaeval Biblical and Talmudic commentaries.

JUBILEE Seventh *Sabbatical year. According to *Leviticus 25*, every seventh year should be a sabbatical year; no agricultural work should be done and all debts should be forgiven. Every seventh sabbatical year is a Jubilee year when slaves are freed and land bought since the previous Jubilee should be returned. Laws on the Jubilee year are contained in the *talmudic tractate *Sheviit* and only ever applied to the land of *Israel. (See also *SABBATICAL YEAR*).

JUBILEES, BOOK OF   *Pseudepigraphic book. The *Book of Jubilees* is supposedly a revelation given to *Moses by an *angel. It dates however from the Second *Temple period. It is so called because the events of the *Bible are dated according to the *Jubilee years. Fragments of *The Book of Jubilees* were found in the *Qumran excavations and the book was influential on later *midrashic literature.

JUDAH   Name of one of the *twelve tribes of *Israel. The land of Judah was situated in the south of the *Promised Land and the name Judah was frequently used for the whole of the *Southern Kingdom. (See *SOUTHERN KINGDOM*).

JUDAH HALEVY   (1075–1141) Spanish poet and philosopher. Judah Halevy was a prolific poet and about eight hundred examples of his work survive. His *Sefer ha-Kuzari* is a philosophic work based on the legend of the King of the Khazars who invited an Aristotelian philosopher, a Christian, a Muslim and a Jew to expound their beliefs before him. It has proved immensely popular and was particularly influential on the *Kabbalists.

JUDAH HA-NASI   (2nd Century CE) Legal expert. Judah ha-Nasi was a descendant of Rabbi *Hillel. As *nasi of the community, he built up the sense of unity of the Jewish people and was a key figure in the redaction of the *Mishnah. Although it is not clear by what principles he made his selection from the *Oral Law, his collection was regarded as fixed and later *halakhah grew out of commentary on the *Mishnah* (see *TALMUD*). Judah was much revered by his contemporaries and known as Rabbi. (See *MISHNAH*).

JUDAH MACCABEE   (2nd Century BCE). Military leader. The son of Mattathias the *Hasmonean, Judah led the revolt against the pagan Syrians. As a result of his campaign, he captured *Jerusalem and purified the *Temple (see *HANUKKAH*). His exploits are recorded in the *Book of Maccabees* (See *MACCABEES, BOOK OF*).

JUDAISM   See *JEW*.

90

JUDEA   Latin form of *Judah. Name of the Southern Kingdom of the Jews which came under Roman rule in 63BCE. At that period, Jews also lived in the north in the region of Galilee. After the *Bar Kokhba revolt was crushed in 135CE, Judea was renamed Palaestina. (See also *SOUTHERN KINGDOM).

JUDGES, BOOK OF   *Biblical book. The *Book of Judges* contains the history of the Israelites after the death of *Joshua until the need was felt for an established king. The judges themselves were charismatic leaders who arose at times of particular need. The exploits of Othniel, Ehud, Shamgar, *Deborah, *Gideon, Abimelech, Tola and Jair, Jephthah, Ibzan, Elon and Abdon and *Samson are recorded. The book itself was the result of a deuteronomic redaction. (See *DEUTERONOMIC HISTORIAN).

JUDGMENT   See *DIN

JUDITH, BOOK OF   Book of the *Apocrypha. The story is set in the Assyrian period and tells how the beautiful Judith deceived the Assyrian general Holophernes. It dates from the period of the Second *Temple and may have been written to encourage the people in the *Maccabean wars. The book only survives in Greek versions.

JUSTIFICATION   Judaism teaches that righteousness is the only way to achieve justification in the eyes of *God. Thus the *prophet *Micah maintains, 'What does the Lord require of you, but to do justice and to love mercy and to walk humbly with thy God'. Because it was understood that human beings were incapable of perfect righteousness (see *YETZER HA-RA), *sacrifice was instituted as *atonement for *sin. Once the sacrificial system disappeared with the destruction of the *Temple in 70CE, *prayer and *fasting were regarded as the means by which the divine-human relationship was restored. (See *FASTING, *SACRIFICE, *YOM KIPPUR).

KABBALAH   Mystical teachings. Kabbalah refers to the Jewish esoteric teachings which have evolved since the Second Temple period. Traditionally it was believed to have been revealed in its full perfection either to the first man *Adam or as a secret part of the *Oral Law to *Moses on Mount Sinai. The aim of Kabbalah was to uncover the hidden life of *God and the secrets of his relationship with his *creation. Characteristic kabbalistic doctrines include the transmigration of *souls, the achievement of *tikkun (cosmic repair) the *sefirot (emanations) and the activities of supernatural powers. These ideas were absorbed into folk belief and popular customs and spread into the Christian community as Jewish magic. (See also *ADAM KADMON, *BAHIR, SEFER HA-, *DEVEKUT, *EMANATION, *EN SOF, *GEMATRIA, *HASIDISM, *LURIA, ISAAC, *MERKAVAH MYSTICISM, *METATRON, *PRACTICAL KABBALAH, *SEFER YEZIRAH, *SEFIROT, *SHABBATEANISM, *TIKKUN, *ZADDIK, *ZIMZUM, *ZOHAR).

KABBALAT SHABBAT (Hebrew. 'Reception of the Sabbath') Evening *synagogue service welcoming the *sabbath. It is customary to put on fresh clothes and recite particular hymns. (See also *SHABBAT).

KABRONIM (Hebrew. 'Buriers') Community gravediggers.

KADDISH (Aramaic. 'Holy') Doxology said to conclude the sections of the liturgical services. The four different types of kaddish include
i)   The whole kaddish said at the end of each *Amidah except in the morning service
ii) The half kaddish which connects the sections of the service
iii) The scholars' kaddish said by mourners after study
iv) The *mourners' kaddish recited by mourners at the end of each *synagogue service. Traditionally the prayer is said standing facing *Jerusalem and dates back to *Talmudic times. The mourners' kaddish is said every day for eleven months after the *death of a parent, spouse, child or sibling and subsequently on each anniversary of death. (See *YAHRZEIT).

KALLAH Months in the year when Jewish scholars gathered to study in the Babylonian *academies. The custom dates back to the 3rd Century CE and ordinary people used to come to listen to the debate. The practice has recently been revived in modern *Israel.

KAL VA-HOMER (Hebrew. 'Light and heavy') A principle by which the *halakha is decided. The Kal va-Homer was the first principle of *hermeneutics in the systems of both *Hillel and *Ishmael.

KANAH, BOOK OF *Kabbalistic book. The *Book of Kanah* is modelled on the *Zohar*. It dates from the 14th Century and is probably of Spanish origin. With its negative attitude to the straightforward meaning of the text, it was influential on the *Shabbatean movement.

KAPLAN, MORDECAI (1881–1983) Founder of the *Reconstructionist movement. Kaplan believed *Judaism to be 'an evolving religious civilization'. His best-known book was *Judaism as a Civilization* (1934). (See *RECONSTRUCTIONISM*).

KAPPAROT (Hebrew. 'Atonements') The practice of transferring an individual's *sins to a bird. On the eve of the Day of Atonement (*Yom Kippur), a fowl is swung over the head of an individual who prays that by its death, his sins will be forgiven. This ceremony has been abandoned by *Progressive *Jews. (See also *YOM KIPPUR).

KARAITES An heretical sect. The Karaites were founded by *Anan b. David in the 8th Century CE who taught that only the *Written Law was authoritative and the *Oral Law could be disregarded. The sect was consolidated in the 9th and 10th Century and was subject to much criticism from such *Rabbanite scholars as *Saadiah Gaon. The Karaites themselves believed that their movement went back to the division of the *Northern and *Southern Kingdoms in the 10th Century BCE and that they were following the traditions of the *Sadducees. The sect spread from Babylonian throughout the Ottoman empire as far as the Crimea. Some rabbanite scholars, such as *Maimonides respected the Karaites. The attitude of the civil authorities also varied – they were not, for example, recognised as *Jews by the German government in the 1930s and '40s, but they are welcomed in the State of *Israel although they are not allowed by either *halakhah or their own laws to intermarry with the Jewish population. (See also *RABBANITES).

KARET (Hebrew. 'Extirpation') Divine punishment. The *Mishnah lists thirty-six offences for which sudden death – karet, is the punishment.

KASHER, KASHRUT (Hebrew. 'Fit', 'Fitness') The body of laws governing food. The original lists of forbidden species in the *Bible were explained and developed in the *Oral law. Animals fit for consumption must both chew the cud and have a cloven hoof (such as sheep and cows). Birds of prey are forbidden. Fish may only be eaten if they have both fins and scales. Animals must be slaughtered in a particular way (see *SHEHITA*) and the meat washed to remove all traces of *blood. Following the Biblical verse, 'thou shalt not seeth a kid in its mother's milk', meat foods and milk foods may not be eaten or even prepared together. The laws are contained in the *Talmudic tractate *Hullin* and the section 'Yoreh Deah' in the *Shulhan Arukh*. They include all the regulations on permitted ('Kosher') and forbidden ('terefah') foods, methods of slaughter, meat preparation, the separation of meat and milk, vegetable foodstuffs and Passover (*Pesah) rules.

KAVOD (Hebrew. 'Glory') The glory of *God. According to the Biblical *prophets, there will come a time when the whole world is full of kavod.

KAVVANAH (Hebrew. 'Intention') Concentration when praying and fulfilling a commandment. The *Shulhan Arukh* teaches that a little *prayer with kavvanah is better than a great deal of prayer without it. Similarly commandments should not be obeyed mechanically, but with the full intention of keeping the *mitzvot.

KEDUSHAH (Hebrew. 'Holiness') Set apart through holiness. According to the *Book of Leviticus* 19:2, the Jewish people are commanded to be holy because 'the Lord your *God is holy'. Holiness is of God's very nature and that holiness can be shared by keeping the *mitzvot (commandments). Most *benedictions use the formula, 'Blessed art thou Lord God. . . who has sanctified us through your commandments' and it is in keeping the commandments that *Israel is set apart from the other nations of the world.

KEHILLAH (Hebrew. 'Congregation') A Jewish community or *synagogue congregation.

KELAL ISRAEL (Hebrew. 'All of Israel') The interrelatedness of all Jews. Traditionally it was taught that all Jews were present at the making of the *Covenant on Mount *Sinai. Today the notion of kelal Israel is invoked to encourage *Orthodox, *Progressive and Secular Jews to work together on communal projects. (See also *KENESET ISRAEL*).

KENESET ISRAEL (Hebrew. 'The Community of Israel') The whole Jewish community. In *rabbinic literature, Keneset Israel was used as a personification of the community in its dialogue with *God. (See also *KELAL ISRAEL).

KERIAH (Hebrew. 'Rending') Rending garments as a symbol of mourning. Traditionally on the death of parent, spouse, child, or sibling, a tear is made in the coat lapel before the funeral takes place. The custom goes back to *Biblical times (eg. *Genesis, 37:34 and *Job 1:20). It is not observed by *Progressive Jews. (See *FUNERAL CUSTOMS).

KEROVAH (Aramaic. 'Precentor') *Piyyutim which form part of the *Amidah prayer. Kerovah were written for *Sabbaths, *festivals and *fast days.

KETER MALKUT (Hebrew. 'Crown of royalty') The mark of *God's sovereignty. The Keter Malkut is the title of a poem by Solomon ibn Gabirol which is recited after the evening service on the Day of Atonement (*Yom Kippur). God's sovereignty is recognised in worship.

KETER TORAH (Hebrew. 'Crown of law') Crowns that decorate the *Torah *scroll covers. The keter torah symbolises the sovereignty of law in the Jewish way of life. (See *SCROLLS, *TORAH ORNAMENTS).

KETUBBAH (Hebrew. 'Writing') The *marriage contract. The ketubbah sets out the obligations between the couple and protects the woman financially in the event of a *divorce. According to Jewish law, husband and wife may not live together until the ketubbah has been made out and they are frequently beautiful, richly decorated documents. (See also *MARRIAGE).

KETUVIM (Hebrew. 'Writings') See *HAGIOGRAPHA.

KHAZAR An Eastern European tribe that converted to *Judaism. The Khazars were an independent nation between the 7th–10th Centuries who converted to Judaism in c.740 CE. They disappeared from history in the 11th Century. Judah *Halevy's Kuzari is an account of their conversion.

KIBBUTZ *Israeli agricultural collective. The first kibbutz was founded in 1921 and the kibbutzim movement was an important element in the pioneering strategy of the *Jews in Palestine. The settlements are organised democratically with all possessions held in common and the weekly general meeting serving as the sovereign body. Originally children lived apart from their parents in children's houses to liberate the women for outside work. Different kibbutzim have different philosophies but, in general, family life has become more important. The proportion of kibbutz members (Kibbutzniks) in the *Knesset and as senior army officers is far greater than their proportion in the general population.

KIDDUSH (Hebrew. 'Sanctification') Prayer recited over wine to sanctify *Sabbaths or *festivals. The prayer consists of four verses from the book of *Genesis followed by a *benediction over wine and a benediction for the day. It is forbidden to eat on a Sabbath or festival until Kiddush has been recited. In the *synagogue, it is often said at the conclusion of Sabbath evening (Friday night) service and in *progressive synagogues after the Saturday morning service. (See also *HAVDALAH, *SHABBAT).

KIDDUSH HA-SHEM (Hebrew. 'The Sanctification of the Name') The glorification of *God. Traditionally God could be glorified through *prayer, conduct and *martyrdom. Martyrdom in particular has been understood as the ultimate expression of Kiddush ha-Shem and is obligatory rather than commit the sins of *idolatry, unchastity and murder. Jewish martyrdom goes back to the time of the *Hasmoneans and includes the martyrs in the *Jewish Wars (see *AKIVA), in the Christian Crusades, in the pogroms of Eastern Europe and in the *Holocaust. Every day, when reciting the *Shema, the pious *Jew should be offering himself for Kiddush ha-Shem.

KIDNAPPING According to *Deuteronomy 24:7, kidnapping is a capital offence and the *sages taught that the eighth of the *Ten Commandments referred to kidnapping rather than stealing property. In fact, the conditions for obtaining a conviction for kidnapping were so stringent that *capital punishment was most unlikely.

KIKE An insulting term for a *Jew.

KINAH A poem of mourning. Kinot were traditionally spoken over the dead (as *David's lament for *Saul and Jonathan in *II Samuel* 1:19–27) and in times of national crisis. Several anthologies have been produced and kinot are frequently recited on *Tishah B'Av.

KINDLING OF LIGHTS See *CANDLES*.

KINGDOM OF HEAVEN The future state of perfection. The *sages taught that after the era of the *messiah, *God will create a new heaven and a new earth which will be a kingdom of perfect peace and harmony. (See *ESCHATOLOGY*).

KINGS, BOOKS OF A book of the *Bible, divided into two parts. The *Books of Kings* contain the history of Kings *David and *Solomon, the division of the kingdom, the destruction of the *Northern Kingdom by the Assyrians, the continued history of the *Southern Kingdom and the Babylonian conquest. The Books are generally thought to have been compiled in the mid 6th Century by a writer profoundly influenced by the thought of the *Book of *Deuteronomy*. He was convinced that both the Assyrian and Babylonian conquests were the results of the *Jews' unfaithfulness to *God. (See *DEUTE-RONOMIC HISTORIAN*).

KINGSHIP, SACRAL The belief that the King was chosen and maintained by *God. After initial reluctance to have a king, the Israelites believed that their monarch was God's chosen, the *anointed one, the *messiah. However he was not an absolute ruler – like his subjects he was bound by the laws of God. Although he was described as the son of God, he was also understood to be a mortal man. As in many Middle Eastern states of the ancient world, the Hebrew King was also a *priest; he burned incense, offered sacrifice and blessed the people. The kingship of the *Northern Kingdom disappeared with its destruction in 721 BCE; the Davidic kingship of the *Southern Kingdom continued until the 6th Century Babylonian conquest. Kingship was briefly revived under the *Hasmoneans and *Herod, but this was rather different from the kingship of the line of David. (See also *MESSIAH*).

KIPAH See *YARMULKE*.

KITTEL (Yiddish. 'Gown') Gown worn for special services. The kittel is a white garment worn by some *Ashkenazi Jews for *Rosh Hashanah (New Year), *Yom Kippur (Day of Atonement), also by the celebrant at the *Pesah (Passover) service, by the bridegroom at his *wedding and by the dead for *burial.

KNESSET (Hebrew. 'Assembly') The Parliament of the State of Israel.

KOHELET See *ECCLESIASTES.

KOHEN A hereditary *priest. After the destruction of the *Temple in *Jerusalem in 70 CE, *sacrifice no longer had a place in the Jewish religion. A priest's duties were restricted to reciting the Priestly *Benediction on *festivals and redeeming the *first-born (*Pidyon ha-Ben). Kohenim continue to exist, but identity depends on folk memory passed down from father to son. To this day kohenim may not marry divorced women or *proselytes; because of the historical questionableness of the continued institution, the *Progressive movements no longer recognise the category. (See *AARON, *AARONIDES, *HIGH PRIEST, *LEVITES, *PRIEST, *SACRIFICE, *SADDUCEES, *TEMPLE).

KOL BO (Hebrew 'All within') Jewish law book. Kol Bo is a book of *halakhic rulings; it is of unknown authorship and was probably compiled in the 13th Century CE.

KOLLEL An advanced *yeshivah.

KOL NIDREI (Aramaic. 'All vows') Prayer at the beginning of the *Rosh Hashanah (New Year) evening service. The prayer declares that all personal *vows made rashly to *God are now cancelled and it is repeated three times. Misunderstanding has arisen over the prayer – *Anti-Semites arguing that it shows Jews do not feel obliged to keep their word. In fact there are strict limitations as to the vows that can be cancelled. So well-known is the prayer, that Rosh Hashanah eve is often called Kol Nidrei. (See *ROSH HASHANAH).

KORBAN Sacrificing all property to God. This practice is mentioned in the New Testament as a means of escaping the duty of supporting parents. It died out with the destruction of the *Jerusalem *Temple at the end of the 1st Century CE.

KOSHER   See *KASHRUT*.

KUPPAH   Charity Box. There is a kuppah in every home and *synagogue and money is put in it on sad, solemn or joyful occasions to be distributed to the poor.

KUZARI   See *JUDAH HALEVY*.

LADINO   Spanish-Jewish dialect. Ladino is written in the Hebrew script and was spoken by *Sephardi *Jews.

LAG BA-OMER   A holiday celebrated on Iyyar 18. It commemorates the thirty-third day of counting the *Omer and it is sometimes known as the scholars' feast because a plague among the pupils of *Rabbi *Akiva was halted on that day. Today bonfires are lit, bows and arrows are played with and three-year old boys have their first haircut.

LAMED VAV ZADDIKIM   (Hebrew. Thirty-six righteous men). According to the *Talmud* in each generation there are at least thirty-six righteous men. There are many legends about the 'lamed-vavniks' (*Yiddish). They are said to be responsible for the state of the world and the coming of the *messiah depends on their righteousness.

LAMENTATIONS, BOOK OF   A Biblical book, numbered among the *five *scrolls. The *Book of Lamentations* is a lament for the destruction of *Jerusalem by the Babylonians in 586 BCE. It was traditionally thought to have been written by *Jeremiah although this is not accepted by most modern scholars. It is closely related to other examples of *wisdom literature and was almost certainly written in the first half of the 6th Century BCE.

LAMPS   See *CANDLES, *MENORAH, *NER TAMID*.

LASHANAH HABA'AH BI YERUSHALAYIM   (Hebrew 'Next Year in Jerusalem'). The concluding words of the *Passover *seder.

LAVER   Basin for ritual *ablution. Lavers were provided in the

*Temple in *Jerusalem. They are still used in some *synagogues before the *priestly *benediction is pronounced. (See also *ABLUTION, *MIKVEH).

LAW   See *CODES, *HALAKHAH, *ORAL LAW, *TORAH, *WRITTEN LAW.

LAW OF RETURN   The law which gives every *Jew the right to immigrate to *Israel. The Law of Return was passed in 1950 and since then there have been various test cases. At present *Progressive *proselytes and their children (who are not recognised as *Jews by the *Orthodox) are covered by the Law of Return, but *apostates are not.

LEAVEN   See *HAMEZ.

LEKHAH DODI   (Hebrew 'Come my friend') Introductory words of a well-known *Sabbath evening hymn. According to the *Talmud, scholars used to greet the *Sabbath and the hymn may have been inspired by this. It contains nine verses and a refrain 'Come my friend to meet the bride; let us welcome the presence of the *Sabbath'.

LEKU NERANANAH   (Hebrew 'O come let us exalt') Opening words of *Psalms 95. Leku Nerananah is the beginning of a group of Psalms (95, 96, 97, 98, 99 and 29) recited in the *Ashkenazi rite at the beginning of the *Sabbath evening service.

LEL SHIMMURIM   (Hebrew 'Night of Watching') The first night of *Passover. It was traditionally believed that no harm could occur on that night so doors were left unlocked. (See *PESAH).

LEONTOPOLIS   A Jewish settlement in Egypt. In the 2nd Century BCE an Egyptian temple was converted into a temple for the Jewish *God. It survived until 73 CE and for much of that period Leontopolis seems to have been under independent Jewish rule.

LEPROSY   A skin disease which made the sufferer unclean. Biblical leprosy is not the same as modern leprosy. *Leviticus 13 describes the signs of leprosy and the *talmudic tractate *Negaim* discusses the laws of leprosy.

LESHON HARA   See *SLANDER.

LETTER MYSTICISM   See *GEMATRIA.

LEVI   Third son of the *patriarch *Jacob by his wife Leah. Levi was the ancestor of the *Levite tribe. (See *LEVITE).

LEVI BEN GERSHOM   (Gersonides) (1288–1344) French philosopher, *biblical commentator and *talmudist. Levi Ben Gershom's major philosophical work was Sefer Milhamot Adonai ('The Book of the Wars of the Lord') written between 1317 and 1329. Although fiercely criticised by his contemporaries, Levi must be numbered with *Maimonides as one of the most influential and creative Jewish philosophers.

LEVIATHAN   A sea monster. In the *Bible, the leviathan often symbolises the forces of chaos.

LEVIRATE MARRIAGE   The marriage of a childless widow and her husband's brother. If a man dies leaving no children, his brother must marry the widow to raise children in his brother's name (see *Deuteronomy 25:5). The ceremony of *halizah described in Deuteronomy 25:7–10 releases the man from the obligation. Nowadays levirate marriage is forbidden and halizah must be given to childless widows. If it is refused, the woman is technically an *agunah (a 'tied woman').

LEVITE   The descendants of *Levi. The Levite tribe lacked land, but instead were appointed to serve in the *tabernacle. They were supported by *tithes from the other Israelites. The Levites were subject to the *priests, the descendants of *Aaron (see *AARONIDES) and during the time of the monarchy, they became state officials. The *aggadic tradition teaches that when at the end of time *God purifies the *twelve tribes, the tribe of Levi will be purified first.

LEVITICAL CITIES   Cities prescribed in the *Bible for the *Levites. The Book of *Numbers specifies that forty-eight cities were set aside including six *Cities of Refuge. This provision was necessary because the Levites had no land of their own, but scholars do not think the numbers of cities in the Book of Numbers is completely accurate. (See *LEVITES).

101

LEVITICUS   The third book of the *Pentateuch. Leviticus* contains the laws concerning *sacrifice, the *sanctuary, impurity and holiness. Called the *Torat Kohenim* ('Priests' Manual') and believed by the *sages to have been written by *Moses, it is now generally recognised as coming from the *priestly source (see *DOCUMENTARY HYPOTHESIS*). It was traditionally the first book to be studied in *heder ('elementary school'). (See also *HOLINESS CODE*).

LIBATION   A liquid offering. A libation of oil or wine was poured out with most *Temple *sacrifices. The laws of libation are described in *Numbers* 15:1–16.

LIBERAL JUDAISM   An English *Progressive movement. Liberal Judaism was founded by Lily Montagu and Claud Montefiore. It is the most radical of the English movements and, arguably, closest to American *Reform. Liberal *synagogues are affiliated to the Union of Liberal and Progressive Synagogues which together with the English Reform Synagogues of Great Britain maintain the Leo Baeck College (the English Progressive *rabbinical seminary).

LIGHTS, FESTIVAL OF   See *HANUKKAH*

LILITH   A mythological female demon. According to the *Midrash, Lilith was created before *Eve, but fell out with *Adam because she would not accept his dominance. She was believed in folk legend to kill new-born babies and in the *Zohar* is described as 'the harlot, the wicked, the false, the black.' Among modern Jewish *feminists, she has become something of a heroine. (See *FEMINISM*).

LITVAK   A Jew from Lithuania.

LITURGY   Pattern of religious services. The liturgy grew out of the practices in Palestine and Babylon in the time of the *geonim. The Italian and *Ashkenazi rite is based on the Palestinian tradition while the *Sephardi rite draws on the Babylonian. Ultimately both are based on the pattern of worship and *sacrifice in the *Temple in *Jerusalem. The liturgies adopted by the *Progressive movements are considerably shorter; several prayers which are now felt to be offensive (eg. 'Blessed art thou O Lord God, King of the universe, who has not made me a *woman') have been removed and much of the service is recited in the vernacular.

LIUBAVICH Russian village. Liubavich was the home of Dov Ber and Menahem Mendel Shneersohn and became the centre of *Habad *Hasidism. The Liubavicher are one of the most powerful hasidic groups: they maintain a high profile within the Jewish community and actively seek new adherents. (See *HABAD, *HASIDISM).

LOANS According to the *halakhah, loans must be repaid within a fixed period otherwise the borrower's property may be taken. Officially the *Sabbatical year cancelled all loans, but *Hillel instituted a system by which the loan could be recovered (see *PROSBUL) The exacting of interest on a loan to a fellow countryman is forbidden, but it is permitted to strangers (*Deuteronomy 23:20–21). (See also *USURY).

LOST TRIBES See TEN LOST TRIBES.

LOTS, FEAST OF See *PURIM.

LULAV (Hebrew 'A shoot') A palm branch. The lulav is one of the *four species which is waved at services on the *festival of *Sukkot. (See *FOUR SPECIES, *SUKKOT).

LURIA, ISAAC BEN SOLOMON (Ari) (1543–1572) *Kabbalist. Luria settled in *Safed, gathered a group of disciples round him and taught them the mysteries of the Kabbalah. He is thought to have received a revelation from the *prophet *Elijah and his teachings were preserved in different forms by his followers. Luria himself wrote a commentary on a section of the *kabbalah and several hymns. His ideas were highly influential on the *Hasidic movement. (For his ideas see *KABBALAH, *SEFIROT, *TIKKUN, *ZIMZUM).

LXX See *SEPTUAGINT.

MA'AMADOT See *COURSES PRIESTLY.

MA'ARAVOT An arrangement of *piyyutim. The ma'aravot piyyutim are said in addition to the usual prayers recited at the ma'ariv (evening) service. (See *MAARIV).

MA'AREKHET HA-ELOHUT (Hebrew. 'The order of God') A *kabbalistic book. The Ma'arekhet Ha-Elohut is an attempt to present

103

the teachings of the Kabbalah systematically. It was composed by an unknown author in the late 13th Century.

MAARIV   (Hebrew. 'Evening Service') The order of evening service. A *minyan is required for the Maariv service. It was supposedly first ordained by the *patriarch *Jacob and includes the *Shema and the *Amidah.

MAASEH   (Hebrew. 'Story') A legal source. *Halakhah is derived from various sources such as *minhag (custom). A maaseh is an event such as a legal judgment or particular act of an eminent authority. Halakhah which stems from maaseh has particular force because the past cannot be changed.

MAASEH BOOK   (Hebrew. 'Story Book') A collection of folk tales first published in 1602.

MAASER   See *TITHES.

MACCABEES, BOOKS OF   Books of the *Apocrypha. The *Books of Maccabees* contain the stories of Simon the *Hasmonean and *Judah Maccabee. The first book covers the history of the Jewish people from 175BCE–135BCE. It is written in Hebrew and is generally regarded as an accurate historical source. The second book is far less objective and more literary. It is written in Greek and concentrates on the heroic exploits of Judah up to his victory over Nicanor in 164BCE. It is thought to be an abridgement of a work composed by one Jason of Cyrene. (See also *HASMONEANS*).

MACHPELAH, CAVE OF   Burial place of the *patriarchs *Isaac and *Jacob. The burials are recorded in the *Book of *Genesis* and the site has been identified with Harem el-Khalil in Hebron. Traditionally it is a place of Jewish *pilgrimage.

MAGEN DAVID   (Hebrew. 'Shield of David.') A six-pointed star. The magen David has become the symbol of *Judaism. The oldest example dates from the 7th Century BCE and it became the badge of the Prague community in 1354. It was used by the Zionists in the 19th Century and by the Nazis. (See *BADGE, JEWISH*). When the State of *Israel was founded in 1948, the magen David design was chosen for the flag of the new nation.

MAGGID (Hebrew. 'One who tells'). A popular preacher. From the 17th Century CE Maggidim were common in the Eastern European communities. Their sermons were simple so that ordinary people could understand them and they often used *mashalim (parables). Many of the early *hasidic leaders became known through their activities as maggidim. Among the *Kabbalists, a maggid was a supernatural spirit who passed on secrets to chosen scholars. Such maggidim were said to have appeared among the disciples of *Shabbetai Zevi.

MAGIC Influencing events by supernatural powers. Sorcery and witchcraft are forbidden in the *Bible, but magic was an important part of Jewish folk religion and *Kabbalah. (See also *AMULETS, *GEMATRIA).

MAHAMAD The governing body of a *Sephardi congregation.

MAHLOKET (Hebrew. 'Division') Difference of opinion. Dissension. Rabbinic discussion encouraged difference of opinion, but dissension was condemned.

MAH NISHTANNAH (Hebrew. 'How is it different') The first of *four questions asked by the youngest capable person at the Passover *seder. (See *PESAH, *SEDER).

MAHZOR (Hebrew. 'Cycle') The *Festival *Prayer Book. The Mahzor is the Prayer Book for festivals in contrast to the *Siddur which is used every day. Both the *Ashkenazi and *Sephardi versions are based on the 11th Century *Mahzor Vitry. The Progressive movements have produced their own festival Prayer Books. (See *LITURGY, *PRAYER BOOK).

MAHZOR VITRY A *festival *Prayer Book. The Mahzor Vitry was compiled in the 11th Century CE by Sumhah b. Samuel of Vitry, a pupil of *Rashi. It forms the basis of the modern *Orthodox Mahzor and gives liturgical rulings on the *Sabbaths and festivals.

MAIMONIDEAN CONTROVERSY   A philosophical controversy. The Maimonidean controversy was initiated by *Maimonides himself against the authority of the *geonim. In turn his *Mishneh Torah* was fiercely condemned by many contemporary scholars and a *herem was pronounced against it. *Nahmanides attempted to defend Maimonides and the controversy was temporarily halted when his books were burnt by Christian friars. However the tension between the rationalists and the anti-rationalists continued at various times throughout the Middle Ages. (See *MAIMONIDES*).

MAIMONIDES   (Moses b. Maimon. Ramban) (1135–1204) Codifier and philosopher. Maimonides' great *Code of Law, the *Mishneh Torah* ('Repetition of the law') was written 'to make the entire *Oral Law. . . accessible to young and old'. His major philosophical work, the *Guide to the Perplexed* shows how the Jewish religion can be understood symbolically as well as literally. It includes the famous thirteen *principles of the Jewish faith. Many commentaries were subsequently written on the *Guide to the Perplexed* and it has been enormously influential not only on the Jewish community, but also on such Christian thinkers as Thomas Aquinas and Meister Eckhardt. (See also *MAIMONIDEAN CONTROVERSY*).

MAIMUNA   Celebration of the last day of *Pesah (Passover). In many eastern communities it is celebrated with picnics.

MAJORITY   See *BAR MITZVAH*.

MAJOR PROPHETS   In classifying the books of the *Bible, the long books of *Isaiah*, *Jeremiah* and *Ezekiel* are reckoned major prophets in contrast to the shorter *minor prophets. (See also *PROPHETS*).

MALACHI   The last of the *Biblical *minor prophets. The *Book of Malachi* contains reproaches against the people and a warning of the coming *Day of the Lord. It also predicts that *Elijah will return before the judgment (see also *MESSIAH*). The book is of unknown authorship, but was probably composed in the mid 6th century BCE. After Malachi, it was believed that *prophecy had departed from *Israel. (See *PROPHETS*).

MALKUYYOT (Hebrew. 'Sovereignty) The beginning of the *musaf for *festivals. The prayer includes verses from the *Psalms, *Pentateuch and prophets. After it is read on *Rosh-HaShanah (New Year), the *shofar (ram's horn) is sounded.

MAMZER (Hebrew 'Bastard'). The child of an adulterous or incestuous union. Children of unmarried mothers are not mamzerim. Although a mamzer has equal rights of inheritance and can hold public office, it is a considerable civil disability since a mamzer may only marry another mamzer or a *proselyte. The child of a mamzer and a legitimate *Jew is also a mamzer. The *progressive movements have abolished the category as being unjust. (See also *AGUNA, *GET).

MANASSEH Son of *Joseph. Because Joseph inherited a double portion (see *FIRST BORN), both his sons, *Ephraim and Manasseh became ancestors of Israelite tribes (See *TRIBES, THE TWELVE).

MANASSEH, PRAYER OF *Apocryphal book. The *Prayer of Manasseh* is supposedly written by Manasseh, the last King of *Judah before the Babylonian conquest. It implores God's mercy, but was probably composed at the end of the 1st Century BCE.

MANNA Food dropped from *Heaven and eaten by the *Israelites on their journey to the *Promised Land. According to *Exodus 16: 26–36, manna and quails were the main items of diet. It is unclear exactly what manna was, but the *sages believed that it was ground by the *angels.

MANUAL OF DISCIPLINE One of the *Dead Sea Scrolls. The *Manual of Discipline* describes the rules and customs of the *monastic community of *Qumran. (See *DEAD SEA SCROLLS).

MAOT HITTIM A Passover (*Pesah) collection. Most hittim were organised to ensure the poor could purchase Passover necessities. The practice continues to this day.

MAOZ TZUR (Hebrew. 'O fortress, rock') Opening words of a well-known *Hanukkah hymn. *Maoz tzur* originated in 13th century Germany and is sung both at home and in the *synagogue.

MAPHTIR (Hebrew. 'The concluder') The final reader of the *Torah portion (see *READING OF THE LAW*). The maphtir can refer either to the reader or to the passage itself.

MAPPAH (Hebrew. 'Cloth') The binding of a *Torah *scroll. (See *SCROLL*). *Mappah* was also the title of Moses *Isserles' commentary to the *Shulhan Arukh*.

MAR (Aramaic. 'Master') Babylonian title for *exilarchs and some *amoraim.

MARI An early Mesopotamian settlement. Excavations at Mari have yielded important documents which cast light on the organisation of early *Israelite society.

MAROR (Hebrew. 'Bitter herb'). A *Pesah (Passover) food. According to *Exodus* 12:8, on *Passover the *Jews were commanded to eat *Mazzah with bitter herb. It is one of the symbolic foods displayed on the *seder table and represents the bitterness of Egyptian slavery. (See *PESAH*, *SEDER*).

MARRANOS *Jews of Spain and Portugal who converted to Christianity. Many Jews were compelled to convert in Christianity in 1391 in Spain and 1497 in Portugal. The Marranos were always suspected of clinging to their old Jewish Ways. Many fled abroad either to countries in the Ottoman Empire or to Northern Europe where they often reverted to Judaism. Some Marrano families rose to great prominence in their new countries. Many became completely *assimilated into *gentile culture and society, but, particularly in Spain, some groups still exist who have retained various Jewish practices without being aware of their origin. (See *ANUSIM*, *APOSTASY*).

MARRIAGE The religious and legal union between man and woman. From *Biblical times, monogamy has been the general rule among the *Jews. Jews must marry within their own religious community (see *INTERMARRIAGE*) and both marriage and having children are a positive duty. The first commandment given to *Adam and *Eve was to be fruitful and multiply. Although a happy marriage is much to be desired, divorce is permitted (see *GET*). The actual ceremony is in two parts:- Kiddushin (betrothal) and Nissuim (the marriage itself), but from the Middle Ages, the two parts were combined. Once the marriage contract is agreed (see *KETUBAH), the bridegroom is led to the bride under the marriage canopy (see *HUPPAH). *Benedictions are said over wine and both the man and woman drink from the same cup. The man gives the woman a ring pronouncing in Hebrew the formula: 'Behold you are consecrated to me with this ring according to the law of *Moses and *Israel.' The ketubah is then read out, seven *blessings are recited and the bridegroom crushes a glass with his foot (the symbolism of this is obscure). Traditionally weddings are a time of great rejoicing. Among *progressive Jews, there is an attempt to make the service more reciprocal, but in any case, different communities follow different marriage practices.

MARSHALIK (Yiddish. Jester) The Jester at Eastern European weddings.

MARTYR An individual who dies for the faith. Although the preservation of life is a duty, the pious *Jew should die rather than commit *murder, sexual impurity or *idolatory. In the Middle Ages, regulations were formulated on how martyrs should behave in response to Christian persecution. (See also *ANTI-SEMITISM *KIDDUSH HA-SHEM).

MASADA A rocky fortress in Southern *Judea. The fortress was built by King *Herod in 4BCE. Subsequently it was the last *Zealot stronghold of the *Jewish War. In 73CE the Zealot defenders en masse committed suicide rather than fall into the hands of the Romans. This heroic episode is described in *Josephus' *Jewish War*.

MASHAL (Hebrew. 'Fable'). A short moral tale often with animal characters. There are many mashalim in the *midrash, *Talmud* and later medieval literature, many of which seem to be derived from Arab sources.

MASHIAH See *MESSIAH.

MASKILIM The proponents of the 18th and 19th Century Enlightenement. (See *HASKALAH).

109

MASORAH   The rules of reading the *Bible in public worship. Scholars, known as the *Masoretes, between 6th–9th Centuries aimed to preserve the authentic text by adding vowel and *cantillation signs. The accepted text is that of Aaron ben Asher, the leader of the Tiberias Masoretes. This also contains indications of the words which are pronounced differently from the way they are written.

MASORET   (Aramaic. 'Tradition') Jewish *custom, law, history and folk beliefs.

MASORETES   See *MASORAH.

MASSEKHET   (Hebrew. 'A web', 'A tractate') A subdivision of a *seder ('Order') of the *Mishnah. Each seder is divided into massekhtot and each massekhet is divided into chapters. Since the 16th century, each massekhet has been printed on an identical number of pages.

MASTEMA   The name of the *Devil in the Book of *Jubilees. According to the Book of Jubilees Mastema is the chief of the evil spirits who tested *Abraham (see *AKEDA) and killed the first-born of the Egyptians.

MATMID   (Hebrew. 'A persistent person') A scholar dedicated to *Talmudic study.

MATTAN TORAH   (Hebrew. 'Giving of the law') Term used for the giving of the *Torah by *God to *Moses on Mount *Sinai.

MATZAH   See *MAZZAH.

MAZAL TOV   (Hebrew. 'Good Luck') Expression used on celebratory occasions, particularly *weddings.

MAZEVAH   A gravestone or monument.

MAZZAH   Unleavened bread eaten at *Pesah ('Passover'). According to *Exodus 12:39, the Israelites took mazzah rather than bread with them when they fled from Egypt because they could not wait for the bread to rise. To commemorate this, mazzah must be eaten on the first night of Passover, which is described in the *Seder as the 'bread of affliction'. For the rest of the Passover season, no *hamez ('leaven') may be eaten. The laws concerning the baking of mazzah are complicated because no trace of fermentation is permitted. So important is the tradition of eating mazzah that Passover is sometimes called the feast of unleavened bread. (See also *AFIKOMEN, *PESAH, *SEDER).

MEDITATION The practice of contemplating spiritual matters. The *Kabbalists in particular strove for a contemplative vision of the divine and instructions on methods of meditation were widespread. Today meditation is an important part of *hasidic prayer and was influenced by the Kabbalists of *Safed. (See also *DEVEKUT, *KAVVANAH).

MEGILLAH (Hebrew 'Scroll'). The five scrolls of the *Bible. The Books of *Ecclesiastes, *Esther, *Lamentations, *Ruth, and *Song of Songs are all referred to as scrolls.

MEGILLAT TA'ANIT (Hebrew. 'Scroll of Fasting') An *Aramaic work listing the days on which it is forbidden to *fast. The Megillat Ta'anit dates from the 1st or 2nd Century CE and is of disputed authorship.

MEHIZAH (Hebrew. 'Separation') The partition between seating allocated for men and seating allocated for women in the *synagogue. In *Orthodox synagogues either women sit in a gallery above the main body of the synagogue or there is a division between the front and the back seats. According to the *Talmud, this division goes back to the days of the *Temple. *Progressive synagogues have abolished the mehizah as discriminatory and families sit together.

ME'IL (Yiddish 'Mantle') The embroidered cloth in which the *Torah *scroll is wrapped before being replaced in the *Ark. (See *SCROLL).

MEIR, RABBI *Sage of the 2nd Century CE. A pupil of *Akiva and *Ishmael, Meir was appointed *hakkam after the revival of the *Sanhedrin. His *halakhic contribution to the *Mishnah was largely anonymous since it was decreed that his statements would not have

111

his name attached after a dispute with the *nasi, *Simeon. Traditionally therefore in the *Mishnah*, an anonymous saying represents the view of Meir and his master Akiva.

MEKHILTA (Aramaic. 'A measure') Work of *halakhic *midrash. The *Mekhilta of R. *Ishmael* is a commentary on the *Book of *Exodus* as is the 5th Century *Mekhilta of Simeon ben Yohai.* (See *MIDRASH).

MELAMED (Yiddish. 'Teacher') Teacher in an elementary school. (See *HEDER).

MELAVVEH MALKAH Final meal of the *Sabbath.

MELCHIZEDEK King of Salem in the time of *Abraham. Melchizedek is described in *Genesis 14:18–20 as 'priest of *God most high.' He is mentioned in the *Dead Sea Scrolls and the Slavonic *Book of *Enoch* as having certain *messianic functions. This probably stems from **Psalm 110:4* where 'the Lord has sworn and will not repent, thou art *priest for ever after the manner of Melchizedek.'

MELDAR Term used in *Sephardi congregations for reading sacred texts.

MEMORBUCH (German. 'Memorial book'). A community *prayer book commemorating the dead.

MEMORIAL PRAYERS See *KADDISH, *YAHRZEIT, *YIKZOR.

MEMRA (Aramaic 'Word') The creative work of *God. The memra is the agent by which *God created the world.

MENDELSSOHN, MOSES (RaMbeMan) (1729–1786) Philosopher. Mendelssohn dedicated his life to improving the civic status of the *Jews and providing a philosophical justification for the Jewish religion. His debate with the Christian clergyman John Lavater was widely discussed since, as a close friend of the philosopher G.E. Lessing, Mendelssohn participated in the German intellectual life of his day. The character of Nathan in Lessing's *Nathan the Wise* is believed to have been based on Mendelssohn and he is seen as the forerunner of *Reform Judaism. He himself remained faithful to the *halakha but in subjecting the Jewish religion to the rational tests of the 18th Century enlightenment the practices of strict *Orthodoxy were bound to be called into question. (See also *HASKALAH).

MENORAH (Hebrew 'Candelabrum') The seven-branch candlestick. The menorah stood on the *tabernacle and in the *Jerusalem *Temple. According to *Exodus 25:40 its pattern was a divine gift to *Moses. In the Arch of Titus in Rome which represents the destruction of the Temple in 70CE, a menorah is plainly visible. It became a common emblem of the Jewish religion and subsequently, in 1948, an official badge of the State of *Israel. The eight branch *candle holder used at Hannukah is also described as a menorah. (See also *HANNUKAH, *MAGAN DAVID).

MENSH (Yiddish. 'A human being') An honourable, trustworthy person.

MENSTRUATION See *NIDDAH.

MERCY SEAT See *ARK OF THE COVENANT.

MERITS OF THE FATHERS The belief that the good deeds of ancestors can bring benefit to their descendants. It was traditionally believed that the virtues of the *patriarchs led to rewards for later generations of the Jewish people. Similarly, on a lesser scale, good deeds performed now can secure benefits for one's descendants.

MERKAVAH MYSTICISM (Hebrew. 'Chariot' mysticism) Speculations based on *Ezekiel's vision of the chariot of *God. Traces of Merkavah mysticism can be found in the *Dead Sea Scrolls, in rabbinic *midrash and in the *Talmud. The speculations were also taken up by Christian *gnostics and the merkavah traditions were preserved and incorporated into *kabbalistic thought. (See also *KABBALAH).

MESHULLAH (Hebrew. 'Shadow') An emissary. Meshullahim travelled from community to community in the *gaonic period carrying the decisions of the *academies. They were an important link in the Jewish world and some left interesting historical accounts of their travels.

MESHUMMAD   *Apostate. A Meshummad is one who has converted to Christianity. (See *APOSTASY).

MESSIAH   (Hebrew. *'Anointed One') A charismatic figure who would restore the Israelite kingdom. Messianic speculation flourished in the inter-testamental period and included an anointed king, a righteous *priest and a *prophet of the final days. The idea of a messiah descended from King *David became central during the Roman occupation and there were several claimants such as Jesus and Simeon *bar Kokhba. The *sages taught that the Davidic messiah would be preceded by the Messiah ben Joseph. When the Messiah ben David established the messianic age, *God's Kingdom would be established on earth and all nations would turn to *Jerusalem. Belief in the coming of the *messiah was included in *Maimonides' *Principles of the Jewish Faith* and *Shabbetai Zevi was believed to have fulfilled the *prophecies. In general the *Progressive movements have rejected belief in a personal messiah and instead focus on some golden age in the future. In some circles, the establishment of the State of *Israel has been understood as the start of the messianic redemption although many secular Israelis reject any form of messianic speculation. (See also *MESSIANIC MOVEMENTS).

MESSIANIC MOVEMENTS   Movements based on the coming of the *messiah. Throughout later Jewish history, the community has yearned for a leader descended from King *David who would restore the Kingdom (see *MESSIAH). At various times charismatic figures have emerged. In the 1st Century BCE, according to the historian *Josephus, Judas the Galilean and subsequently Theudas attempted to lead opposition against the Roman overlords. The followers of Jesus believed him to be the promised messiah. In 132 CE *Akiva, the most eminent religious authority of the day, recognised Simeon *bar Kokhba as the promised king. Further claimants arose both in Christian Europe (e.g. the *Karaite Kohen Solomon in the 12th Century) and in the Islamic world where much excitement was generated by *Shabbetai Zvi. Even after his conversion to Islam, many of his followers persisted in believing in his claims. After the 18th Century, messianic expectations tended to be sublimated into hopes of social and political reform and they were later secularised into the aspirations of modern *Zionism. (See SIMEON *BAR KOKHBA, *MESSIAH, *SHABBETAI ZEVI, *ZIONISM).

METATRON Angel. Metatron is mentioned in Jewish *apocalyptic literature. In the *Talmud*, he is said to have a name like that of his master and he is associated both with *Enoch and the archangel *Michael. Because his name can be spelt with either six or seven Hebrew letters, the *kabbalists believed him to be both the supreme *sefirah and Enoch.

METEMPSYCHOSIS See *GILGUL*.

METURGEMAN (Aramaic. 'Interpreter') The spokesman for a scholar. When giving lectures, the *sages used to speak to the meturgeman who delivered the message to the listeners.

MEZUMMAN (Yiddish. 'Ready cash') One of three people. Three people must be present for the public recitation of *grace after meals.

MEZUZAH (Hebrew 'Door Post') Parchment scroll attached to the doorpost. According to *Deuteronomy* 6:9, the children of *Israel must write *God's words upon the doorposts of their houses. In order to fulfil this, the words of *Deuteronomy* 6:4–9 and 11:13–21 are written on parchment and placed in a small container. One of these is attached to the right hand doorpost of every room in the house. This is a very ancient custom – a mezuzah was found in the excavations at *Qumran – and is the means by which every Jewish house can be recognised.

MICAH One of the *minor prophets of the *Bible*. The prophet Micah lived in the *Southern Kingdom and his prophecies reflect the political situation of the late 8th Century BCE. The book condemns the leaders of *Israel who ignore *God's laws and it promises future victory and the *ingathering of the *tribes. Ch. 6:8, 'What doth the Lord require of thee, but to do justly and to love mercy and to walk humbly with thy God' was seen by the *sages as a summary of Jewish law.

MICHAEL Archangel. With *Gabriel, Michael is the only *angel mentioned in the *Bible. in the *Aggadah, he is seen as the guardian of *Israel. (See also *ANGEL*).

MIDRASH (Hebrew. 'Interpretation'). The interpretation and explanation of Biblical texts. *Aggadic midrashim derive moral principles or explain theological ideas from the text while *halakhic midrashim explain Biblical law. Various rules were formulated for deriving a midrash between the 1st and 12th centuries CE. The best-known examples of midrash include *Midrash Rabbah* on the *Pentateuch and *megillot, the *Tanhuma*, which explains the weekly *synagogue *Torah* reading and the *pesiktot, which were collections of homilies for *Sabbaths and *festivals. Various collections of midrashic ethical teaching are associated with particular *sages and from the 12th century, anthologies were drawn up from earlier sources.

MIKVEH (Hebrew. 'A collection'). A ritual bath. The mikveh is used for ritual cleansing after *menstruation (see *NIDDAH*) or contact with the dead. *Proselytes to *Judaism are immersed in it as part of the conversion ceremony and vessels are dipped in it. A mikveh must contain enough water to fill a square cubit up to the height of three cubits and the water must come directly from a spring or be rainwater – it cannot have been previously drawn into a receptacle. Provided the minimum amount of water is present that has not been drawn, extra drawn water may be added to it. The historian *Josephus in the 1st century CE describes the obligation of visiting a mikveh before attending *Temple worship and there are many archaeological remains of mikvaot. Regulations concerning the mikveh are to be found in the tractate *Mikva'ot* of the *Talmud*. (See also *ABLUTION*, *NIDDAH*, *PROSELYTE*, *PURITY*).

MILAH See *BRIS*

MILK Milk may only be drunk from permitted animals and milk or milk derivatives may not be eaten with any meat foods. In an *Orthodox Jewish household, all utensils and preparation areas used for milk are kept completely separate from meat utensils and preparation areas. (See *KASHRUT*).

MIN (Hebrew. 'Heretic'.) A sectarian or heretic. A min can be either a *gentile or a *Jewish heretic. In the *Amidah, a *benediction is said against the minim (probably the Judaeo-Christians in this case). An animal slaughtered by a min is not *kosher and *scrolls written by minim cannot be used.

MINHAG (Hebrew. 'Custom') Binding customs. The *sages relied on established custom particularly in civil law. The minhag must be widespread, common and unrequired if it is to be incorporated into the *halakha although some minhagim only have force in a particular location. A minhag can only be disregarded if it is in fundamental opposition to the principles of Jewish law. Collections of minhagim have been drawn up since the 8th century CE.

MINHAH The afternoon service. Minhah is a substitute for the *Temple afternoon *sacrifice and the service includes the *Ashrei, *Amidah, Tahanum prayers and the *Aleinu. Traditionally the service dates back to the time of the *patriarchs when, according to *Genesis 24:26, *Isaac meditated in the field in the evening. Nowadays *ma'ariv (the evening service) is recited directly afterwards.

MINIM See *MIN*.

MINOR PROPHETS The collection of shorter prophetic books in the *Bible. The minor prophets include *Hosea, *Joel, *Amos, *Obadiah, *Jonah, *Micah, *Nahum, *Zephaniah, *Haggai, *Zechariah and *Malachi. (See also *MAJOR PROPHETS, *PROPHECY).

MINYAN (Hebrew. 'Number') The necessary quorum for public services. The *Amidah, *Priestly *Benediction and *Kaddish cannot be recited unless ten adult (post *bar mitzvah) men are present. In the *Progressive movements, women as well as men are counted as part of the minyan. (See also *MINYAN MAN).

MINYAN MAN An individual paid to come to *synagogue to make up the necessary quorum. In order to hold services and particularly to fulfil the duty of saying *kaddish, a minyan is necessary. Occasionally individuals are paid to come to make up the necessary ten adult males.

MIRACLE A divine sign. Several *Biblical events such as the parting of the Red Sea and *Elijah calling down fire from *Heaven are regarded as miracles. The *sages emphasized that normal daily life was a series of miracles and later philosophers found the supernatural element of miracles difficult to accept. Nonetheless miracles which apparently break the laws of nature are part of traditional Jewish belief.

MI SHE-BERAKAH (Hebrew. 'He who blessed') A *benediction recited for the *Torah reader. The *cantor recites the Mi She-Berakah after each reading. Other forms of the prayer are used after the birth of a child, by a bridegroom and on behalf of the sick.

MISHMAROT   See *COURSES, PRIESTLY.

MISHNAH   The *Oral law. The term 'mishnah' can mean the entire corpus of oral law. It is also the title of *Judah Ha Nasi's great compilation of oral law. This *Mishnah* was a combination and selection of existing mishnah and was compiled in the 2nd century CE. It is divided into six sedarim ('Orders') namely Zeraim ('seeds'), Moed ('Festivals'), Nashim ('Women'), Nezikin ('Damages'), Kodashim ('Holy Things') and Tohorot ('Purities'). Each seder was divided into *'massekhtot' ('tractates') which are in different orders in the different manuscripts. The *Mishnah* contains many different views as well as those of Judah HaNasi. The first surviving printed edition dates from 1492. (See also *ORAL LAW, *TALMUD).

MISHPAT IVRI   (Hebrew. 'Hebrew Law') *Halakhah which parallels secular law. Mishpat Ivri arose in the 20th century. In the State of *Israel, the halakhah applies in all matters of marriage and divorce. When legislating on difficulties of personal status, Article 46 of the Israeli constitution insists that traditional Jewish law must be explored before the final legislation is formulated.

MITNAGDIM   (Hebrew. 'Opponents') Opponents of *hasidism. The Vilna Gaon, *Elijah b. Solomon Zalman, led the opposition to hasidism and insisted that *Judaism rested on disciplined study and *Orthodox practice. Later in the 19th century however, the mitnagdim joined forces with the hasidim to resist secularism, assimilation and the *Haskalah. Nonetheless the mitnagdim follow a different rite from the hasidim – they use the *Ashkenazi Polish liturgy, while the hasidim use the *Sephardi *prayer book of Isaac *Luria.

MITZVAH   A duty, commandment or good deed. All male Jews over *bar mitzvah age are expected to keep the mitzvot while women are excused the time-bound positive commandments. A *benediction should be recited before performing a mitzvah and holiness is to be found in their observation. The pious will be rewarded for keeping the mitzvot in the hereafter. (See also *ORAL LAW, *WRITTEN LAW).

118

MIXED MARRIAGE   See *INTERMARRIAGE*.

MIZRAH   (Hebrew. 'East') Direction to be faced when praying. Also ornament placed to indicate the direction for *prayer. *Jews pray facing towards *Jerusalem. In *Orthodox households, a mizrah is often placed on the wall nearest Jerusalem to mark which direction to face. (See also *ARK, *SYNAGOGUE).

MOADIM LE-SIMHAH   (Hebrew. 'Holidays for rejoicing') *Sephardi *festival greeting.

MODEN ANI   (Hebrew. 'I give thanks') Opening words of the prayer to be said on rising in the morning.

MOHEL   The performer of the circumcision ceremony. (See *BRIS).

MONASTICISM   Although *Judaism does not have a monastic tradition (see *ASCETICISM), in the past ascetic groups such as the *Essenes and *Nazarites have led quasi-monastic lives.

MONTEFIORE, SIR MOSES   (1784–1885) English Jewish leader. Montefiore was elected Sheriff of London in 1873 and subsequently received both a knighthood and baronetcy. President of the Board of Deputies of British Jews from 1835–1874, he was an active humanitarian in his efforts for Jews both in England and abroad. He also supported several Jewish projects in *Israel.

MONTHS   See *CALENDAR, *ROSH HODESH.

MOON, BLESSING OF THE   Prayer said at the time of the New Moon. The Jewish *Calendar is based on lunar months and the new moon is understood as a symbol of both the renewal of nature and *Israel's *redemption. (See also *ROSH HODESH).

MOREH NEVUKHIM   (Hebrew. 'The *Guide to the Perplexed*'). Philosophical treatise explaining the tenets of the Jewish religion. The *Moreh Nevukhim* was composed by *Maimonides in the twelfth century. (See also *MAIMONIDEAN CONTROVERSY).

MORE JUDAICO   Oath imposed on Jews involved in legal pro-

119

ceedings with non-Jews. Used in Central and Eastern Europe from the Middle Ages on, it was abolished in Germany in 1846. The oath was sworn on the *Torah and curses were invoked on those who broke it.

MORENU (Hebrew. 'Our Teacher') Title given to distinguished *rabbis in the late Middle Ages and later.

MORNING SERVICE See *SHAHARIT*.

MOSER (Yiddish. 'Betrayer') An informer who denounces fellow Jews. The *Ladino term is malsin.

MOSES c.13th century BCE. *Prophet and lawgiver. The stories of Moses are found in the Books of *Exodus*, *Leviticus*, *Numbers* and *Deuteronomy*. After being brought up in the Egyptian court, he fled to Midian, having killed an Egyptian. There he encountered *God in a burning bush. He was commanded to lead the Jewish people from slavery in Egypt to liberation in the *Promised Land. During the course of the journey, he received God's revelation of the *Torah on Mount *Sinai. In the tradition, Moses has a unique status. He is described as 'Moshe Rabbenu' (Moses, our Master) and the rabbis taught that the whole world owes its existence to the merits of Moses and *Aaron. Besides receiving the written Torah, he was said to have been given the entire *Oral Law. One of *Maimonides *Principles of the Jewish Faith* was that the *revelation to Moses was superior to that of any other prophet. According to the Christian tradition, he appeared with the prophet *Elijah at the Transfiguration of Jesus and the Muslim *Koran* teaches that he predicted the coming of the prophet Mohammed. However the rabbis were anxious to avoid a personality cult of Moses; they recognised his faults and the *Book of Deuteronomy* stresses that because of his sin, he was not himself allowed to reach the Promised Land.

MOSES, ASSUMPTION OF *Apocryphal text dating from the 1st century CE. It contains the supposed *prophecy of *Moses for his successor *Joshua. Originally written in Greek, it survives in a Latin version.

MOSES, BLESSING OF The blessing of Moses described in *Deuteronomy* 33. It describes each of the *twelve tribes of Israel with the exception of Simeon and probably dates from the 11th century BCE.

MOSES BEN MAIMON See *MAIMONIDES.

MOSES BEN NAHMAN See *NAHMANIDES.

MOTHER According to Jewish Law, the mother should share equal respect with the father. A child inherits his or her Jewish status from the mother and the child of an unmarried Jewish mother is Jewish in every respect. A *mamzer is the child not of unmarried parents, but of a prohibited relationship. The mother is responsible for the maintenance of the home and family life. The four matriarchs of the *Bible, Sarah, Rebekah, Leah and Rachel are to be revered equally with *Abraham, *Isaac and *Jacob, the three *patriarchs.

MOUNT SINAI See *SINAI.

MOURNING Lamentation for the dead or for a calamity. The Bible describes wearing sackcloth, the rending of garments, sitting on the ground, putting dust on the head, *fasting and abstaining from washing as mourning customs. In modern times, the bereaved stay at home for seven days (sit *shiva) after the *funeral and receive visitors sitting on a low stool. Parents and children should be mourned for thirty days, and, in a modified manner, for a year. A *yahrzeit lamp is lit and *kaddish recited on the anniversary of the death.

MUKTZEH (Hebrew. 'Set aside things'). Objects that may not be touched on the *Sabbath. According to the *Talmud, there are four categories of Muktzeh:- objects connected with work, objects not normally used, objects that came into existence on the Sabbath day and objects which supported objects connected with work. Money and tools are obvious examples of muktzeh.

MUMAR (Apostate.) See *APOSTASY.

MURDER If a murder is premeditated and witnessed by two individuals, according to Jewish law, the penalty is beheading. If the killing was not premeditated, in Biblical times, the perpetrator could flee to one of the *Cities of Refuge. In fact the standard of proof was so meticulous, that *capital punishment became impracticable to impose and imprisonment was the usual penalty.

MUSAF Additional *synagogue service for *Sabbath and *Festivals. It is usually recited after the *Torah and *haftarah readings and corresponds to the additional *sacrifices that were made in the *Temple on Sabbaths and Festivals.

MUSAR (Hebrew. 'Ethics') Moral instruction. A distinct branch of ethical literature grew up in the Middle Ages which was extensively studied particularly in the 19th century. (See *MUSAR MOVEMENT*).

MUSAR MOVEMENT An educational movement particularly in 19th century Lithuania. Among the *Mitnaggedim, threatened by the Enlightenment (see *HASKALAH*), *musar was studied extensively in the *yeshivot. Students intoned ethical works in unison and were expected to participate in disciplinary activities to subdue their natural instincts.

MUSIC The music of the *Temple was organised by the *Levites. In the *synagogue, the traditional chant was sung by the *hazzan (cantor) who sometimes added his own embellishments. According to Jewish law, mixed choirs are forbidden although they are used in *Progressive synagogues.

MYRTLE One of the *species which are waved on the *festival of *Sukkot. (See *LULAV*).

MYSTICISM See *KABBALAH*.

NAGID Jewish community leader in a Muslim country. In the Middle Ages the office of nagid existed in Yemen, Egypt and Spain and from the 16th–19th Centuries Nagadim were appointed in Algeria, Morocco and Tunisia. The nagid was appointed by the Muslim ruler and frequently he held a high office at Court. He represented the Jewish community, was responsible for the community's payment of tax to the State and oversaw religious duties. He had the power to imprison or flog his opponents and he could also ensure *excommunication from the community. In Babylon the *exilarch performed similar duties, but, unlike the negadim, it was a hereditary office. The position was discontinued in the 19th century.

NAHALAH See *YAHRZEIT*.

NAHMANIDES (Moses ben Nahman, Ramban) (1194–1270) Spanish philosopher and *Talmudist. Nahmanides was the founder of a highly prestigious talmudic academy at Gerona. He defended *Maimonides against the *ban of *excommunication pronounced on him by the French rabbis and tried to find a compromise in the *Maimonidean controversy. He was the leading speaker in the formal disputation against the apostate Pablo Christiani in 1263 at *Barcelona and was subsequently tried for blasphemy and was compelled to leave Spain. About fifty of his works survive including commentaries, *prayers, *piyyutim and theological treatises. His writings were highly influential and much studied and in his own lifetime he was described as 'the trustworthy rabbi'.

NAHMAN OF BRATLAV (1772–1811) *Hasidic leader. Nahman was a direct descendant of *Israel b. Eliezer and spent much of his life engaged in controversy with other Hasidic leaders. He introduced several innovations including the particular elevation and veneration of the one true *zaddik (namely himself). His biographer and disciple Nathan Stemhartz organised his followers after his death and groups of hasidim still follow Nahum's teachings today.

NAHUM, THE BOOK OF Minor *prophetic book of the *Bible. The *Book of Nahum* was probably composed in the late 7th Century BCE just before the fall of the Assyrian Empire. The prophet rejoices in the destruction of Nineveh and *God is praised as the avenger of all wrong.

NAKDANIM (Hebrew. 'Punctuators') Scholars who provided *Biblical manuscripts with vowels and accents. The Nakdanim were active between 9th–14th Centuries and were the successors of the *Masoretes.

NAME, CHANGE OF In the *Bible, names are changed to mark a significant event e.g. Abram to Abraham, Jacob to Israel. The *Talmud* teaches that if a person's name is changed when they are very ill, this might mislead the *Angel of Death who would turn his attention elsewhere. The change of name is usually accomplished in a short service in which renewed life is asked for the person newly named.

NAMES OF GOD   It was forbidden to pronounce the *Tetragrammaton so consequently substitute titles were used. These include El (God), El Elyon (Most High), El Olam (Eternal God), El Shaddai (God Almighty), El Brit (God of the Covenant), *Elohim (God), *Adonai (Lord), *Hashem (The Name), Ha-Makom (The Place), Shekhinah (The Presence), Ha-Kadosh (The Holy One), Ha-Rahaman (The Merciful One), Attik Yomim (Aramaic. The Ancient of Days).

NASHIM   (Hebrew. 'Women') The third order of the *Mishnah. Nashim deals with the laws of sex and marriage.

NASI   (Hebrew. 'Ruler') Leaders of the 2nd–4th centuries. The title was used in preference to that of King. *Simeon bar Kokhba used the title on his coins, but the first time the title was used for certain by rabbinic leaders was for *Judah haNasi in the late 2nd Century. The nasi presided over the *Sanhedrin, kept in touch with the various Jewish community and led prayer. His authority was recognised by the Roman overlords. The title survived in some of the *diaspora communities and the *Karaites described their leaders as nasim until the 18th century.

NATHAN OF GAZA   (1643–1680) A *Kabbalist and *Shabbatean leader. As a result of a vision, he was convinced that Shabbetai Zevi was the *messiah and dedicated himself to working for the cause. He travelled constantly around the eastern Mediterranean and ultimately his grave became a place of *pilgrimage. His letters were much copied and his disciples believed him to be a reincarnation of Isaac *Luria.

NATURE   The Book of *Genesis teaches that nature is part of *God's *creation. Subsequently the *rabbis insisted that the regularity of the natural laws are as much an expression of God's will as are *miracles and supernatural occurrences.

NAZIRITE   An Ascete. Nazirites vowed to abstain from wine, from touching a corpse and from cutting their hair. The laws of the Nazirite are described in *Numbers 6:1–21 and in the tractate 'Nazir' in the *Mishnah. Nazirite vows can only be taken in *Israel and were discouraged by the *rabbis as being contrary to the spirit of Judaism. In the *Bible both *Samson and *Samuel are described as Nazirites.

NEHEMIAH, BOOK OF *Biblical book. The *Book of Nehemiah* was perceived as the second part of the *Book of *Ezra* by the rabbis. It describes the rebuilding of the walls of *Jerusalem, the renewal of the *covenant under Ezra and Nehemiah's own reforms. (See also *EZRA, BOOK OF*).

NEILAH (Hebrew. 'Closing') Closing prayer for the *Day of Atonement. Originally the Neilah was recited every day in the *Temple one hour before sunset. Today it is believed to symbolize the closing of the Gates of Heaven after the Day of Judgement.

NEO-ORTHODOXY A Modernist movement within *Orthodoxy. Neo-Orthodoxy was founded in the late 19th Century by Samson Raphael *Hirsch. Accommodation with modern society was accepted together with a full secular education, while remaining true to the principles of *halakhah. (See also *HIRSCH, SAMSON RAPHAEL*).

NEPHESH (Hebrew. 'Soul') The spiritual part of a human being. The word 'nephesh' derives from the word meaning 'breath' and 'wind' and the *Book of *Genesis* Ch.2 describes how *God breathed into the nostrils of the first man *Adam and Adam became a living soul. Traditionally it was believed that the soul led a shadowy existence in *Sheol after death, but subsequently the Jews were influenced by the Hellenistic doctrine of the immortality of the soul. The *Kabbalists taught the idea of *Gilgul, the transmigration of the soul from one body to another. (See also *GILGUL*).

NER TAMID (Hebrew. 'Eternal Light') The Light that burns constantly before the *Ark in the *synagogue. The ner tamid is a symbol of the golden *menorah which burned constantly in the *Temple and was understood as a sign of *God's presence and as a symbol of the spiritual light emanating from the Temple.

NESEKH Wine used for heathen worship or wine made by a *gentile. Nesekh is forbidden to Jews because there is always the suspicion it has been used in the worship of pagan gods.

NESHAMAH YETERAH (Hebrew. 'Additional Soul') Folk belief that an additional *soul is given for the *Sabbath. The belief is found in both the *Talmud* and *kabbalistic literature and the use of spices in the *Havdalah ritual is probably connected with the need to revive the original soul after the departure of the neshamah yeterah.

NETUREI KARTA (Aramaic. 'Guardians of the City') Ultra *Orthodox Jews who do not recognise the political state of *Israel. The Neturei Karta consists of a group of families living in the Mea Shearim quarter of *Jerusalem. They take no part in Israeli society, carry no Israeli identity card and vote in no elections.

NEVI'IM See *PROPHETS.

NEW CHRISTIANS See *MARRANOS.

NEW MOON See *ROSH HODESH.

NEW YEAR There are four different new years in the Jewish tradition:- Nisan I is the beginning of the religious *calendar; Elul I is the new year for tithes; Tishri I – see *ROSH HASHANAH; Shevat I is the new year for trees. (See *TU BI-SHEVAT).

NEW YEAR IN JERUSALEM See *LASHANAH HABA'AH BI YERUSHALAYIM.

NEZIKIN (Hebrew. 'Torts'). Fourth order of the *Mishnah. Nezikin deals with legal procedures and civil law and includes the tractate *'Avot'.

NIDDAH (Hebrew. 'Menstruating Woman') The laws relating to menstruating women which are found in the order of *Tohorot in the *Mishnah. A woman is considered unclean and is forbidden to her husband from the time a woman's menstrual period begins until seven days after it is finished. After childbirth, she is unclean for thirty-three days if she has a boy and sixty-six if she has a girl. When the unclean period is over, she must immerse herself in the ritual bath or *mikveh. These laws are explained as maintaining sexual interest in married life and their origin lies in the *sin of *Eve. Although traditionally it was considered more important to build a mikveh than a *synagogue, the laws of niddah have fallen into disuse except among the strictly *Orthodox.

NIGHT PRAYER   Prayers recited before going to sleep. Traditionally the first paragraph of the *Shema and other *blessings taken from the *evening service are recited before settling oneself for sleep.

NIKKUR   (Hebrew. 'Separating the fat') *Removing the fat from *sacrificial animals. According to the *Book of Leviticus* Ch. 7, fat from the sacrifices might not be eaten, but instead was burnt on the *altar.

NINTH OF AV   See *TISHA B'AV.*

NOACHIDE LAWS   Laws given to *Noah and thought to be relevant to all human beings. The Noachide laws include prohibitions against theft, sexual immorality, *blasphemy, *idolatry, eating from a living animal and the injunction to formulate a system of laws. Although *Jews are expected to keep the *Torah in its entirety, *gentiles are only expected to keep the seven Noachide laws. *Maimonides taught that such a gentile has a share in the world to come. There is some dispute as to whether Christians with their trinitarian beliefs keep the Noachide prohibition against idolatry.

NOAH   Survivor of the *Biblical *flood. The *Book of *Genesis* describes how *God saved Noah, his family and a breeding pair of each species in a great *ark. After the flood, God made a *covenant with *Noah, giving him the *Noachide laws and promising that never again would he seek to destroy the world he had made. The *aggadic tradition gives several additional instances of Noah's righteousness.

NORTHERN KINGDOM   See *ISRAEL.

NOTARIKON   System of shorthand. In Notarikon words are shortened or one letter stands for the whole. Notarikon is also used as a tool for interpreting the *Bible and is one of the *hermaneutical rules for the interpretation of scripture. (See also *HERMANEUTICS*).

NUMBERS, BOOK OF   Fourth book of the *Pentateuch. The *Book of Numbers* includes a census of the twelve tribes and describes the Israelites' travels through the wilderness from the revelation of *Sinai until the stay at Shittim. It also includes the laws of the *Nazarite, the *Levites and the red *heifer. Traditionally believed to have been written by *Moses, most scholars place it considerably later. (See also *DOCUMENTARY HYPOTHESIS).

NUSAH Musical term used in the Jewish *liturgy. Nusah sometimes refers to the traditional tune and sometimes it indicates a particular musical mode.

NUSAKH (Hebrew. 'Version') The different *liturgical rites used in the various Jewish communities. The term can also refer to different traditions of melody in different *synagogues.

NUZU Ancient city in Mesopotamia. Nuzu was the site of important archaeological discoveries which cast light on the life and times of the *patriarchs. The modern town Yoghlan Tepe in Iraq is built over the original site.

OATHS A self curse if certain obligations or conditions are not met. The *Bible records many instances of oaths being taken and fake oaths were strongly condemned. According to the *Talmud, oaths could be used as evidence in civil cases, but the oaths of minors, the insane, the deaf and known liars could not be accepted. Taking an oath involved touching a *Torah scroll and swearing by *God or by one of his attributes. From the 14th Century, *witnesses swore oaths that they were speaking the truth although this was not a practice for which there was universal approval. (See also *MORE JUDAICO).

OBADIAH, BOOK OF *Biblical book of *prophecy. The *Book of Obadiah* is generally dated in the late 7th/early 6th century BCE. It includes oracles of woe against Edom, particularly for the Edomite's support of the Babylonians. The final section which may be a later addition, promises the future triumph of the *Israelites. There are many similarities between the work of Obadiah and that of *Jeremiah.

ODEL (18th Century) Daughter of the *Baal Shem Tov and mother of several *zaddikim. In *Hasidic legend Odel is held to be the ideal type of woman.

OHEL (Hebrew. 'Tent') Structure over a grave. Particularly among the *Hasidim, an ohel is constructed over the graves of *zaddikim and a *ner tamid is kept burning at its foot. Such graves serve as places of *pilgrimage.

OIL Oil was used to anoint Kings and *High Priests and was used in the *Temple's sacrificial ritual. Among oriental *Jews, it is still the custom to use only oil in the *ner tamid. (See also *HANUKKAH).

OLAM HA-BA (Hebrew. 'The World to Come') The hereafter. Olam ha-ba will begin with the *resurrection of the dead and a final judgment. The righteous will be rewarded and the wicked will be punished. (See also *AFTERLIFE, *EDEN, *GEHENNA, *HEAVEN, *HELL, *MESSIAH, *NEPHESH, *RESURRECTION).

OLD TESTAMENT See *BIBLE.

OLEH (Hebrew. 'One who ascends') An immigrant or *pilgrim to the land of *Israel.

OMER (Hebrew. 'Sheaf') An offering brought to the *Temple in *Jerusalem on Nisan 16. An omer was defined as one tenth of an ephah of barley. On Nisan 16 (the Second day of *Passover), it was burnt on the *altar by the *priests to ensure a safe harvest. Subsequently forty-nine days were counted which were traditionally observed as days of semi-mourning. After the forty-nine days had passed, the *festival of *Shavuot was celebrated. (See also *LAG B'OMER).

OMER, COUNTING THE See *OMER, *SHAVUOT.

ONANISM Interrupted sexual intercourse or masturbation. In *Genesis 38, Onan was condemned for 'spilling his seed on the ground'. Following this, most *rabbis condemn any form of contraception which creates a barrier to the seed and other methods (such as the contraceptive pill) are only really accepted for medical reasons.

ONEG SHABBAT (Hebrew. 'Sabbath delight') A celebratory gathering on the *Sabbath day. Many *synagogues hold an oneg Shabbat after the Friday night or Saturday morning service.

ONKELOS Translator of the *Bible into *Aramaic. Onkelos is often associated with Aquila who translated the *Bible into Greek and he may even have been the same person. He was said to be a *proselyte to Judaism and was though to have had a close relationship with the *rabbis of his time.

ORACLE See *URIM and THUMMIM.

ORAL LAW The oral interpretation of the *Written Law. Among *Orthodox *Jews, it is believed that both the written and the oral law were given to *Moses on *Mount Sinai. Originally, however, the oral law was rejected by the *Sadducees. It was studied in the *academies and collected together and recorded by *Judah haNasi in the *Mishnah. Oral commentary on the *Mishnah* was recorded in the Babylonian and Palestinian *Talmuds. The *Karaites rejected the authority of the oral law although it has remained the main subject of study in the *yeshivot to this day. Among *progressive Jews who reject the belief in the absolute *God-given authority of *Torah, the oral law is less studied. (See also *MISHNAH, *TALMUD, *TORAH, *WRITTEN LAW).

ORDINATION See *SEMIKHAH

ORPHAN The care for the widow and orphan has always been regarded as an important duty in Judaism (see *Deuteronomy 24:19–21).

ORTHODOX JUDAISM Traditional Judaism. The Orthodox believe that both the *Written and *Oral Law were given by *God to *Moses on Mount *Sinai. The term was first coined in 1795 to make a distinction between Traditional Jews and *Progressive Jews. The latter are regarded by the Orthodox as sinners; their *rabbis are perceived as laymen and their *converts as non-Jews. For the Orthodox, only a literal observance of *Torah and the subsequent *Codes of Law is adequate. Some Orthodox leaders try to isolate their followers from the outside world while others try to integrate with modern culture while remaining true to the principles of *halakhah. Although many Orthodox communities have been destroyed by the *holocaust, thriving groups exist particularly in *Israel, the United States and the British Commonwealth. (See also *HASIDISM, *MITNAGDIM, *NEO-ORTHODOXY).

PACIFISM   See *WAR.

PAIS   Ringlets of hair worn in front of the ears by strictly *Orthodox men. Pais are left uncut in fulfilment of the commandment in *Leviticus 19:27.

PALESTINE   The territory of the land of *Israel. The country was so called from late Roman times, but the name was officially changed in 1948 with the founding of the State of Israel. The term Palestinian is used for the non-Jewish previous inhabitants of the land and their descendants.

PALESTINIAN TALMUD   See *TALMUD.

PARABLE   A comparison. Parables are often stories which make a moral or religious point by drawing a comparison. They were used by the *Biblical *prophets and many are to be found in the *aggadic tradition.

PARADISE   See *GARDEN OF EDEN, *HEAVEN.

PARASHAH   (Hebrew. 'Section') The weekly portion of the *Torah read in the *synagogue. The parashah may refer to the whole portion or to a division of it. If to a division, each shorter section is read by a different person.

PARENTS   According to the *Ten Commandments, children are required to honour their father and their mother. According to the *Talmud, children must support their parents in their old age and must obey their parents at all times unless obeying them would involve transgressing the *Torah.

PARNAS   (Hebrew. 'Supporter') Head of the Jewish community. In the Middle Ages, the Parnas was elected to the office generally for a limited period. In the modern era, the term refers to the President of a congregation or head of a particular local community.

PAROCHET   The curtain veiling the sanctuary of the *tabernacle. According to *Exodus 26:31, it was made of scarlet, purple and fine linen and had a woven design. Today the *Ashkenazim use the term to refer to the curtain hanging in front of the *Ark in the *Synagogue.

PARTITION See *MEHIZAH*.

PARVE (Yiddish. 'Neutral') Food that contains neither milk nor meat products. Under the rules of *kashrut parve foods can be eaten at both milk and meat meals.

PASCHAL LAMB The lamb *sacrificed in the *Temple at the *Passover *Festival. Traditionally the Paschal lamb was sacrificed on Nisan 14, was roasted whole and eaten by the community. This custom ended with the destruction of the *Temple in 70 CE although a bone is still put on the *seder plate to symbolise the paschal lamb. The *Samaritans continue to sacrifice a lamb at Passover time on Mount *Gerizim.

PASSOVER See *PESAH*.

PATRIARCHS AND MATRIARCHS The *Biblical ancestors of the Jewish people. *Abraham, *Isaac, *Jacob and their wives, Sarah, Rebekah, Leah and Rachel are considered to be the patriarchs and matriarchs. Their stories are recorded in the *Book of *Genesis* and the *rabbis taught that because of their merits, *God hastened the liberation of the *Israelites from slavery in Egypt.

PEACE OFFERING *Sacrifice given in fulfilment of a *vow or as a free-will offering. Although the rules for such sacrifices are laid down in the *Talmud*, no more sacrifices were made after the destruction of the *Temple in *Jerusalem in 70CE.

PEAH (Hebrew. 'Corner') See *GLEANINGS*.

PENITENCE, THE TEN DAYS OF The period of ten days from *Rosh Hashanah to *Yom Kippur. The *rabbis taught that individuals are judged at Rosh Hashanah and the judgment is announced at Yom Kippur. It is possible however to reverse the judgment through severe penitence during the ten day period. During the Ten Days of Penitence, *Selihot are said every day and a special *liturgy is followed in the *synagogue.

PENITENTIAL PRAYERS See *SELIHOT*.

PENTATEUCH   The first five books of the *Bible. The Pentateuch contains the books of *Genesis, *Exodus, *Leviticus, *Numbers and *Deuteronomy. It covers the history of the *Jews from the *creation of the world until the death of *Moses. Among *Orthodox Jews it is an article of faith that the Pentateuch is a single document and was revealed by *God to Moses who wrote it down. The Pentateuch is written on a single *Scroll and a portion is read week-by-week in the *synagogue (see *SIDRA). The entire text is completed in a year and the Scroll is dressed and kept in the *Ark of the synagogue. The Pentateuch, the *Written Law of the Jewish people, is known as the *Torah. It is the ultimate authority of the Jewish religion and the source of all subsequent *Oral Law. (See also *DOCUMENTARY HYPOTHESIS, *TORAH, *WRITTEN LAW).

PENTECOST   See *SHAVUOT.

PEREK SHIRAH   (Hebrew. 'Chapter of a Song') An anonymous collection of hymns of praise. The Perek Shirah dates from as early as the 10th Century BCE and is preserved in several manuscripts. It is sometimes recited after *Morning Service.

PERSECUTION   See *ANTI-SEMITISM.

PERUSH   *Rashi's commentary as printed in editions of the *Talmud.

PERUSHIM   (Hebrew. 'Separated Ones') See *PHARISEES.

PESAH   (Passover) The *Festival of unleavened bread (*Mazzah). Pesah is one of the three *pilgrim festivals and takes place in the spring. It begins on Nisan 15 and lasts for seven days in *Israel and eight in the *diaspora. It is a festival of freedom; the story of the *exodus is remembered at the *seder meal which is generally eaten at home. In the days of the *Temple, the *paschal lamb was *sacrificed on Passover eve commemorating how the *Israelites killed a lamb and smeared its blood on their doorposts so that the *angel of death would 'pass over' their houses. At the *seder, a particular order of service is followed which is found in the *Haggadah. During the seven or eight days of the festival, no leaven (*hamez) must be kept in the house and no leaven products may be eaten. Traditionally it is believed that the *prophet Elijah, as the herald of the *messiah, would return during the Passover season and the seder looks forward to the messianic *redemption. The counting of the *omer is begun on the second night of the festival. (See also *SEDER).

PESHAT The literal meaning of a text. Peshat is frequently set in contrast with *derash, the symbolic interpretation. This distinction was used by *Rashi in his *Bible commentaries.

PESHITTA (Syrian. 'Simple') The Syriac translation of the *Bible. The Peshitta dates back to the late 1st Century CE.

PESHER (Hebrew. 'Interpretation') The application of *prophecy to future events. In particular Pesher is the name given to a number of *biblical commentaries among the *Dead Sea Scrolls.

PESIKTA (Aramaic. 'Section') *Midrashic homilies. Pesikta are homilies, dating back possibly to the 5th Century CE, on *Torah and *haftarah *Bible readings. The two best known are the Pesikta de-Rav Kahana and the Pesikta Rabbati.

PETIHAH (Hebrew. 'Opening') The ritual of opening the *synagogue *Ark. Petihah is performed to take out or to replace the *Torah scrolls or when reciting particularly solemn *prayers: It is usual to stand when the Ark is open.

PHARISEE (Hebrew. 'Perushim') A religious sect of the Second *Temple era. The Pharisees are first mentioned c.160 BCE. Their name means 'the separated ones' and they were scrupulous in their observance of both *written and *oral law. They taught in the *synagogues and their beliefs, particularly in the *resurrection of the dead and the coming of the *messiah, affected that of the vast majority of the Jewish people. At times they came into conflict with the *Sadducees and at one stage they were excluded from the *Sanhedrin. After the destruction of the *Temple in 70CE, the sacrificial system came to an end. It was the Pharisaic interpretation of the law that survived and was continued in the work of the *rabbis. Although the New Testament paints an unflattering picture of the pharisees, there is no doubt that they had high standards of moral integrity.

PHILISTINES The ancient people of Southern *Palestine. The Philistines became the chief enemies of the *Israelites in the time of the *Judges and, because of their threat, the Israelites felt it necessary to have a king to rule over them.

PHILO (c.20 BCE – 50 CE) Ancient philosopher. Philo lived in Alexandria and interpreted the Jewish faith in the light of contemporary philosophical thinking. He wrote on such subjects as *creation, *allegory, the *soul and *providence but his work was probably more influential on early Christianity than on Judaism.

PHILOSOPHY Throughout history Jewish philosophers have tried to explain the Jewish faith in the light of current philosophical understanding. *Philo of Alexandria was influenced by stoicism and neo-Platonism; medieval philosophers such as *Maimonides and *Saadyan Gaon had read the Greek philosophers in Arabic translation and Maimonides, in particular, was profoundly affected by the thought of Aristotle. In the modern period the process has continued:- Moses *Mendelssohn for example had a close friendship with the German philosopher Lessing and Franz *Rosenzweig and Martin *Buber were influenced by existentialism.

PHYLACTERIES See *TEFILLIN.

PIDYON HA-BEN (Hebrew. 'Redemption of the Firstborn') The ceremony of 'buying back' the *firstborn son from *God. According to *Exodus 13:11–16, every first-born son belongs to God, *Redemption is accomplished by paying to the *priests the equivalent of five shekels on the baby's thirty-first day of life. Today this sum is paid to a *kohen and it is accompanied by the recital of special prayers.

PIKKU'AH NEFESH (Hebrew. 'Regard for human life') The obligation to save life. Pikku'ah nefesh is based on the command in *Leviticus 19:16 that 'thou shalt not stand idly by the blood of thy neighbour' and the duty to save life supersedes any other law except those against *murder, *idolatry and *incest. Further than this, *Sabbath laws must be put aside in cases of illness or childbirth, so, for example, it is permitted to ignite a fire on the *Sabbath to keep an ill person warm, or to extinguish a light to help them to sleep.

PILGRIMAGE   The practice of visiting a holy place. According to the *Torah, all Jews should go up to *Jerusalem for the three *pilgrim festivals. After the destruction of the *Temple, the practice continued, but it was to mourn at the *Western Wall at the ruins of the Temple. Since the reunification of Jerusalem in 1967, particularly, visiting *Israel has become an important element in modern Judaism. The *hasidim also visit the tombs of their *zaddikim and it is customary to visit the graves of eminent scholars.

PILGRIM FESTIVALS   See *PESAH, *SHAVUOT, *SUKKOT.

PILPUL   A method of interpreting the *Talmud. Traditionally a distinction is made between 'pilpul' and 'girsah' – the straightforward meaning of the text. Pilpul was intended to resolve contradictions and make the text relevant to changing historical circumstance. Latterly it became more and more casuistic and many critics believed that it had become less than conducive to serious study.

PIRKE AVOT   See *AVOT.

PIRKE DE RABBI ELEAZAR   *Aggadic work. The *Pirke de Rabbi Eleazar* was composed in the 8th Century and is a story about Rabbi Eleazar b. Hyrcanus. The book reflects many of the customs prevalent in *Israel at the beginning of the *geonic period and has been frequently reprinted.

PIYYUT   A poem which is used as a *prayer either privately or during the course of the *liturgy. The earliest examples of piyyutim go back to the 6th Century and they continued to be produced until the time of the *Enlightenment. Examples include the 'kerovah' which were written to be included in the *Amidah and the 'yozer' which were said with the *Shema. Piyyutim were also composed to be sung at *Sabbath meals and to accompany private prayer. Over the centuries many anthologies of piyyutim have been produced.

POGRAM   An attack, often against the *Jews, in nineteenth and twentieth century Russia and Poland. Pograms were often an important spur to emigration particularly to the United State. They also inspired the desire for a Jewish homeland and encouraged many European Jews to join *Zionist groups.

POLEMIC   Controversial dialogue between religious groups. Jewish polemic was produced against heretics in the *rabbinic period and in the Middle Ages, Christians encouraged anti-Jewish polemic. This reached its climax with the public disputations between the Christians and the *Jews which took place in Paris in 1240 and *Barcelona in 1263 (see *NAHMANIDES). Further disputes occurred within the Jewish community (see *MAIMONIDEAN CONTROVERSY) particularly in later years between the *Hasidim and the *Mitnaggdim and the *Orthodox and the *Reform.

POLYGAMY   Marriage to several wives. Although polygamy seems to have been common in *Biblical times, it was formally forbidden by Gershom b. Judah in c.1000 CE. In fact his ban only reflected the current state of affairs. Polygamy has not been practised among the *Jews for at least two thousand years.

POSEKIM   *Halakhic scholars. Traditionally the heads of *yeshivot, the *rabbis and the *avot battei din were regarded as posekim. They were asked by their local communities to lay down halakhic rulings on practical matters. These rulings were only regarded as locally binding. After the various *Codes of law had been produced, the role of the posekim was to interpret the precise application of the Code.

PRACTICAL KABBALAH   See *KABBALAH.

PRAYER   Public or private communication with *God. In the *Jerusalem *Temple a pattern of prayer was laid down by the men of the *Great Assembly which followed the pattern of the Morning, Afternoon, Evening and Additional *sacrifices. After the destruction of the Temple in 70 CE, the same pattern – *Shaharit, *Minhah, *Maariv and *Musaf – was maintained. From the *geonic period daily *prayerbooks (*siddurim) and *festival prayerbooks (*mahzorim) were compiled. (See also *AMIDAH, *LITURGY, *NIGHT PRAYERS, *PIYYUT, *SHEMA, *TEFILLIN).

PRAYER BOOK   Books containing the text of set *prayers. Before the *geonic era, all prayers were known by heart and prayer books do not seem to have existed. A book containing the daily prayers is known as a *Siddur and one containing the *Festival prayers as a *Mahzor. The earliest known prayerbook, that of Rav Amram Gaon,

137

dates back to the 9th Century. The *Ashkenazim use four main types of prayerbook:- *Ha-Mahzor ha Gadol* ('the Great Festival Prayer Book') which contains all the yearly prayers; the *Mahzor* which contains the prayers for each individual festival; the *Siddur* for individual daily use and the fuller *Ha-Siddur ha-Shalom*. The *Sephardim use the *Tefillat ha-Hadesh* for daily and *Sabbath prayer and individual books for the festivals. The *Hasidim and the *Progressive Movements have their own prayer books.

PRAYERS FOR THE DEAD   See *KADDISH, *YAHRZEIT*.

PREACHER   See *MAGGID*.

PRIEST   A hereditary caste within Judaism. (See *AARON, *HIGH PRIEST, *KOHEN, *LEVITE, *PIDYON HA-BEN, *PRIESTLY BLESSING, *SACRIFICE, *TITHE*).

PRIESTLY BLESSING   Formula for *blessing the people. The Priestly Blessing is found in the *Book of *Numbers* 6:24–26 and was given by *Moses to the *priests. It was recited each day in the *Temple and became part of the daily *synagogue *liturgy.

PRINCIPLES OF THE FAITH   See *IKKARIM*.

PROFANATION   Desecration of sacred things. In the days of the *Temple, acts of profanation had to be *redeemed through *sacrifice. In a wider context, particularly after the destruction of the Temple, profanation was used for breaking *God's law as in profanation of the divine name (see *HILLUL HA-SHEM) or profaning the *Sabbath.

PROGRESSIVE JUDAISM   Non-*Orthodox movements within Judaism. Progressive Judaism is a product of the *Haskalah. (See *CONSERVATIVE JUDAISM, *RECONSTRUCTIONISM, *REFORM JUDAISM*).

PROMISED LAND   Land promised to the *patriarch *Abraham. According to the *Book of *Genesis*, *God promised Abraham that the land would belong to his descendants for ever. (See also *CANAAN, *EREZ ISRAEL, *PALESTINE*).

PROPHET, PROPHECY   One who speaks the word of *God. The early prophets are described in the *Bible as 'seers' or 'men of God'. Prominent among these preclassical prophets were *Samuel, *Nathan, *Elijah and *Elisha. Also mentioned are groups of prophets who dwelt together in bands. These early prophets gave advice, were believed to be able to foretell future events and were involved at the highest level with the political life of their times. The classical prophets are those whose sayings are preserved in the Bible, namely the three major prophets (*Isaiah, *Jeremiah and *Ezekiel) and the twelve minor prophets (*Hosea, *Joel, *Amos, *Obadiah, *Jonah, *Micah, *Nahum, *Habakkuk, *Zephaniah, *Haggai, *Zechariah and *Malachi). The writing prophets shared many of the characteristics of the early prophets although they tended to emphasize the importance of loyalty to *God rather than correct ritual and foretelling the future. According to the *Book of *Deuteronomy*, the criterion of a real prophet was whether his words came true. It was generally agreed that prophecy ended after the Babylonian *exile and that one of the signs of the coming *messiah would be the return to earth of the prophet Elijah.

PROSBUL   A legal formula for reclaiming debts after the *Sabbatical Year. The prosbul was introduced by the *sage *Hillel, but by the Middle Ages it was abandoned because the Sabbatical Year was no longer operative.

PROSELYTE   Convert to Judaism. Conversion seems to have been relatively common in the Second *Temple period and a set procedure was laid down by the *tannaim. The disadvantages of being Jewish were explained to the prospective proselyte and if he or she replied, 'I know of this and am not worthy', he or she was to be accepted immediately. *Circumcision and ritual *immersion were required for male converts, ritual immersion alone for female. Once converted, the proselyte was given a new name as 'son' or 'daughter of *Abraham' (the first proselyte). He or she must be regarded as a *Jew in every respect except that a female proselyte may not marry a *Kohen and, unlike a born-Jew, may marry a *mamzer. After the Christian Church had forbidden 'judaizing' on pain of death, attitudes towards proselytes became increasingly negative. In addition, it was felt that there was no need to try to convert Christians and Muslims because both groups kept the *Noachide laws and therefore had a place in the

*World to Come. In modern times however, with the increase of *intermarriage, conversion to Judaism has again become common, particularly in the *Progressive movements. However Progressive conversions are not regarded as valid by the *Orthodox.

PROSTITUTION, SACRED   Sexual intercourse as part of the cult. Sacred prostitution was common in ancient Middle Eastern religions but was associated with *idolatry and was strictly forbidden in the *Book of *Deuteronomy* and by the *Biblical prophets (eg. *Ezekiel.* 23:37).

PROSTRATION   Lying face down in submission. Prostration was practised in the *Temple at certain points during the *Yom Kippur service and this tradition is continued by the *Ashkenazim.

PROVERBS, BOOK OF   *Biblical book and part of the *Hagiographa. The *Book of Proverbs* consists of a collection of moral maxims many of which are traditionally ascribed to King *Solomon.

PROVIDENCE   The foreseeing care of *God for his creation. The *Bible teaches that God is the Lord of history and guides the destiny of humanity – particularly that of his *Chosen People. Providence is a subject much discussed by both Jewish and Christian *philosophers.

PSALMS, BOOK OF   *Biblical book and part of the *Hagiographa. The *Book of Psalms* consists of a collection of a hundred and fifty songs. They include poems of praise and thanksgiving, war songs, songs in honour of the king, *festivals or historical events and songs which relate to particular experiences. Many of them are traditionally ascribed to King *David. They are much used in the *liturgy and a different psalm is recited on each day of the week at the end of the *morning service. This practice may well date back to the days of the *Temple when the *Levites used to recite the psalms.

PSEUDEPIGRAPHA   Books mainly dating from the time of the Second *Temple which are not included in the *Canon of Scripture. Well known examples of pseudepigrapha include the *Book of *Enoch*, the *Book of *Adam and Eve* and the *Assumption of Moses.* (See also *APOCRYPHA).

140

PUMBEDITA   Centre of Jewish learning from 2nd–4th Century CE. The academies of Sura and Pumbedita were the two centres of Babylonian scholarship.

PURIFICATION AFTER CHILDBIRTH   After childbirth, a woman is ritually unclean for thirty-three days if she has a boy and sixty-six if a girl. After this, the *Book of *Leviticus* prescribes a *sacrifice of purification. Today it is customary for a woman to visit the *synagogue after her period of ritual impurity is finished. (See also *NIDDAH*).

PURIM   (Hebrew. 'Lots') The *Feast of *Esther. Purim commemorates the deliverance of the *Jews by Esther and Mordecai from Haman's plot to destroy them. It is celebrated on Adar 15 and the *Book of Esther* is read in the synagogue. It is customary to dress up and there is a general carnival atmosphere. (See also *SCROLLS*).

PURIM, SPECIAL   Annual celebrations instituted by particular Jewish communities to commemorate times when their community was delivered from danger. Examples include the Purim of Narbonne (Adar 21), the Purim of Cairo (Adar 23), the Purim of Buda (Elul 10) and the Purim of Livorno (Shevat 22).

PURITY   The state of ritual acceptability. Traditionally the three causes of ritual impurity are *leprosy, sexual emissions and contact with the dead. *Leviticus* lays down provisions for the purification of lepers, but these laws are no longer observed because modern leprosy is not considered to be the same disease as the leprosy in the *Bible. (For the laws of purification from sexual emissions see *NIDDAH*). Contact with the dead renders a person ritually impure for seven days and, to this day, *kohenim avoid all contact with the dead. The laws of ritual purity are laid down in the *Mishnah*, but many have fallen into disuse and the *Progressive movements have abandoned them completely. (See also *KOHEN*, *MIKVEH*, *NIDDAH*, *TOHORAH*).

QABBALAH   See *KABBALAH*.

QUMRAN COMMUNITY   A monastic group who lived near the shores of the Dead Sea in the 1st Century BCE/CE. Major archaeological excavations have taken place in the area and the Qumran site consists of a large building complex with extensive store rooms and a cemetery. The community which lived there is believed to be identical with the *Essene community described by Pliny the Elder. There are signs that the buildings were destroyed by fire in the late 1st Century CE, presumably by the Romans in the Jewish war described by *Josephus. Near the site are the caves where the *Dead Sea Scrolls were discovered. These give a remarkable picture of the beliefs and practices of a monastic community – presumably the one living at Qumran. (See also *DEAD SEA SCROLLS, *ESSENES, *YAHAD).

RABBANITES The opponents of the *Karaites. From the 10th Century, Rabbanite was used to describe a *Jew who accepted the authority of the *Oral Law.

RABBI A learned man who has received *ordination. 'Rabbi' literally means 'my master' and the title has been used since the time of *Hillel for those who have received *semikhah. This was only granted in Israel so the learned men of Babylon were known as *Rav. Rabbis were not *priests and had no sacramental duties. In the early days they devoted themselves to interpreting and expounding the *Written and *Oral Law. It was only in the Middle Ages that rabbis became spiritual leaders of particular communities and initially there was reluctance to accept money for teaching *Torah. The role of the medieval rabbi was to give *responsa, serve on *battei dinim and, frequently, to be rosh *yeshivah (head of the talmudic academy). Since the *Enlightenment, the traditional yeshivah training has been regarded as less than adequate for the modern rabbi and nowadays most rabbis are graduates of specific *rabbinical seminaries. The modern rabbi's role is broadly analogous to that of a Christian minister in that he leads services, preaches sermons, educates children and counsels his congregants. In *Israel the rabbi serves on the rabbinical courts which have important jurisdiction in matters of personal status. All the *Progressive movements now allow *women to be rabbis, but this is anathema to the *Orthodox.

RABBINICAL CONFERENCES Gatherings of *rabbis convened to make authoritative rulings. From the mid 19th Century, *Progressive rabbis felt the need to meet together to provide definitive guidance. This was hotly opposed by the *Orthodox who insisted that none of the traditional religious laws could be changed. *Reform

Conferences were held in Europe in the 19th Century. In the United States the Pittsburgh platform was adopted in 1887 which was partially modified at the annual convention in Columbus in 1937. In 1961 the Federation of *Reconstructionist Congregations also laid down its programme at a conference. Since the founding of the State of Israel, there has been some agitation for the restoration of the *Sanhedrin among the *Orthodox.

RABBINICAL SEMINARIES   Academies for the training of *rabbis. Since the time of the *Enlightenment, traditional *yeshivah training has been regarded as less than adequate as a preparation for the modern rabbinate. In 1829, the first rabbinical seminary was founded in Padua. This was followed by the École Centrale Rabbinique in 1830, the Juedisch-Theologisches Seminar of Breslau in 1854, Jews' College of London in 1855, the Berlin Jeudische Hochschule in 1872 and the Orthodox Hildesheimer's Seminar in 1873. In the United States the *Jewish Theological Seminary (*Conservative) was founded in 1886, the Hebrew Union College (*Reform) in 1875, the Elchanan Theological Seminary (*Orthodox) in 1897 and the *Reconstructionist College in 1968.

RANSOM   Compensation paid to avoid *death, *slavery or punishment. In Ancient Israel, ransom was frequently paid to avoid corporal punishment and eventually set amounts for each offence were established. It was also regarded as an important religious duty to ransom Jewish captives taken in war.

RAPHAEL   An *angel. Raphael is mentioned in the *Apocrypha and, according to the *Talmud, he is one of the three angels who visited *Abraham after his *circumcision.

RASHI   (Solomon ben Isaac) (1040–1105) *Biblical and *Talmudic commentator. Rashi's academy in France became one of the most famous in Europe. He wrote commentaries on all the books of the *Bible* except *Ezra, *Nehemiah and *Chronicles which were largely based on *midrashic sources. They were hugely popular and his work influenced Christian as well as Jewish readers. His commentary on the *Pentateuch* was the first Hebrew book ever to be printed. He also produced commentaries on the *Talmud. To this day Rashi's Commentaries remain among the most studied Jewish works.

143

RAS SHAMRA   Site of archaeological excavations. Ras Shamra is the site of the ancient city of Ugarit and excavations there have greatly added to our knowledge of *Canaanite customs.

RAV   (Abba Arikha) (3rd Century CE) Babylonian *amora. Rav founded the great academy at Sura and many of his discussions are recorded in the Babylonian *Talmud*.

RAV   Babylonian title for *Rabbi in *talmudic times.

RAZIEL, BOOK OF   A mystical collection. The *Book of Raziel* is an anthology of mystical works dating back to the 13th Century and the *Hasidei Ashkenaz movement. Possession of the *Book of Raziel* was believed to protect the owner's house from danger.

READING OF THE LAW   See *TORAH, READING OF*.

REBBE   (Yiddish. 'Teacher') Teacher. Title given by the *hasidim to their spiritual leader (see also *ZADDIK*) also by *yeshivah pupils to their teachers.

RECHABITES   A Jewish sect mentioned by the *prophet *Jeremiah. The Rechabites were said to be tent-makers who did not drink wine. According to the *Mishnah*, they had a fixed day in the year for bringing wood to the *Temple and they were described in the *Midrash as 'water-drinking sacrificers'.

RECONSTRUCTION   A *Progressive movement. Founded by Mordecai *Kaplan and disseminated from 1935 by the *Reconstructionist* Magazine, Reconstructionism maintains that Judaism is an evolving religious civilization. The Reconstructionist *Prayer Book avoids all notions of a personal *messiah, the *chosenness of the *Jews or the specific revelation by *God to *Moses. Kaplan's ideas have been highly influential and most major American cities have a reconstructionist congregation.

REDEMPTION   Rescue from destruction. The *Bible describes *God as the source of human redemption. He liberated the *Jews from slavery in Egypt and ultimately he will establish an everlasting *covenant. The *Talmud* teaches that redemption will come about through good deeds and *repentance. The agent of God's redemption will be the *messiah; the land of *Israel will be restored to the Jewish people and, after a final judgment, all the righteous, both Jew and *gentile will be saved to live in God's light forever. Although these beliefs in redemption are part of the *principles of the Jewish faith, in modern times redemption is more frequently understood in terms of the triumph of good over evil in this world. *Progressive Jews in particular tend to emphasize individual salvation as part of earthly human growth and development.

RED HEIFFER The creature used in ancient *purification ceremonies. The *Book of *Numbers* describes how the red heiffer must be slaughtered, burned and its ashes combined with spring water. This solution was used for purification on the third and seventh day after defilement. After the destruction of the *Temple, no more red heiffers could be *sacrificed and, although the *Talmud* discusses the laws of the red heiffer, the ritual died out.

REFORM JUDAISM A *Progressive denomination within mainstream *Judaism. From the time of the *Enlightenment, there was an attempt to make Judaism more relevant by introducing new *prayers in the vernacular and abbreviating the traditional liturgy. Reform Judaism developed differently in different countries. In Great Britain, Reform Judaism became very much like the *Conservative movement in the United States and a more radical movement, Liberal Judaism, was founded in the late 19th Century. In Germany, despite the reform of the liturgy, congregations remained theologically conservative. In the United States, at the Pittsburgh Platform, the Reform *rabbis pledged themselves to accepting only the laws and customs which 'elevate and sanctify our lives'. This position was modified by the Columbus platform in 1937 and in recent years American Reform Judaism has become more traditional. In the United States, Reform rabbis are trained at the Hebrew Union College and in Great Britain, the Leo Baeck College trains both Liberal and Reform.

REJOICING IN THE LAW See *SIMHAT TORAH*.

REMNANT A faithful group who will survive all tribulations and punishments. According to the *Biblical *prophets, as a result of their unfaithfulness, the Jewish people would be driven into exile and many would be destroyed. Nonetheless a faithful remnant would be saved. This theme is prominent in the work of *Isaiah, *Jeremiah, *Micah and *Joel. To this day, the traditional liturgy includes the petition to 'guard the remnant of *Israel and suffer not Israel to perish'.

RENDING OF GARMENTS   See *KERIAH.

REPENTANCE   See *TESHUVAH.

RESH KALLAH   The leading sages of the Babylonian *academies. At any one time there were seven resh kallah and they were expected to preach publicly in the academies.

RESPONSA   Authoritative answers to *halakhic queries. Letters of responsa were sent between the *academies in *talmudic times and from the *geonic period, responsa were the major source of the dissemination of the *Oral Law throughout the *Diaspora. Queries were sent to the *yeshivot; they were discussed and the final letters of responsa were signed by all the senior *rabbis of the *yeshivah. Collections of responsa were also made and circulated. *Orthodox authorities continue to give responsa to this day which frequently deal with problems arising from modern technology such as whether it is permissable to open the refrigerator on the *Sabbath.

RESURRECTION   The belief that the *dead will be raised. Although there is no doctrine of resurrection in the *Bible, by *talmudic times the belief in the resurrection of the dead had become an important tenet of the Jewish faith. It was never accepted by the *Sadducees, but it was preached by the *Pharisees and was incorporated into the *synagogue *liturgy. The precise details and chronology are not exactly clear, but it is believed that the resurrection will take place 'in the days of the *messiah'. *Maimonides incorporated the doctrine in his *Principles of the Jewish faith, although there is some doubt as to whether he believed in the literal resurrection of the body. *Progressive Judaism has largely abandoned the belief preferring the doctrine of the immortality of the *soul.

RETALIATION   Retribution. The idea of retaliation is enshrined in the *Bible – an 'eye for an eye and a tooth for a tooth'. Nonetheless from ancient times, monetary compensation was considered not only an acceptable, but a desirable substitute for literal retribution.

REVELATION *God's disclosure of himself. The ultimate revelation for the Jewish people is the *Torah which God revealed to *Moses on Mount *Sinai. He also revealed himself through the *prophets, the *writings and through the *Oral Law. It remains a fundamental tenet of *Orthodox Judaism that he who denies that the Torah was revealed by God has no place in the *World to come.

RIGHTEOUSNESS Living in accordance with the law of *God. Righteousness is the goal of every pious Jew and traditionally it was taught that in every generation there are only thirty-six perfectly righteous men and, for their sake, the world continues to exist. The Hebrew word for righteousness also is used for *charity and alms-giving. (See also *ZEDAKAH and *ZADDIK).

RIMMONIM (Hebrew. 'Pomegranates') Sephardic term for the finials on the staves on which the *Scroll of the Law is rolled. Traditionally the finials were shaped like pomegranates though later other designs were used.

RISHON LE-ZION (Hebrew. 'First of *Zion') Title of the *Sephardic *Chief Rabbi of *Israel.

RISHONIM (Hebrew. 'Authorities') Earlier scholars. The *Talmud uses the term 'rishonim' to describe scholars who have gone before. Today the term is used for the authorities who succeeded the *geonim until those of the mid 15th Century when the practice of rabbinic *semikhah was revived.

RITUAL SLAUGHTER See *SHEHITA.

ROBBERY Theft of property. The traditional penalty for robbery was full restitution either of the object itself or of its full value.

ROSENZWEIG, FRANZ (1886–1929) German theologian. Rosenzweig's *Star of Redemption* (1921) was highly influential on the Jewish community of the mid twentieth century. He collaborated with

Martin *Buber in translating the *Bible into German, despite his increased disability from a paralysing disease.

ROSH HA-SHANAH (Hebrew. 'New Year') The Jewish *New Year. Rosh ha-Shanah is celebrated on Tishri 1. Traditionally it is believed that all human beings are judged on Rosh ha-Shanah; the virtuous are inscribed in the *Book of Life, the wicked in the Book of Death and the in-betweens have a ten day period of grace until *Yom Kippur. (See *TEN DAYS OF REPENTANCE). The *shofar is blown during the Rosh ha-Shanah services to call the people to repentance and it is customary to eat something sweet in the hope of a sweet year ahead. Among the *Orthodox, the *tashlikh ceremony is performed in the afternoon of the first day (in the *Diaspora, Rosh Ha-Shanah is celebrated for two days).

ROSH HA-SHANAH A tractate of the *Talmud dealing with the laws and customs of the *calendar's various *new years.

ROSH HODESH (Hebrew. 'Head of the month') The celebration of the appearance of the New *Moon. In the days of the *Temple, a special *sacrifice was offered on this day. In the *talmudic period, a proclamation of the new moon's appearance was communicated throughout the Jewish world by means of beacons. Today the half *Hallel is recited and the *Musaf service is added to the *Amidah on the first day of the month. (See also *MOON, BLESSING OF THE).

ROSH YESHIVAH (Hebrew. 'Head of the *yeshivah') The title bestowed on the principals of *yeshivot.

RUAH (Hebrew. 'Spirit') See *NEFESH.

RUTH, BOOK OF One of the *Five Scrolls and a book from the *Hagiographa section of the *Bible. the Book of Ruth tells the story of a Moabite woman who makes a *levirate marriage with her husband's kinsman, Boaz and subsequently becomes the ancestress of King *David. The book was probably written in the time of *Ezra and in the *aggadic literature, Ruth is regarded as a prototype of a righteous *proselyte.

SAADIAH GAON (882–942) Babylonian Jewish leader. Saadiah Gaon was head of the academy at *Sura although he came into conflict with the *exilarch of the time. He was a prolific author, producing works on *halakhah, *philosophy, *liturgy and grammar. In his lifetime he was recognised for his learning and piety. He was the first mediaeval Jewish *philosopher to try to reconcile *Biblical revelation with current philosophical thinking and he was tireless in his efforts to persuade the *Karaites that the *Oral Law was indispensable to the understanding of the text of the Bible.

SABBATH The seventh day of the week and the day of rest. According to the *Book of *Genesis*, on the seventh day of *creation, *God rested and, in consequence, he blessed the seventh day and made it holy. The *Ten Commandments include the command to keep the Sabbath day holy. From early times, keeping the Sabbath was seen as a symbol of the uniqueness of the *Israelite people and the *rabbis laid great stress on Sabbath observance. They defined thirty-nine occupations as work which must be avoided and suggested that three meals should be eaten in celebration. The Sabbath begins on the Friday evening with the lighting of the *candles and concludes on Saturday evening with the *havdalah ceremony. (See also *KIDDUSH*, **HAVDALAH*).

SABBATH, GREAT See *SHABBAT HA-GADOL*.

SABBATH LAMP Oil lamp kindled to greet the *Sabbath. Today *candles are frequently used. The *mother of the household lights the candles, reciting a special blessing. Normally two candles are lit to fulfil the two *commandments 'Remember the Sabbath day' (*Ex*. 20:8) and 'Observe the Sabbath day' (*Deut*. 5:12). (See also *CANDLE*).

SABBATH PRAYER Prayers said only on the *Sabbath. The Sabbath evening *Maariv service in the *synagogue is preceded by a short service known as the *Kabbalat Shabbat. At home, *kiddush is recited before the Sabbath evening meal and songs are often sung after. In the synagogue daily services, the *Amidah consists of only seven *benedictions and a *musaf service is added. At the end of the Sabbath, after *Maariv, the *havdalah ritual is performed. Different communities use different *psalms and *piyyutim for different Sabbaths.

SABBATH, SPECIAL *Sabbaths on which special rituals are performed. The Sabbath before each new month (see *ROSH

149

HODESH) is known as Shabbat Mevarekhin and special *benedictions are recited. Shabbat Shuvah is the Sabbath that occurs during the *Ten Days of Penitence. Shabbat Hol ha-Moed is the Sabbath that occurs during the *Passover and during the *Sukkot festival. Shabbat Hanukkah is the Sabbath that falls during the eight days of *Hanukkah. On Shabbat Shira, the Song of *Moses (*Ex.15) is recited. Other Sabbaths are also regarded as special. These include the four Sabbaths before the month of Adar, the Sabbath before *Purim, the Sabbath before and the Sabbath after *Av.9 and the Sabbath immediately preceding the month of Nisan. All these have their own slightly different *liturgies. (See also *SHABBAT HA-GADOL).

SABBATICAL YEAR The seventh year on which all land should be fallow. According to Jewish law, no agricultural work should take place on the Sabbatical year and all debts should be remitted. The seventh Sabbatical year (or possibly the fiftieth year) was called the *Jubilee Year. The Sabbatical Year only applied in the land of *Israel and Rabbi *Hillel instituted the provision of *prosbul so that the rich would continue to lend money over the Sabbatical Year. Provisions for the Sabbatical Year had fallen into disuse by the Middle Ages. (See also *PROSBUL).

SABBETAIANS Followers of the false *messiah *Shabbetai Zevi.

SACRIFICE Offering to *God. Worship in the *Temple in *Jerusalem centred round the offering of sacrifices. *Sin offerings were made by the priests on the *festivals as a propitiation for the nation's *sin and were also made for individuals (see *TRESPASS OFFERING). Burnt offerings of animals were made twice daily with two additional lambs offered each *Sabbath. To accompany the animal offerings, meal offerings were also made and *libations were poured out. Details of the Temple ritual are preserved in the *Talmud. Although the Temple was thought to be the only legitimate place for sacrifice, the *high places of the *Southern Kingdom continued their rituals and sacrifices were offered in the *Northern Kingdom at Bethel and Dan. After the *Exile, the *Samaritans offered their sacrifices on Mount *Gerizim. After the destruction of the Temple in 70CE, *prayer and *fasting took the place of sacrifice. The *synagogue liturgy is based on the times of the Temple sacrifices (see *SHAHARIT, *MINHAH, *MUSAF). However, the hope of the restoration of the

Temple and the sacrificial system is preserved to this day in the *Orthodox liturgy. The *Progressive movements do not look forward to the restoration of sacrifice.

SACRILEGE   Violation of the sacred. The tractate Meilah in the *Talmud* is concerned with the subject of sacrilege in the *Temple. Today *Torah *scrolls, *tefillin, *siddurim, *synagogues and their furnishings and cemeteries should all be treated with respect. (See also *GENIZAH*).

SADDUCEES   Sect of the Second *Temple period. The Sadducees were the hereditary *priests of the *Temple and supervised the *sacrifices. The name is probably derived from *Zadok, King *Solomon's *High Priest. They dominated the *Sanhedrin and were in frequent conflict with the *Pharisees. They rejected the *Oral Law and only accepted the authority of the written *Torah. In the *Talmud*, they are also called *Boethusians, but after the destruction of the Temple in 70CE, they had no clear role and disappeared from history (see also *KOHEN*).

SAFED   A town in Galilee. In the 16th Century, Safed was an important *Kabbalistic centre of learning.

SAGES   Wise men. Sages were Jewish leaders from the time of the Second *Temple until the Arab conquest of the Eastern Mediterranean. The Sages upheld the *Oral Law and, after the destruction of the Temple, were highly influential in the schools of *Bet *Hillel and Bet *Shammai and then through the *academies. The term is frequently used in the later period as an alternative to *Rav or *Rabbi.

SALE   Transfer of property in exchange for money. According to Jewish Law, a sale only becomes binding when an article of agreement, a 'kinyan' has been drawn up and exchanged.

SALT   Salt was used in all ritual *sacrifices. After the destruction of the *Temple, salt continued to be used in home rituals. Bread is dipped in salt after the *benediction and all meat must be washed and salted before being cooked.

SAMAEL A name for *Satan. Samael appears in the *Book of *Enoch* and is a prominent character in the *Zohar and other *kabbalistic literature.

SAMARIA Capital of the *Northern Kingdom. Occasionally Samaria is used to refer to the whole of the Northern Kingdom. Subsequently, in the Second *Temple period, Samaria referred to the land between *Judea and Galilee which was inhabited by the *Samaritans. The city itself was known as Sebaste by the Romans.

SAMARITANS A tribe descended from the *Jews of the *Northern Kingdom. The Samaritans themselves claim to be descendants of the tribes of *Ephraim and *Manasseh. They were believed to have intermarried with the Assyrian conquerors after 721 BCE and were rejected by the Jews who returned from the Babylonian *exile under *Ezra and *Nehemiah. Because they were not permitted to worship in the *Temple in *Jerusalem, they built an alternative shrine on Mount *Gerizim. Throughout their history they have been persecuted by Roman, Christian and Muslim alike. Today only a small community survives near the town of Nablus. Nonetheless they are recognised as *Israeli citizens under the *Law of Return. They retain their own *liturgy and customs and have developed their own Codes of Law. They keep all the *Biblical festivals and *sacrifice the *paschal lamb at *Passover. They keep the *Sabbath very strictly, they practise *circumcision and they keep the laws of ritual *purity. Until the 17th century their *High Priests were direct descendants of *Aaron and, after the last descendant died, they are now descended from Uzziel b. Veliat, the Uncle of Aaron. *Intermarriage between Jew and Samaritan is only allowed if the Jew is willing to keep all the Samaritan customs.

SAMARITAN PENTATEUCH The Samaritan version of the Five Books of *Moses. The *Samaritans claim that their most ancient *scroll dates back to the thirteenth year of the *Israelite Settlement of *Canaan.

SAMBATYON A legendary river. The *ten lost tribes of Israel were said to be stranded on the other side of the river Sambatyon after the Assyrian conquest of the *Northern Kingdom in 721BCE.

SAMSON   One of the *Biblical *Judges. Samson was a *Nazarite and possessed of extraordinary strength. His adventures are to be found in the *Book of *Judges*, Chs. 13–16.

SAMUEL   (c. 11th Century BCE) Biblical *judge and early *prophet. Samuel was closely involved with the founding of the monarchy in *Israel and *anointed both *Saul and *David. His exploits are recorded in the *First Book of *Samuel*, Chs. 1–16. In the *aggadic tradition, he was said to be the author of the *Book of *Judges* and to be the father of the prophet *Joel. His tomb near *Jerusalem was a place of *pilgrimage in the Middle Ages.

SAMUEL, BOOKS OF   A *Biblical book. Originally the *Book of Samuel* was a single composition, but was subdivided in the *Septuagint. It covers the history of the Jewish people from the days of the last *judge *Samuel, through the reign of King *Saul until the last days of *David. It contains oracles, lists and poetry as well as history and was produced in its final form by the *Deuteronomic historian in the 6th Century BCE.

SANCTIFICATION   See *KIDDUSH*.

SANCTUARY   A place of refuge (See also *CITIES OF REFUGE*).

SANCTUARY   The central place of Jewish worship. The shrines at *Shiloh and Bethel were described as sanctuaries when they contained the *Ark of the Covenant. The *Holy of Holies in the *Temple in *Jerusalem was also seen as a sanctuary. Today the term is used to describe the area around the *Ark in a modern *synagogue.

SANDAK   One who holds the baby at the rite of *circumcision. It is reckoned a great honour to serve as sandak and the duty is normally performed by one of the grandfathers.

SANHEDRIN   The supreme religious and political body of the Jews in the period of the Second *Temple and later. It was referred to as the 'court of seventy-one' and *talmudic sources describe it as a permanent assembly of *sages. Different sources give different pictures as to its function and composition. The *High Priest may have served as its president. After the destruction of the *Temple in

153

70CE, the Sanhedrin was reformed initially at *Jabneh and subsequently in Galilee. It was re-established after the *Bar Kokhba revolt at the Synod of *Usha. The Romans withdrew their recognition of it in the 5th Century and it fell into disuse. Since the establishment of the State of *Israel, there have been moves to re-establish the Sanhedrin, but as yet nothing has come of them. (See also *BET DIN).

SANHEDRIN   Tractate the *Mishnah dealing with judicial procedure.

SANHEDRIN, THE GREAT   Body convened by Napoleon I. The Great Sanhedrin met in 1807 to confirm the decisions of Napoleon's newly formed Assembly of Jewish Notables.

SARAH   Wife of the *patriarch Abraham and mother of *Isaac. (See also *PATRIARCHS AND MATRIARCHS).

SATAN   The Devil. In the *Bible, Satan refers to merely an adversary, but in the *Apocrypha, Satan represents the forces of evil. The *rabbis taught that he was responsible for all the *sins recorded in the Bible and, according to legend, the *shofar is blown on *Rosh Hashanah in order to confuse him.

SATMAR   A *Hasidic sect, with centres in both *Israel and the United States.

SAUL   The first King of *Israel. Saul was *anointed by the last *judge, the *prophet *Samuel. The people felt the need for a king in face of the increasing threat from the *Philistines and his exploits are recorded in the First Book of *Samuel Chs. 9–31. Ultimately he fell out with Samuel who anointed the young *David in his place. He eventually killed himself after his defeat by the Philistines on Mount Gilboa where his sons also died.

SAVORAIM   Babylonian scholars. The savoraim succeeded the *amoraim in c. 500CE and were in their turn succeeded by the *geonim in c.689CE. A few savoraic decisions were included in the *Talmud.

SCAPEGOAT   A *sin-offering *sacrificed on *Yom Kippur. On Yom Kippur, lots were cast between two goats. One was slaughtered and the other, the scapegoat, was dedicated to *Azazel and released into the wilderness. After the destruction of the *Temple in 70CE, the sacrificial system came to an end and the scapegoat ritual was no longer practised.

SCHNEUR ZALMAN (1745–1813) Founder of the *Habad *Hasidic movement.

SCHOOLS See *EDUCATION.

SCRIBE A legal scholar and copier of documents. *Biblical scribes such as *Ezra were attached to official government or *Temple offices. Later they were responsible for the inscribing and transmission of *Torah *scrolls, *gittim, *tefillin and *mezuzot. When a scribe inscribes a document, he should be in a state of ritual purity. The *Tikkun Soferim was composed to give official guidance to the rules of the scribal arts.

SCIENCE OF JUDAISM See *WISSENSCHAFT DES JUDENTUMS.

SCROLL Length of parchment or vellum on which holy books are written. It is composed of strips which are sewn together to form a roll. Each end is attached to a wooden stave and rolled towards the middle. Scrolls are written by qualified scribes. Today the *Pentateuch is written on a scroll to be read in the *synagogue (see *SEFER TORAH) and several *biblical books are customarily written on scrolls (see *SCROLLS, FIVE).

SCROLLS, FIVE Five books of the *Hagiographa. The five scrolls are the *Song of Songs (read on *Passover), *Ruth (read on *Shavuot), *Lamentations (read on *Av.9), *Ecclesiastes (read on *Sukkot) and *Esther (read on *Purim). They are customarily written out by *scribes on individual *scrolls.

SCROLL OF THE LAW See *SEFER TORAH.

SECOND DAY OF FESTIVALS The second day on which *festivals are celebrated in the *diaspora. It became customary to celebrate all festivals except *Yom Kippur for two consecutive days to make sure they were was definitely celebrated on the correct day. Although this practice has been abandoned by *Progressive Jews, it is still maintained by the *Orthodox and various customs have grown up connected with the second days of festivals. (See also *ROSH HODESH).

SECRETS OF ENOCH   See *ENOCH.

SEDARIM   (Hebrew. 'Order') The six divisions of the *Mishnah.

SEDAROT   Portions of the *Scroll of the law which are read in the *synagogue on the *Sabbath. The *Pentateuch is divided into fifty-four sedarot so all Five Books of *Moses are read out each year. Each sidrah is identified by a key word taken from the first line of the text.

SEDER   (Hebrew. 'Order') The order of service particularly at *Passover. The seder usually refers to the home Passover ritual which is described in the *Haggadah. In the *diaspora it takes place on two consecutive nights (see *SECOND DAY OF FESTIVALS) and includes recitation of the *kiddush, the hiding of the *afikomen, the sharing of special foods, a festival meal, songs, the recitation of the *Hallel and the drinking of four cups of *wine. The structure and order of the ritual is laid down in the *Mishnah.

SEDER OLAM   (Hebrew. 'Order of the World') Two written chronicles. The *Seder Olam Rabbah* is a *midrashic history from the days of the *creation to the *Bar Kokhba revolt in 132CE. The *Seder Olam Zuta* records the generation from *Adam until the ending of the Babylonian *exilarchate.

SEFER HASIDIM   (Hebrew. 'Book of the Pious') Mediaeval German devotional work. The *Sefer Hasidim* was influential on the *Hasidei Ashkenaz movement and incorporated the teachings of Samuel ben Kalonymus, Judah ben Samuel and Eleazar ben Judah.

SEFER HA-YASHAR   (Hebrew. 'Book of Jashar') Ancient book. The *Sefer ha-Yasher* is now lost, but is mentioned in the *biblical books of *Joshua, II *Samuel and I *Kings. A mediaeval volume of biblical legends bore the same title.

SEFER TORAH   (Hebrew. 'Book of the Law') The *Scroll of the *Pentateuch kept in the *Ark of the *synagogue and read week by week. (See *PENTATEUCH, *SCRIBE, *SCROLL, *SEDAROT, *TORAH).

SEFER YETZIRAH (Hebrew. 'Book of *Creation') *Kabbalistic work. The *Sefer Yetzirah* dates from between 3rd – 6th centuries CE. It contains the theory that the universe is derived from the Hebrew alphabet and from the ten *sefirot of the Creator. It was highly influential and from the time of the *geonim, many commentaries were written on it.

SEFIROT The emanations of *God. According to *kabbalistic teaching, ten sefirot emerge from the divine. All together they form a dynamic unit and each one points to a different element in God's *creative nature. They are sometimes portrayed as a tree. The three highest are the Supreme Crown, Wisdom and Intelligence. The seven lower are Love, Power, Beauty, Endurance, Majesty, Foundation and Kingdom. The theory of the sefirot was outlined in the *Sefer Yetzirah* and was clearly influenced by *gnostic thought.

SELAH Word found in the *Book of *Psalms* of unknown origin and meaning.

SELIHOT Additional *synagogue service for *fast days and the season of penitence. Different selihot have been devised in the different communities although the *Mishnah* outlines six additional *benedictions to be recited with the *Amidah. The *Sephardim recite Selihot for the forty days before *Yom Kippur while the *Ashkenazim only start on the Sunday before *Rosh Hashanah. Both traditions recite selihot on official fast days.

SEMIKHAH (Hebrew. 'Laying on of hands') Rabbinical *ordination. In the time of the *sages in *Israel, religious leaders were ordained as *rabbis by the laying on of hands. Membership of the *Sanhedrin was restricted to those who had undergone this ceremony, but any teacher could ordain his students by using the formula 'Yoreh, yoreh. Yaddin, yaddin.' (May he decide? He may decide! May he judge? He may judge!). In the early days, rabbinical ordination did not occur outside Israel and Babylonian teachers were called *Rav rather than Rabbi. From the 5th Century licence to judge was often given in a written document and from the 12th Century this document came to

157

be called semikhah. Today all the *rabbinical seminaries and some *yeshivot grant semikhah using the ancient formula.

SEPHARDIM *Jews of Spanish origin. Although the term 'Sephardim' is frequently used to mean 'non-Ashkenazim', technically the Sephardim are those Jews descended from those who lived in Spain before the expulsion of 1492. After the expulsion, the Jews of the Iberian peninsula scattered through North Africa, Italy, the Ottoman Empire and subsequently with the later expulsion of the *Marranos to Holland, England, France, Germany and the New World. The customs and liturgy of the Sephardim differ in many respects from that of the Ashkenazim and they follow Joseph *Caro's *Shulhan Arukh without the additions of Moses *Isserles. Despite the decimation of the Ashkenazim in the *holocaust, today there are still many fewer Sephardim. Because of conditions in Muslim countries, many have emigrated to *Israel where there is a Shephardic as well as an Ashkenazic *Chief Rabbi. The traditional language of the Sephardim is *Ladino.

SEPTUAGINT Greek translation of the *Bible. The *Septuagint* is so called because it is supposed to have been translated by seventy scholars. It dates from the 3rd Century BCE and some early manuscripts (e.g. the Codex Sinaiticus and the Codex Alexandricanus) still survive.

SERAPH An *angel or a species of serpent. In *Isaiah's vision in the *Temple, he sees seraphim surrounding the throne of *God, each wearing three pairs of wings. Clearly in this instance they are angelic beings but in the *Book of *Numbers*, seraph-snakes are sent to punish the *Israelites.

SERMON A religious discourse generally given during the course of a formal service. (See also *DARSHAN*, *HOMILETICS*, *MAGGID*).

SERVANT SONGS Poems found in the *Book of *Isaiah*. The Servant Songs tell of a faithful servant of *God who suffers on behalf of the people. They are to be found in *Isaiah* 42:1–4; 49:1–6; 50:4–9; 52:13–53:12. They have been interpreted as referring to the *Jewish people as a whole or to particular historical individuals.

SE'UDAH (Hebrew. 'Meal') A celebratory meal. A Se'udah can be held in conjunction with a *circumcision, a *wedding, a *festival or the *Sabbath and it is a religious duty to enjoy such festivities. According to the rabbinic tradition, at the end of time, *God will give a glorious final se'udah at which the meat of *leviathan will be eaten. It is particularly meritorious if *Torah is discussed during the course of a se'udah.

SE'UDAH SHELISHIT (Hebrew. 'Third Meal') The third meal eaten in honour of the *Sabbath.

SE'UDAT HAVRAAH (Hebrew. 'Community Meal') Meal provided by friends and neighbours for mourners.

SE'UDAT MAFSEKET (Hebrew. 'Final Meal') Last meal eaten before the *fasts of *Yom Kippur and *Av.9.

SE'UDAT MITZVAH (Hebrew. 'Meal associated with a Commandment') Meal eaten after religious ceremonies and celebrations.

SEVEN BENEDICTIONS See *SHEVA BERAKHOT*.

SEVORAH See *SAVORAIM*.

SEVENTEENTH OF TAMMUZ See *TAMMUZ, FAST OF*.

SEXUAL MORALITY According to Jewish law, sexual intercourse may only take place within *marriage, but refusal of sexual intercourse within marriage is grounds for a *divorce. All *homosexual activity is strictly forbidden. (See also *NIDDAH*).

SHABBOS GOY (Yiddish. *'Sabbath *gentile'). A non-Jewish person who is hired to carry out tasks on the Sabbath which are forbidden to *Jews.

SHABBAT (Hebrew. 'Sabbath') See *SABBATH*.

SHABBAT (Hebrew. 'Sabbath') The first tractate of the *Mishnah* and *Talmud. Shabbat discusses the laws of the *Sabbath and explores the thirty-nine forbidden categories of work.

159

SHABBAT HA-GADOL (Hebrew. 'The Great Sabbath'). The *Sabbath immediately before *Passover. In the afternoon service, the *Haggadah is read and the *Sermon normally deals with the laws of *leaven. It may be called the great Sabbath because the *haftarah reading from the *Book of *Malachi* looks forward to the return of the *prophet *Elijah who will bring in the 'great and terrible day of the Lord'.

SHABBATEANISM The doctrines and beliefs preached by *Shabbetai Zevi.

SHABBETAI ZEVI (1626–1676) False 'messianic' leader. After meeting *Nathan of Gaza. Shabbetai declared himself to be the *messiah. He appointed representatives of the twelve tribes and announced his messiahship by circling the city of *Jerusalem on horseback. Nathan sent out letters to all the communities of the *diaspora, calling the people to *repentence. The whole community was in ferment and it was thought Shabbetai would depose the Turkish Sultan and take over his earthly rule. However he was *excommunicated in Jerusalem and subsequently arrested in Constantinople. In 1666, he was given the choice between death and conversion to Islam. To the great scandal of the Jewish world, he chose the latter and finally died in 1676. Many of his followers continued to believe in him including Nathan. His *kabbalistic ideas continued to circulate and inspired later popular movements. (See also *DONMEH, *FRANK, JACOB, *NATHAN OF GAZA).

SHADDAI (Hebrew. 'Almighty') See *NAMES OF GOD.

SHADKHAN A match-maker. Arranged *marriages were the norm in Judaism until the time of the *Enlightenment. The Shadkhan was paid a proportion of the dowry for his or her services. It was considered a great virtue to arrange successful marriages and, although the shadkhan is often a figure of fun in popular legend, the shadkhan had an important role in the community.

SHAHARIT The Morning Service in the *liturgy. The Shaharit service replaced the morning *sacrifice after the *Temple in *Jerusalem was destroyed in 70CE. It consists of the morning *benedictions, the *Shema, the *Amidah and, on particular mornings, the set *Torah reading. It can only be recited in full if a *minyan of ten adult men are present and on weekdays both *tallit and *tefillin are worn. It must be recited after daybreak and on the *Sabbath, tefillin are not laid.

SHALI'AH (Hebrew. 'Messenger'). Messenger. Another name for a *meshullah.

SHALOM (Hebrew. 'Peace') A common Hebrew salutation.

SHALOM ALEIKHEM (Hebrew. 'Peace to you') A common Hebrew salutation.

SHALOM BAYIT (Hebrew. 'Peace in the home') The desirable harmonious relationship between a married couple. (See also *MARRIAGE).

SHAMMAI (c.50BCE – c.30CE) *Sage. Shammai was a contemporary of *Hillel and together they were reckoned the last of the *zugot. He was the founder of *Bet Shammai which was known for its stringency in its interpretation of the law as compared with *Bet Hillel.

SHAMMASH *Synagogue beadle. The duties of the Shammash are many and various. He is a salaried official who ensures the practical smooth-running of the institution to which he is attached.

SHAS The *Talmud. Shas was originally an abbreviation of the 'Shishah Sedarim' (Six Orders) of the *Mishnah and *Talmud*.

SHATNES Forbidden cloth. According to Jewish law it is forbidden to wear clothing woven of linen and wool together. Today shatnes laboratories exist to test the precise composition of new fabrics.

SHAVING According to Jewish law it is forbidden to shave the corners of the head and beard. Shaving is understood to mean removal of hair with a knife or razor. Other methods such as depilatories or scissors are not forbidden and the authorities differ as to exactly where the corners are. Shaving is definitely forbidden on Holy days, when *mourning, during the counting of the *Omer and for three weeks before *Av.9. (See also *BEARD, *PAIS).

SHAVUOT (Hebrew. 'Weeks') The *festival of Pentecost. Shavuot is celebrated on Sivan 6, fifty days after the first day of *Passover. Originally it was an agricultural celebration, marking the end of the barley and the beginning of the wheat harvest. Subsequently it became the anniversary of the giving of the *Torah to *Moses. In the *synagogue the *Book of *Ruth* is read as well as the *Ten Commandments. Traditionally small children begin Hebrew School at Shavuot and in *Progressive congregations it is the time for *Confirmation. The synagogue is decorated with green plants and dairy foods are normally eaten because, according to the *Song of Songs*, the Torah is compared to milk. In the *Diaspora the festival is celebrated for two days. (See *ROSH HODESH).

SHECHEM Ancient city in *Canaan. Shechem was the centre of the House of *Joseph and when the kingdom divided after the death of *Solomon, Jeroboam was declared king there. In the *Northern Kingdom it was the second city after *Samaria.

SHEHITA (Hebrew. 'Slaughter') Ritual slaughter of animals for food. Since c.1220, it has been necessary to pass an examination before practising as a shohet (ritual slaughterer). Animals must be killed as quickly and painlessly as possible, by a single uninterrupted cut across the throat. The knife must be completely smooth and clean and the act of killing must be preceded by a *benediction. Only *kosher creatures may be slaughtered and women, the handicapped, minors and the irreligious are barred from acting as shohetim. It is believed that meat eating was only introduced after the great *flood and when the *messiah comes humanity will revert to its original condition of vegetarianism. (See *KASHRUT).

SHEITEL (Yiddish. 'Wig'). Wig worn by married *Orthodox women to obey the injunction to cover their hair.

SHEKINAH (Hebrew. 'Dwelling'). *God's presence. The Shekinah may refer to God himself, but more usually to God's presence in the world. It is often described as a light or a radiance which illuminates the world, rests on the people of *Israel and sustains the *angels in

*Heaven. The *kabbalists identified the Shekinah with the tenth of the sefirot and it represents the feminine principle.

SHELI'AH ZIBBUR   (Hebrew. 'Messenger of the Community') Leader of worship in a *synagogue. The Sheli'ah Zibbur repeats certain *benedictions, reads some doxologies, leads the *Amidah and recites the intermediary *kaddish *prayers. (See also *HAZZAN).

SHELOSHIM   (Hebrew. 'Thirty') The thirty day period of mourning following a death in the family. (See *FUNERAL CUSTOMS, *MOURNING, *SHIVA).

SHEM, HA-   (Hebrew. 'The Name') Term used when referring to *God. 'Ha-Shem' is used to avoid pronouncing the divine *tetragrammaton. It is used in such phrases as 'Barukh ha-Shem' (Blessed be God). (See also *NAMES OF GOD).

SHEMA   (Hebrew. 'Hear!') Central *prayer of the Jewish *liturgy. The Shema is made up of three Biblical passages, *Deuteronomy 6:4–9, *Deuteronomy* 11:13–21 and *Numbers* 15:37–41. It should be recited twice everyday, once in the morning and once in the evening and is a declaration of the oneness of *God. It should also be recited just before death. After the first sentence ('Hear O *Israel, the Lord our God, the Lord is one') it is usual to insert the phrase 'Blessed be the name of His glorious Kingdom for ever and ever'.

SHEMINI ATZERET   The eighth day of *Sukkot. In *Israel it is celebrated on the same day as *Simhat Torah, but in the *diaspora Simhat Torah is celebrated on the second day of Shemini Atzeret. It is observed as a day of solemn assembly and is kept on Tishri 22/23. A special *prayer for rain is recited and the *yikzor memorial prayer is said among the *Ashkenazim.

SHEMONEH ESREH   (Hebrew. 'Eighteen *Benedictions') See *AMIDAH.

SHEOL   Dwelling place of the dead. Sheol appears as the place of the dead in the *Bible and was thought to be located somewhere below the earth. (See *DEATH, *GEHENNA, *RESURRECTION).

SHEVA BERAKHOT (Hebrew. 'Seven *benedictions') Benedictions recited at a *wedding. The sheva berakhot are said after the man has put the ring on the woman's finger. For seven days after the marriage, the sheva berakhot are also recited during *grace after meals.

SHEWBREAD Bread laid out on the *altar in the *Temple. Twelve loaves were laid out and were changed every week and eaten by the *priests. After the destruction of the Temple in 70CE, shewbread was no longer offered.

SHIDDUKHIN (Hebrew. 'Betrothal') The first stage in the *marriage ceremony. At Shiddukhin the woman is promised as the wife of the man. (See also *MARRIAGE, *WEDDING).

SHILOH Ancient *shrine. Shiloh in the territory of *Ephraim was the *Israelite's first cultic centre after they conquered the *Promised Land.

SHIRAYIM (Hebrew. 'Leftovers') Food left over by the *zaddik at *Sabbath and *festival meals. The shirayim is competed for among the *Hasidim.

SHIVAH (Hebrew. 'Seven') Seven days of *mourning. After the death of a close relative, it is customary to sit without shoes on a low stool while friends and relations come to visit to pay their condolences. Work is forbidden during this period. (See also *MOURNING, *SHELOSHIM).

SHO'AH See *HOLOCAUST.

SHOFAR An animal horn blown like a trumpet. The shofar which is made from a ram's horn is blown every day from Elul 2 until the end of *Rosh Hashanah and then again at the last service on *Yom Kippur. In *biblical times it was also blown to declare the *Jubilee Year. It is meant to call people from sleep, to examine their lives, to *repent and to turn again to *God.

SHOHET (Hebrew. 'Slaughterer') see *SHEHITA*.

SHRINE Sacred Place of Worship. After the conquest of the *Promised Land, the *Israelites kept the *Ark of the Covenant at several shrines e.g. *Shiloh, *Shechem. Once the *Temple in *Jerusalem was built in the days of King *Solomon, it was felt that the Temple was the only proper place for *sacrificial worship although the *High Places continued to exist. Once the Temple was destroyed in 70CE, the sacrificial system came to an end. Worship continued in the *synagogue, but they were regarded more as community centres than as sacred places.

SHROUD Wrapping for the dead. Traditionally corpses are wrapped in a plain linen cloth before *burial. (See *FUNERAL CUSTOMS).

SHTETL (Yiddish. 'Small town') Eastern European small town with a largely Jewish population. The life of the shtetl has become known through the paintings of Marc Chagall and the stories of Shalom Aleichem. This way of life was initially eroded by the *Enlightenment, economic depression, *anti-semitic *pogroms and the possibility of emigration to the United States and it was completely destroyed by the *holocaust.

SHTIBL (Yiddish) Small Jewish village in Eastern Europe. Also a small chapel. (See also *SHTETL).

SHTREIMEL See *STREIMEL.

SHUL (Yiddish) *Yiddish word for *synagogue.

SHULHAN ARUKH (Hebrew 'The Prepared Table'). *Code of Jewish Law written by Joseph *Caro. The Shulhan Arukh summarises the commandments governing daily and *Sabbath activities, the laws of everyday life (e.g. *purity, *mourning, *kashrut), the laws of *marriage and *divorce and civil and criminal law. It was amended for the Ashkenazim by Moses *Isserles and is generally accepted as the most authoritative code. First printed in 1565, it has been the subject of many commentaries and is much studied.

SICARII (Latin 'Men with daggers') Jewish freedom fighters in the 1st Century rebellion against Rome.

SICK, PRAYERS FOR   The Eighth *benediction of the *Amidah is a *prayer for the sick. Prayers for the sick may be offered at any time and, if the illness is serious, the name of the person may be changed to confuse the *angel of death. (See *NAME, CHANGE OF).

SICK VISITING   Visiting the sick is an important duty in Judaism. (See *BIKKUR HOLIM).

SIDDUR   The daily *Prayer Book. (See *PRAYER BOOK).

SIDELOCKS   See *PAIS.

SIDRAH   See *SEDAROT.

SIFRA   (Aramaic 'Book') *Halakhic *midrash on the *Book of *Leviticus. The *Sifra* was probably compiled in the 4th Century CE and may go back to the school of *Akiva in *Israel.

SIFREI   (Aramaic. 'Books') *Halakhic *midrash on the *Books of *Numbers and *Deuteronomy*. The *Sifrei* was probably compiled in the 4th Century CE, but it is thought to go back to different schools.

SIFREI ZUTA   (Aramaic. 'Books of Zuta') *Halakhic *midrash on the *Book of *Numbers. It goes back to the 4th Century CE, but was lost despite being frequently quoted. It was subsequently rediscovered in the Cairo *Genizah.

SILENT PRAYER   It is customary for members of a congregation to make silent *prayers at certain points in the *synagogue *liturgy.

SIMEON BAR KOKHBA   See *BAR KOKHBA, SIMEON.

SIMHAT TORAH   (Hebrew. 'Rejoicing in the Law'). The final day of the *festival of *Sukkot. In *Israel, it is celebrated on the same day as *Shemini Atzeret, but in the *diaspora, it takes place on the day after. On Simhat Torah, the annual cycle of *Torah readings is completed and a new start is made. This is accompanied by much rejoicing. The Torah is carried in procession seven times round the *bimah of the synagogue and hymns of praise are sung. In *Hasidic worship, the celebration involves dancing as well as music.

SIN Breaking the *commandments of *God. The *rabbis taught that the main cause for sin was the *yetser ha-ra (the evil inclination) and in general sins of commission are taken more seriously than sins of omission. The cure for temptation is thought to be the study of the *Torah. In the days of the *Temple, guilt for sin could be removed by *sacrifice, but after the Temple's destruction, *redemption could only be found through *prayer and *fasting. (See also *FORGIVENESS, *REDEMPTION, *REPENTANCE, *SACRIFICE).

SINAI, MOUNT The Mountain on which *Moses received the *Torah of God. (See *Exodus 20). In the *Bible, Sinai is also called Horeb. (See also *TORAH MI SINAI).

SIN OFFERING See *SACRIFICE.

SION See *ZION.

SIRAH See *ECCLESIASTICUS.

SIX HUNDRED AND THIRTEEN COMMANDMENTS The total number of laws found in the *Pentateuch. Two hundred and fourteen of the commandments are positive ('Thou shalt. . .') and three hundred and sixty-five are negative ('Thou shalt not. . .'). (See also *WRITTEN LAW).

SIYYUM (Hebrew. 'Termination') The completion of writing out a *Torah *Scroll or of studying a *talmudic tractate. A siyyum is frequently celebrated by a special meal known as a *seudat mitzvah.

SLANDER False report about another person. The *rabbis strongly condemned slanderous utterances and rabbinic courts were empowered to impose fines and even *excommunication.

SLAUGHTER See *SHEHITA.

SLAVERY Condition of human being under the ownership of another. According to the *Bible, an *Israelite can only own an Israelite slave for seven years. After that he or she must be freed. *Jews could own foreign slaves and in the Middle Ages some participated in the slave trade. In the 19th Century, many Jews were prominent in the abolitionist movement.

SODOM AND GOMORRAH   Two cities in ancient *Palestine. According to the *Book of *Genesis*. Sodom and Gomorrah were destroyed by *God because of their great wickedness. Later they became prototypes of truly evil places and there are several tales in the *aggadic tradition of the horrible things that occurred there.

SODH   (Hebrew. 'Secret') A method of *biblical exegesis. Sodh is an esoteric method based on the idea that Scripture has more than one level of meaning. It was used to explain the account of the *Creation in *Genesis* and the *chariot vision in the *Book of *Ezekiel*.

SOFER   See *Scribe.

SOLOMON   (10th Century BCE). King of *Judah and *Israel. Solomon was the son of King *David by his wife Bathsheba and he was *anointed by *Zadok the *priest and *Nathan the *prophet. His kingdom extended from Egypt to the River Euphrates and through foreign alliances and judicious marriages, his wealth and splendour were renown. He initiated several building projects including the *Temple in *Jerusalem, but he was condemned by later commentators for his tolerance of his foreign wives' *idolatry. After his death, his kingdom split in two. (See *NORTHERN KINGDOM, *SOUTHERN KINGDOM).

SOLOMON, PSALMS OF   A *Pseudepigraphical book. The *Psalms of Solomon* consists of eighteen *Psalms supposedly composed by King *Solomon, but probably dating from the 1st Century BCE.

SOLOMON, SONG OF   See *SONG OF SONGS*.

SOLOMON, WISDOM OF   See *WISDOM OF SOLOMON*.

SONG OF SONGS   A *Biblical book and one of the *Five Scrolls*. The *Song of Songs* is composed of a series of love songs supposedly composed by King *Solomon. It probably dates c.400BCE and is traditionally understood as an allegory of the love of *God for the *Israelite people. It is used as part of the *liturgy for the *festival of *Passover and as a voluntary reading before the *Sabbath evening service.

SONG OF THE THREE CHILDREN   Addition to the *Book of *Daniel* now found in the *Apocrypha. The *Song of the Three Children* dates back to c.100BCE and contains the *prayer of Azariah, a description of the fiery furnace and the Song of Shadrach, Meshag and Abednego. (see *Daniel* Ch. 3).

SONS OF LIGHT   Characters from the *Dead Sea Scrolls. The sons of Light were presumably the members of the community at *Qumran and they are contrasted with the evil 'Sons of Darkness'.

SOUL   See *NEPHESH*.

SOULS, TRANSMIGRATION OF   See *GILGUL*.

SOUTHERN KINGDOM   The ancient kingdom of *Judah. The *Israelite kingdom was divided after the death of King *Solomon in 930BCE and the two southern tribes, Judah and Benjamin remained loyal to the *Davidic kingship in contrast to the ten northern tribes (see *NORTHERN KINGDOM*). In 586 the Southern kingdom was conquered by the Babylonians and the inhabitants were taken into *exile. Later the exiles were allowed to return and under *Ezra and *Nehemiah, the *temple was rebuilt and the kingdom restored under foreign rule.

SPINOZA, BARUCH   (1632–1677). Philosopher. Spinoza's major works were the *Tractatus Theologico Politico* and his *Ethics*. He was put under a *ban of excommunication by the Jewish community for his 'abominable heresies'. He denied the divine origin of the Law of *Moses and the doctrine of the immortality of the *soul. He taught of a pantheistic, impersonal *God and he remained alienated from the community for the latter part of his life.

STAR OF DAVID   See *MAGEN DAVID*.

STERILIZATION   The *rabbis taught that it is forbidden to impair the organs of reproduction of any living creature. (See also *BIRTH CONTROL*, *ONANISM*).

STRANGER   The *Bible teaches that strangers must be shown every consideration (e.g. *Lev.*19:33). The rabbis believed that for a

169

stranger to be part of the *World to Come, he or she must keep the *Noachide laws. (See also *GER TOSHAV, *HOSPITALITY, *PROSELYTE).

STREIMEL (Yiddish) Fur hat worn by the *Hasidim.

SUFFERING The *Bible teaches that suffering is an essential part of human life (e.g. *Gen. 3:19). The problem of the suffering of the innocent has exercised theologians; suffering tends to be understood as a means of purification or it is believed that compensation for suffering will be made in the *World to Come. The mass destruction of the European Jewish community in the *Holocaust has made the problem acutely difficult.

SUICIDE Taking one's own life is regarded as a *sin equal to *murder.

SUKKAH (Hebrew. 'Booth') A ritual booth used in the *festival of *Sukkot. It is open to the sky and hung with fruit. (See *SUKKOT).

SUKKOT (Hebrew. 'Booths') One of the *Pilgrim festivals. Sukkot begins on Tishri 15 and ends with *Shemini Atzeret and *Simhat Torah. During the eight days, the Jewish community is commanded to 'dwell in booths' to commemorate the *Israelites' wandering in the wilderness before they reached the Promised Land. At the time of the Second Temple a ceremony of water libation was held during the festival. On Tishri 15 (and Tishri 16 in the *diaspora), the *lulav is waved in every direction in the *synagogue and the congregation walks in procession round the *bimah. The seventh day is celebrated as *Hoshana Rabbah when harvest prayers are recited. In *Israel and in the *Progressive community, Shemini Atzeret and Simhat Torah are celebrated together on the eighth day, but in the *diaspora, the eighth day is Shemini Atzeret and the ninth day is Simhat Torah. In colder climates it is not considered necessary actually to live in the Sukkah. Sukkot is clearly a harvest festival; the Sukkah is decorated with fruits and the *four species are held during the *liturgical services. (See also *ETROG, *FOUR SPECIES, *LULAV, *SHEMINI ATZERET, *SIMHAT TORAH).

SUN, BLESSING OF *Benediction recited every twenty-eight years. The blessing of the sun is recited when the sun is believed to be in the same place it was at the time of the *Creation.

SUPERCOMMENTARY A commentary on the famous commentaries of the *Pentateuch. Supercommentaries have been produced on the works of *Rashi and *Nahmanides.

SUPERSTITION Credulity about supernatural beliefs. Although the *Bible forbids all forms of magic and many later theologians have condemned such beliefs as nonsense, many superstitions have persisted in folk belief.

SURA Place of one of the Babylonian academies. Sura was established by *Rav in the 3rd Century CE and several important figures became head of it, e.g. *Saadiah Gaon. In the 10th Century, the academy was moved to Baghdad and within two hundred years the town of Sura was in ruins. (See also *PUMBEDITA).

SUSANNA AND THE ELDERS Book of the *Apocrypha. *Susanna and the Elders* tells the story of the virtuous Susanna. It was a popular tale in the Middle Ages though scholars do not agree on its original date.

SYNAGOGUE House of worship. The institution of the synagogue may date back to the 6th Century BCE and the *exile in Babylon. After the destruction of the Second *Temple in 70CE, the synagogue became the focus of Jewish community life. Many Temple rituals were incorporated into synagogue worship and the times of the services (*Shaharit, *Minhah, *Maariv and *Musaf) reflect the times of the Temple *sacrifices. A synagogue is built pointing towards Jerusalem. The *scrolls of the *Torah are kept in the *Ark. Generally a reading desk is placed in front of the Ark and the *bimah (dais) is in the centre. In *Orthodox synagogues, men and women sit separately – the women generally behind a *mehiza (screen) but in *Progressive synagogues, men and women sit together. Frequently a synagogue will have a smaller chapel – known as a *bet ha-midrash for study and weekday services and in modern times synagogues tend to be large complexes with community halls, classrooms, offices and counselling rooms. In the United States, *Reform synagogues are known as Temples. Salaried officials belonging to the synagogue include the

171

*rabbi, the *hazzan and the *shammash, but *liturgical services are often led by the lay members of the congregation. Most synagogues belong to a larger group which controls rabbinical training, but they are self-governing institutions with an elected council. Attendance at synagogue is meritorious and most services cannot even take place unless a full *minyan of ten adult (post *bar mitzvah) males are present. The *rabbis taught that *God becomes angry when he comes to the synagogue and does not find a minyan.

SYNAGOGUE, THE GREAT   Institution of the Second *Temple period. The Great Synagogue was probably a body which met periodically to pass resolutions. It is believed to have instituted the ceremonies of *kiddush and *havdalah and the *festival of *Purim.

SYNOD   Religious Council. Several synods have been held throughout Jewish history. In 138 the Synod of Usha was convened to organise Jewish life after the persecutions of Hadrian. Local synods were held throughout the Middle Ages and from the 16th–18th Centuries the Council of the Four Lands was the central governing authority for Polish and Lithuanian Jewry. (See also *RABBINICAL CONFERENCES).

SYNOD OF USHA   See *USHA, SYNOD OF.

TAANIT   Tractate of the *Talmud dealing with *fasts.

TABERNACLE   The portable *sanctuary made by the *Israelites after the *exodus. The construction of the tabernacle is described in *Exodus Chs. 25–31 and 35–40. It was divided into two parts. The inner part, the *Holy of Holies contained the *Ark of the Covenant and the presence of *God was thought to dwell there. The whole was surrounded by curtains and was carried from place to place until the *Temple in *Jerusalem was built in the reign of King *Solomon.

TABERNACLE   See *SUKKAH.

TABERNACLES, FEAST OF   See *SUKKOT.

TABLETS, FEAST OF   See *SUKKOT.

TABLETS OF THE LAW   The two stone tablets brought down by
*Moses from Mount *Sinai. The *ten commandments were inscribed
on the tablets of the law and according to the *Book of *Exodus*, Moses
was given them when he was given the *Torah. Later he smashed
them in his anger at the Israelites' construction of the *golden calf and
they had to be reinscribed. The tablets were kept in the *Ark of the
Covenant in the *Holy of Holies in the *tabernacle. According to the
*aggadic tradition, they were created in the first week of *creation and
they contained the *Oral as well as the *Written Law.

TADSHE   A 2nd Century *midrashic work dealing with the symbolism of numbers.

TAG   (Aramaic. 'Crown') A short vertical stroke added to the top of
particular Hebrew letters when they are written in *Torah scrolls or
*Biblical manuscripts.

TAHANUN   (Hebrew. 'Supplication') A prayer in the *liturgy for
*forgiveness. The tahanun is recited every day except on *Sabbaths
and *festivals after the morning and afternoon *Amidah.

TAKKANOT   (Hebrew. 'Directives') Rulings given by scholars.
Takkanot are directives made by particular scholars which have the
force of *halakhah. Takkanot are thought to have been enacted since
the time of the patriarch *Abraham and the *amoraim issued guide-
lines for the issuing of takkanot. They continued to be given until the
time of the *Enlightenment particularly in areas where the halakhah
had to be applied to modern situations such as the rules of inheritance,
personal status and the position of the *agunah. After the Enlightenment, because of the increased role of the secular government,
fewer takkanot were issued until the foundation of the State of *Israel.

TALION   A fitting punishment. *Biblical punishments tended to
follow the principle of talion ('An eye for an eye. . .') but later
monetary compensations and fines were substituted.

TALLIT   Prayer Shawl. The tallit is worn by adult males at
*Shaharit, at *Minhah on *Av 9 and at all services on *Yom Kippur.
It is an oblong piece of cloth with knotted fringes on each corner. It
may be adorned with silver or gold thread and the area which is

173

draped over the head is sometimes called the 'atarah' (Crown). Before putting it on, a special *benediction is said. It may be made of wool or silk.

TALLIT KATAN (Hebrew. 'Small tallit') A garment with fringes at each corner. The tallit katan is worn by *Orthodox *Jews under their secular clothes. It is to fulfil the commandment of *Zitzit (see *Numbers* 15) and it is worn with the fringes visible.

TALMID HAKHAM (Hebrew. 'Disciple of the wise') A scholar. A talmid hakham must be familiar with both *Oral and *Written Law, he must have studied with a distinguished teacher and he must be personally pious. Traditionally he is regarded as the most desirable type of *Jew and, according to the *rabbis, a talmid hakham, even if he is a *mamzer, takes precedence over a *High Priest who is an ignoramus.

TALMUD The record of the discussions of the *amoraim on the *Mishnah*. The *Jerusalem Talmud* was compiled in the late 5th Century CE and the *Babylonian Talmud* in the late 6th Century. It includes the *Mishnah* with its commentaries which are known as *Gemara*. The *Babylonian Talmud* was recognised as the supreme authority by the 11th century. It consists of discursive discussions and includes *halakhah, *aggadah, folk-law, *customs, *prayers, proverbs and accounts of ceremonial. Altogether the entire text, written in *Aramaic, consists of approximately two and a half million words. It is the major subject of study in the *yeshivot and its study is regarded as an important religious duty for Jewish men.

TALMUDIC COMMENTARIES Commentaries on the text of the *Talmud*. Commentaries on the *Talmud* were composed from the time of the *geonim in the 10th Century CE. The best known talmudic commentary is that of *Rashi which was completed by the *tosafists in the 12th Century. Commentaries on the *Talmud* have continued to be produced until the present day.

TALMUD TORAH Religious study. The term Talmud Torah is applied to Jewish religious schools attended beyond the elementary level (*heder) and before going on to advanced studies in the *yeshivah.

TAMID   A tractate in the *Mishnah* describing the work of the
*priests in the *Temple.

TAMMUZ, FAST OF   A *fast day. The Fast of Tammuz takes
place on Tammuz 17 and commemorates the Babylonians breaching
the walls of *Jerusalem in 586 BCE and the Romans breaching them
in 70 CE. The *liturgy follows that of other fast days.

TANAKH   The Hebrew *Bible. Tanakh is an acronym for *Torah
(*Law), Nevi'im (*Prophets) and Ketuvim (*Hagiographa).

TANHUMA   A collection of *aggadic *midrashim. The Tanhuma
contains many midrashim attributed to the 4th century Rabbi
Tanhuma bar Abba, but since it also contains anti-*Karaite material,
the collection cannot be dated before the 9th Century. It is also known
as Yelammedenu from the opening word of each midrash.

TANNA   A *sage of the 1st and 2nd Centuries CE. *Johanan ben
Zakkai, *Akiva, *Ishmael ben Elisha and *Judah ha-Nasi are counted
among the Tannaim. In the *Talmud they are distinguished from the
later *Amoraim. During the era of the Tannaim, the *Temple in
*Jerusalem was destroyed by the Romans in 70 CE and the *Bar
Kokhba revolt was suppressed in 135 CE. Despite these disasters the
Tannaim succeeded in maintaining the Great *Sanhedrin, codifying
the *Oral Law (see *MISHNAH) and establishing several
*academies of higher learning.

TAPPUHIM   (Hebrew. 'Apples') Fruit shaped ornaments used to
decorate *Torah scrolls. (See *TORAH ORNAMENTS).

TARGUM   (Hebrew. 'Translation') *Aramaic translations of the
*Bible. Well-known targumim include the *Targum *Onkelos*, the
Targum Jonathan (of the *prophets) and the *Targum Yerushalmi* (a
*midrashic translation of the *Hagiographa).

TARYAG MITZVOT   See *SIX HUNDRED AND THIRTEEN
COMMANDMENTS.

TAS   (Hebrew. 'Plaque') A silver plaque placed on the *Torah Scroll.
A different tas is used for each *festival. (See *TORAH ORNAMENTS).

TASHLIKH   A ceremony connected with *Rosh Ha-Shanah. The Tashlikh ceremony is performed by running water and the participants' *sins are symbolically cast into the sea, following *Micah 7:18–20. There is no mention of Tashlikh in the *Talmud and the practice may be pagan in origin.

TAXATION   Levies exacted from the people for a communal purpose. *Exodus 30 records a poll tax levied on the people and subsequently there was a complicated system of *tithes which was used to maintain the *Temple establishment. When *Judea was part of the Roman Empire, a tax known as the Fiscus Judaicus was exacted and in the *diaspora it was common for governments to demand a special tax from the Jewish community. In modern times this practice has largely disappeared.

TEACHER OF RIGHTEOUSNESS   Title given to a leader of the *Qumran community in the *Dead Sea Scrolls. The teacher of righteousness is in the *Zadokite fragments and in various *Biblical commentaries. He is said to have suffered at the hands of a 'wicked *priest', but scholars dispute as to whether he is to be identified with a specific historical figure. Suggestions have included the *Scribe *Ezra, Onias III (the last Zadokite *High Priest), Judah b. Jedidiah (*martyred *sage) or Menahem b. Judah (a martyr of the Jewish rebellion against the Romans).

TEFILLAH   (Hebrew. 'Phylacteries') Phylacteries. The *Book of *Exodus* Ch. 13 and *Deuteronomy Chs. 6 and 11, teach that *Jews must bind the *commandments upon their hands and between their eyes. This is fulfilled by binding special boxes containing the *Biblical passages with leather straps over the forehead and round the arm. The practice is an ancient one and mentioned in the New Testament. The commandment of Tefillin is observed by all *Orthodox Jewish men of *bar mitzvah age and over and is performed every weekday. Among the *Ashkenazim, the tradition is to wind the straps round the arm anticlockwise while the *Sephardim wind them clockwise. The *Talmud stresses the importance of the commandment and declares that even *God lays tefillin.

TEL AVIV   City in modern *Israel. Tel Aviv was founded near Joppa in 1909 and, from the founding of the State of *Israel in 1948 until the reunification of *Jerusalem was the new nation's capital.

TEL EL AMARNA   City in Ancient Egypt. Tel el Amarna has been the site of archaeological excavations which yielded letters from *Canaanite kings complaining of attacks from the *Habiru.

TEMPLE   The focus of Jewish worship in ancient times. The First Temple was built in *Jerusalem by King *Solomon and by the era of King *Josiah was regarded as the only legitimate place of *sacrifice. It was destroyed by the Babylonians in 586 BCE on *Av 9. It was then rebuilt after the *exile under *Zerubbabel and was subsequently enlarged by King Herod I in the 1st Century BCE. The building was organised around courtyards. Through the first wall was the Temple Court which was open to everyone even *gentiles. Beyond that lay the Court of *Women which was part of the consecrated area. Through that was the Court of the *Israelites which was open to all male *Jews. From there could be seen the Court of *Priests where *sacrifices were enacted on the *altar. Within the Court of Priests was the *sanctuary with the altar of *incense, the *shewbread table and the *menorah. Finally, beyond the outer room of the sanctuary was the *Holy of Holies. The building of the First Temple is described in *I *Kings* Ch. 5 and *II *Chronicles* Ch. 2 and the structure of the Second Temple is described in the *Mishnah* and in *Josephus' *Antiquities*. Temple rituals are described in the *Mishnah*. It was finally destroyed by the Romans in 70CE and the Arch of Titus in Rome shows Roman soldiers sacking the Temple and looting the golden candlesticks. The only part that remains today is the *Western Wall. Although Jerusalem was believed to be the only place for a Temple, the *Samaritans conducted their own *sacrifices on Mount *Gerizim and there seems to have been a temple in *Elephantine on the Nile delta. It is believed that in the days of the *messiah, the Temple will be restored.

TEMPLE   A Reform *synagogue (United States).

TEMPLE MOUNT   Site of the *Temple in *Jerusalem. The Temple was built on Mount Moriah where *Abraham was supposed to have almost *sacrificed *Isaac. Later, after the Temple's destruction in 70CE, the *prophet of Islam, Mohammed, is thought to have ascended to *Heaven from the same spot. *Orthodox *Jews will no longer walk over the Temple Mount because the *Ark of the Covenant is presumed to have been buried there in the destruction of 70CE.

TEMPLE SCROLL   One of the *Dead Sea Scrolls. The Temple Scroll dates from the 2nd Century CE and includes laws concerning ritual *purity and the *festivals. Since its discovery, it is housed in the Shrine of the Book in *Jerusalem. (See also *DEAD SEA SCROLLS*).

TEMPLE TAX   Tax levied on the *Israelites for the maintenance of the sanctuary. The tractate 'Shekalim' in the *Mishnah* deals with the laws concerning the tax. (See also *TAXATION*).

TEMUNAH, BOOK OF   *Kabbalistic work. The *Book of Temunah* was produced in the late 13th Century and is attributed to Ishmael the *High Priest.

TENANT   One who hires land or property from a landlord. Jewish law recognises the possibility of paying rent either in produce from the land or in money.

TEN COMMANDMENTS   The ten laws given to *Moses on Mount *Sinai as recorded in *Exodus* 20:2–14 and *Deuteronomy* 5:6–18. The Ten Commandments were said to have been inscribed on *tablets of stone which were preserved in the *Ark of the Covenant. They include the edict to worship only one *God, to avoid *idolatry, to keep the *Sabbath and to honour *parents; they forbid making graven images, *theft, *murder, *false witness and covetousness.

TEN DAYS OF PENITENCE   See *PENITENCE*.

TEN LOST TRIBES   The tribes in the *Northern Kingdom who were conquered by the Assyrians in 721 BCE. The ten Northern tribes almost certainly intermarried with the surrounding peoples and lost their separate identity. II *Kings* Ch. 17 maintains they were exiled by the river Gozan and the *rabbis taught that they dwelt beyond the River *Sambatyon. The *Samaritans are probably descended from some of the tribes and, during the course of history, various other groups have been identified with ten lost tribes including the British, the Japanese, the Afghans and certain Red Indian tribes.

TEN MARTYRS   Ten *sages martyred by the Romans. The different sources do not agree on the names of the ten, but the legend of the ten martyrs has persisted particularly in *mystical circles.

TEN PLAGUES The plagues sent by *God to persuade the Egyptians to release the *Israelites from slavery. The plagues are recorded in *Exodus* Chs. 7–12 and include the Nile turning to blood, infestations of frog, lice and flies, cattle disease, boils, hailstorms, a swarm of locusts, darkness and the death of the firstborn. (See also *EXODUS*, *PESAH*).

TENT OF MEETING The tent where *Moses encountered *God while the *Israelites wandered in the wilderness towards the *Promised land.

TEPHILLIN See *TEFILLIN*.

TERAFIM Household gods. The terafim are mentioned in the story of *Jacob and Rachel (*Gen* 31:34) and *David and Michal (*I *Sam* 19:13). They seem to have been used for divination (see *Judges* 17:5), but were ultimately condemned as *idolatrous by King Josiah when he purged the *Temple of all images (see II *Kings* 23:24).

TERUMOT (Hebrew. 'Heave Offering') See *SACRIFICE*, *TITHES*.

TESHUVAH (Hebrew. 'Repentance') Sorrow for *sin and the return to *righteousness. Teshuvah is the theme of the *ten days of penitence and an important concept in scripture. *God's forgiveness will only be given after true *repentance and restitution. During the course of history, there have been various movements within Judaism to encourage repentance and amendment of life. (See also *MUSAR*). A Baal Teshuvah is one who has repented from his sin and is living a new observant life.

TESTAMENT OF THE TWELVE PATRIARCHS
*Pseudepigraphical work. The *Testament of the Twelve Patriarchs* gives an account of the final testament of the twelve sons of the *Patriarch Jacob to the *twelve tribes and is based on Jacob's *blessing of his sons in *Genesis* 49. The work dates from the time of the Second *Temple.

TETRAGRAMMATON (Greek. 'Four letters') The four letters which compose the name of *God. Traditionally the name is so sacred that it is never articulated and the letters JHWH are read in the text as

179

*Adonai ('the Lord') or *Ha-Shem ('the name'). In English the tetragrammaton is sometimes pronounced as Jehovah.

TETRATEUCH   The first four books of the *Bible. The Tetrateuch is composed of the Books of *Genesis, *Exodus, *Leviticus and *Numbers.

TEVET, THE FAST OF   A *fast day which commemorates the besieging of *Jerusalem by King Nebuchadnezzar of Babylon in 586 BCE.

THANKSGIVING PSALMS   One of the *Dead Sea Scrolls. The manuscript dates back to the 1st Century BCE and contains a number of *psalms all beginning either 'I thank thee O Lord' or 'Blessed be thou O Lord'. It was first published in 1955 and is now housed in the Shrine of the Book in *Jerusalem.

THANK OFFERING   *Sacrifices made as gestures of gratitude to *God. The laws governing thank offerings are found in *Leviticus Ch. 7.

THEATRE   The *sages disapproved of the theatre although *Purim plays were performed in medieval Europe. From the 16th Century however *Jews took an active part in secular drama. In Eastern Europe and the United States, Yiddish theatre became an important part of Jewish life and in Hollywood, Jews have been very prominent in the film industry.

THEFT   The appropriation of another person's property. Jewish law distinguishes between theft and robbery. Theft is done secretly and robbery openly. According to *Exodus Ch. 22, the thief must pay back double the value of the stolen property.

THERAPEUTAE   (Greek 'Healers') Sect of the 1st Centuries BCE/AC. *Philo describes the therapeutae as leading ascetic lives and living near Alexandria in Egypt. Their practices may have been similar to those of the *Essenes and it is probable that the monks of the Early Christian Church copied much of their lifestyle.

THIRTEEN ATTRIBUTES OF MERCY   The attributes of *God

recorded in *Exodus* 34. The thirteen attributes include being the Lord, God, merciful, gracious, long-suffering, full of loving-kindness and truth, faithful, forgiving iniquity, transgressors and sin and willing to clear the guilty. The attributes are used in the *liturgy particularly on *fast days, *Rosh Hashana and *Yom Kippur.

THIRTEEN PRINCIPLES OF THE FAITH The principles of the faith listed by *Maimonides. The thirteen principles include *God's existence, his unity, his incorporeality, his eternity, his hearing of *prayer, his inspiration of the *prophets, that *Moses is the supreme prophet, that the *Pentateuch was given in toto to Moses, that the *Torah is immutable, that God is omniscient, that the good will be rewarded and the bad punished, that the *Messiah will come in the future and that there will be a *resurrection of the *dead.

THIRTY-TWO PATHS OF WISDOM Mystical concept based on the twenty-two letters of the Hebrew alphabet and the sefirot from which the world was *created. The idea of the thirty-two paths of wisdom is found in the *Sefer Yetzirah. Later *kabbalists identified the paths as the means by which the highest *sefirah eminates through to the lower sefirot.

THREE WEEKS The period between the *fasts of *Tammuz 17 and *Av 9. The three weeks are a solemn period in which there is no music or entertainment. Some *Orthodox Jews also abstain from meat and *wine except on the *Sabbaths.

THRONE OF GOD The supposed location of *God. God is described as sitting on a throne by *Isaiah (Ch. 6), *Ezekiel (Ch. 1) and *Daniel (Ch. 7). The *Ark of the Covenant is also understood as God's throne. The *kabbalists frequently identified his throne with the chariot, the *merkavah. Most philosophers however interpret such language as *allegorical and maintain that God's throne signifies his power and grandeur.

TIK The case in which the *Scroll of the law is kept (*Sephardic).

TIKKUN Passages instituted by the *kabbalists for reading on special occasions.

TIKKUN   (Hebrew. 'Repair') Kabbalistic term for cosmic repair. The concept of tikkun is much used in the writings of Isaac *Luria.

TIKKUN SOFERIM   (Hebrew. 'Repair of the Scribes') Changes in the *Biblical text. According to the *sages, the men of the *Great Synagogue made eighteen tikkunim to the text.

TISH   (Yiddish. 'Table') A meal taken by a *zaddik with his followers. Three tishim are held every *Sabbath and *festival when the zaddik speaks, sings hymns and distributes *shirayim.

TISHA B'AV   *Fast Day commemorating the destruction of the *Temple in *Jerusalem in 586 BCE and 70 CE. The *Three Weeks lead up to Tisha b'Av and in the *synagogue the *Book of *Lamentations* is read and *kinot are recited. (See also *FASTING).

TITHES   Money or goods levied for the maintenance of religious institutions. The following types of tithe are mentioned in the *Bible: the 'first tithe' given to the *Levites after the *heave offering, the 'second tithe' which was one tenth of the first tithe, the 'poor tithe' which was given to the poor in the third and sixth year and the 'animal tithe' which was levied three times a year. The laws of tithe are compiled in the tractate 'Ma'aserot' in the *Mishnah* and the tractate 'Terumot' deals with the laws of heave offering.

TOBIT, BOOK OF   Book of the *Apocrypha. The *Book of Tobit* tells the story of the righteous Tobit and dates from the Persian period.

TOHORAH   (Hebrew. 'Purification') The ceremony of washing the *dead before *burial. The dead are laid on a board and are washed with lukewarm water while certain *Biblical verses are recited. Then nine measures of water are poured over the body; it is then dried and wrapped in a *shroud. This practice is still followed by the *Orthodox, but has been abandoned by *Progressive Jews.

TOLEDOT YESHU   (Hebrew. 'The life of Jesus') A Jewish biography of Jesus. The *Toledot Yeshu* dates back to the 10th Century, but was almost certainly copied from more ancient sources. The book maintains that Jesus was the product of a rape. Although he had supernatural powers, many of his miracles are given a natural

explanation and it suggests that Jesus' powers were exorcised by the
*sages.

TORAH (Hebrew. 'Teaching') The teaching of *God to the *Jews.
The term 'Torah' is used in several ways. Firstly it can refer to the
*Pentateuch, the five books of Moses (see *TANAKH). It can mean all
the laws on a particular subject; it can mean the total of all Jewish law,
both *Written and *Oral. Although the *sages taught that *Moses
received the Torah from God on Mount *Sinai (see *TORAH
MISINAI), they also taught that the Torah was pre-existent to the
*Creation of the World. The philosopher *Philo identified it with the
divine logos and Rav Hoshaiah equated it with the *Wisdom dis-
cussed in the Book of *Proverbs. Rabbi *Hillel summarized the entire
Torah by saying 'What is hateful to you, do not do to your fellow'.
According to the Book of *Deuteronomy, Ch. 33, the purpose of
Torah was to make the *Israelites a holy nation and a kingdom of
*priests. One of *Maimonides' *thirteen principles was that the Torah
was given in its entirety to *Moses and it can never be changed. The
*Orthodox still insist on the absolute authority of both the Written and
Oral Law; the *Karaites however rejected the validity of the Oral Law
and *Progressive Jews, who accept the findings of *biblical criticism,
(see *DOCUMENTARY HYPOTHESIS) tend to distinguish between
the moral and the ritual law. The *synagogue *liturgy emphasizes the
joy and sweetness in keeping the Torah.

TORAH MI SINAI The doctrine that the *Written and *Oral Law
were given in their entirety by *God to *Moses. The doctrine of Torah
mi Sinai remains the touchstone of *Orthodoxy. (See also *DOCU-
MENTARY HYPOTHESIS and *TORAH).

TORAH ORNAMENTS The covering and decoration of the *Torah
*Scroll. Normally the scroll is rolled on two staves known as *azei
hayyim ('trees of life') and is fastened with a *mappah ('binder') and a
*me'il ('mantle') is placed over the whole. Over the me'il is placed a
*keter or *atarah ('silver crown') to indicate the role of the Torah in the
life of the Jewish community. In Spain, the ends of the staves are often
decorated with *tappuhim ('apples') or *rimmonim ('pomegranates').
Among the *Sephardim the scroll is kept in a *tik ('metal or wooden
case'). Among the *Ashkenazim a *tas ('silver plaque') is placed on the
scroll and a *yad ('pointer') used to aid the reading of the law.

TORAH, READING OF The public reading of the *Torah *Scroll. Although the *Talmud* refers to a cycle of readings which enabled the entire *Pentateuch to be read over the course of three years, by the 12th Century, it became usual to read the whole in an annual cycle. It is divided into fifty-four *sedarot and the first is read on the *Sabbath after *Sukkot and the last on *Simhat Torah. It can only be read if a *minyan is present. Normally before and after the reading, the scroll is taken in procession around the *synagogue and at some point the Torah is raised (*hagbahah) to show the congregation. Each reader recites a *benediction before and after his reading and normally at least seven men are called up (*aliyyot) to read. After the reading, the Scroll is dressed again in its *Torah ornaments and returned to the *Ark. The second reading in the service, the *Haftarah, from the *prophets, is chosen because it has some connection with the Torah reading.

TORAH, STUDY OF The study of *Torah is an important religious duty for every *Jewish man. The *rabbis stressed that when a group met together for study, the *Shekinah was in the midst of them. (See also *EDUCATION*).

TORTOSA, DISPUTATION OF A debate between Christians and *Jews held in 1413 in Tortosa. It was presided over by the Pope who always allowed the Christian speakers to conclude the discussions. In consequence of the disputation, many Jews were baptized into Christianity.

TOSAFOT (Hebrew. 'Additions') Anthologies of comments on the *Talmud*. The Tosafot are records of discussions in the *yeshivot of France and Germany in the 12th Century. Its aim was to develop the commentary of *Rashi and leading practitioners included his son-in-law and grandsons. Today the *Talmud* is printed to include *Mishnah*, *gemara, Rashi's commentary (known as *Perush) and the Tosafot (often called *GaPaT). Later the study of Tosafot was associated with *Pilpul particularly in Poland and Germany.

TOSEFTA Works by the *tannaim. The *Tosefta* dates from the 2nd Century CE and has the same six orders as the *Mishnah*. Some passages, the *Beraitot, parallel passages found in the *Mishnah*, but the *Tosefta* also includes new material. The origin of the work is unknown, but it was presumably intended as a supplement to the *Mishnah*.

TRADITION The doctrines and practices of *Judaism. In the *Talmud* the term for tradition is *masoret which refers to history, *custom, law and folk belief. (See also *AGGADA, *HALAKHAH, *KABBALAH, *MASORET, *MINHAG, *ORAL LAW, *WRITTEN LAW.)

TRAYF (Yiddish 'Non-Kosher') Non *Kosher food.

TRESPASS OFFERING *Sacrifice made to compensate for certain offences. A trespass offering had to be made for perjury, *sacrilege and violation of a *betrothed woman. It was also offered by a *Nazarite and by a cleansed *leper. Normally it consisted of a two-year old ram. After the destruction of the *Temple in 70 CE, no more sacrifices of any kind were offered. (See also *SACRIFICE).

TRIBES, THE TWELVE See *TWELVE TRIBES.

TRIBUNAL See *BET DIN.

TRITO-ISAIAH See *ISAIAH.

TWELVE MINOR PROPHETS See *MINOR PROPHETS.

TWELVE TRIBES OF ISRAEL The traditional division of the *Israelites. According to the *Pentateuch, each tribe was descended from one of the sons of *Jacob, except for *Ephraim and Manasseh who were the two sons of Joseph. Each tribe except *Levi had a particular territory – Reuben, Issachar, Zebulun, Simeon, Dan, Naphtali, Gad, Asher, Ephraim and Manasseh (see *TEN LOST TRIBES) were in the *Northern Kingdom. Judah and Benjamin were in the *Southern Kingdom. Most modern scholars do not accept the traditional explanation for the origin of the tribes, but the tribal structure was important to the Israelites' understanding of themselves as a nation.

TSADDIK See *ZADDIK*.

TU B'AV (Av 15) *Festival marking the beginning of the *wine *harvest. At the time of the Second *Temple, Tu B'Av was celebrated on Av 15. There was dancing in the vineyards and offerings of wood were brought to the Temple.

TU BI-SHEVAT (Shevat 15) *Festival celebrating the *New Year for trees. Tu Bi-Shevat is celebrated on Shevat 15 and, among the *Ashkenazim, it was usual to eat fifteen types of fruit. Since the State of *Israel was established in 1948, the festival has become an occasion of rejoicing in the revival of the land and its fertility.

TZEDAKAH See *ZEDAKAH.

TZEDAKAH BOX See *ZEDAKAH BOX.

TZIMTZUM See *ZIMZUM.

TZITTZIT See *ZITZIT.

UGARIT Ancient Middle Eastern city. Archaeological excavations have yielded new light on the *Canaanite civilization of the late Bronze Age.

ULPAN (Hebrew. 'Study') Institute for advanced study. Also intensive *Hebrew courses for new *Israeli immigrants.

U-NETANNEH TOKEF (Hebrew. 'Let us declare the importance') *Piyyut recited on *Rosh Ha-Shanah and *Yom Kippur. The U-Netanneh Tokef was composed in the 11th Century and declares that *prayer and *charity avert *judgment.

UNION OF AMERICAN HEBREW CONGREGATIONS (U.A.H.C.) Association of American *Reform Congregations founded in 1873.

UNION OF ORTHODOX JEWISH CONGREGATIONS OF AMERICA (U.O.J.C.A.) Association of American *Orthodox Congregations founded in 1898.

UNION OF SEPHARDIC CONGREGATIONS Association of American *Sephardic Congregations founded in 1929.

UNITED SYNAGOGUE   (US) An Association of British *Ortho-dox *Ashkenazic congregations founded by Act of Parliament in 1870.

UNITED SYNAGOGUE OF AMERICA   Association of American *Conservative Congregations founded in 1913.

UNIVERSALISM   The claim that a religion is true for all human beings. Judaism is a universalist religion in that *God is believed to be the ruler for all and that everyone can have a part in the *World to Come (see *NOACHIDE LAWS). However it is particularist in that it teaches that the Jews are the *Chosen People and have greater responsibilities than the other nations of the world.

UNLEAVENED BREAD   See *MAZZAH.

UR   Ancient Middle Eastern city. According to the book of *Genesis, Ur was the birthplace of the *patriarch *Abraham.

URIEL   *Angel mentioned in I *Enoch and IV *Ezra. In the *midrash, Uriel is said to be one of the four guardians of *God's throne.

URIM AND THUMMIM   An ancient device for telling oracles. The Urim and Thummim were kept on the *breastplate of the *High Priest and it seems to have given a yes-or-no answer. The practice seems to have disappeared after the Babylonian *exile.

USHA, SYNOD OF   Convention of *sages in the 2nd Century CE. The Synod met after the *Bar Kokhba revolt to reestablish the *Sanhedrin. Simeon b. Gamaliel was appointed *nasi, Nathan ha-Bavli *av bet-din and Meir was *hakham. (See also *SANHEDRIN, *TANNAIM).

USHPUZIN   (Hebrew. 'Visitors') The seven guests who, in *kabbalistic teaching, visit the *sukkah of every pious *Jew. The idea of the guests is found in the *Zohar. They are *Abraham, *Isaac, *Jacob, *Joseph, *Aaron, *Moses and *David. These seven are sup-posed to visit the sukkah and share a meal during the *festival of *Sukkot.

USURY Lending money on interest. The *Book of *Deuteronomy* forbids usury between *Jews, but allows it in transactions with *gentiles. In the Middle Ages, money lending became a common source of livelihood among Jews because Christians could not lend money on interest and Jews were excluded from the craft and trade guilds. This was the origin of the stereotype of the Jew as an avaricious financier eg. Shakespeare's Shylock.

U-VA LE ZION (Hebrew. 'And a *redeemer shall come to *Zion') Opening words of a *prayer used in the *synagogue services. It is generally said at the conclusion of the service.

VA-ANI TEFILLATI (Hebrew 'And as for me may my *prayer') Opening words of a prayer recited at the beginning of the *Sabbath afternoon service.

VAKHNAKHT (Yiddish. 'Watchnight') Celebration on the night before a *circumcision.

VA-YEKHULLU (Hebrew 'And they were completed') Opening words of the final paragraph of the *Genesis* account of the *creation of the world. This paragraph (*Genesis* 2:1–3) is recited after the *Amidah in the Friday evening service (see *SHABBAT*) and when making *kiddush at home.

VEGETARIANISM Rejection of meat eating. According to the *sages, *Adam was a vegetarian and permission was only given to eat meat in the time of *Noah. They taught that humanity would return to vegetarianism in the days of the *messiah. (See also *SHEHITA*).

VE-HU RAHUM (Hebrew. 'And he being merciful') Opening words of Psalm 78:38. This verse is used as the introduction to the weekday evening service in the *synagogue.

VENGEANCE In general vengeance is regarded as the prerogative of God and forbearance is to be commended in human beings.

VE-SHAMERU (Hebrew. 'And they shall keep') Opening words of *Exodus* 31:16–17. The Ve-Shameru *prayer is said before the *Amidah at the Friday evening service, during the *Amidah on

Saturday morning and also at the *kiddush after the *synagogue service.

VESSELS, SACRED   Furnishings of the *tabernacle and *Temple. The sacred vessels included the *Ark, the *menorah, the veil, *altar, *laver and shovels. Today the term is often used for ritual objects in a *synagogue.

VIDDUI   See *CONFESSION.

VILNA   Capital of Lithuania. In the 18th Century, Vilna or Vilnius became a centre of *rabbinic study and also the *Haskalah movement. All signs of Jewish activity were destroyed in the *Holocaust.

VILNA GAON   See *ELIJAH BEN SOLOMON ZALMAN.

VIMPEL   (Yiddish. 'Wimpel') Fabric strip used to bind the *Torah scroll. Frequently the vimpel is made from swaddling clothes which are subsequently remade, embroidered and given to the *synagogue. (See *TORAH ORNAMENTS).

VISITING THE SICK   Visiting the sick is regarded as an important duty. (See also *BIKUR HOLIM).

VOCALIZATION   The indication of vowel sounds by means of marks placed above or below Hebrew consonants. Originally Hebrew script only consisted of consonants, but by the end of the *talmudic period, a distinctive system of pointing vowels was established. (See also *MASORAH).

VOWS   A promise to *God. Reservation was expressed in the *biblical books about making vows because there was no way to annul a rash or foolish promise. In the *talmudic period, the *rabbis devised an elaborate system for the annulment of vows which is recorded in the tractate 'Nedarim'. (See also *KOL NIDREI, *NAZARITE, *OATHS).

VOWELS   See *VOCALIZATION.

WAGES   Payment for work rendered. Both *Biblical and *talmudic teachings stress the importance of paying wages promptly.

WAILING WALL   Western wall of the *Jerusalem *Temple. The wailing wall was all that remained after the destruction of the *Temple in 70 CE. It is the most sacred place in the Jewish world and a place of *pilgrimage.

WANDERING JEW   A legendary figure. The wandering Jew, Ahasuerus, taunted Jesus on his way to the cross and was condemned to wander the earth forever. The legend was current in Christian medieval circles.

WAR   The settlement of national or international disputes by armed force. The *Israelites participated in wars against their neighbours from the time of settlement in the land of *Canaan. Jews have also fought for their adopted nations in the *diaspora and, since 1948, in the Israeli army to defend the State of *Israel.

WAR SCROLL   One of the scrolls discovered at *Qumran (see *DEAD SEA SCROLLS). The War Scroll describes the final *apocalyptic war between the sons of darkness and the *sons of light.

WATCHER   A heavenly being in the Book of *Daniel. A watcher gives a strange dream to King Nebuchadnezzar. Watchers also appear in later *mystical works.

WATER   See *ABLUTION.

WEDDING   See *MARRIAGE.

WEEKS, FEAST OF   See *SHAVUOT.

WESTERN WALL   See *WAILING WALL.

WHOLE OFFERING   A *sacrifice that was wholly consumed by fire. Normally the whole offering was an offering of grain.

WICKED PRIEST   The opponent of the *Teacher of Righteousness in the *Dead Sea Scrolls.

WIDOW   A woman whose husband has died. According to Jewish

law, she is entitled to the payment of a sum stipulated in her
*ketubbah or she must be maintained by her husband's family.

WIG See *SHEITEL*.

WILLOW See *FOUR SPECIES*, *LULAV*.

WINE Wine plays an important part in Jewish ritual. In the days of
the *Temple, it was poured over the *altar with the *sacrifices. Today
it is used in the *Kiddush and *Havdalah *liturgy and during the
*Passover seder and *circumcision ceremony. At *Purim, even over-
indulgence is tolerated.

WISDOM A quality much advocated in the *Bible. Wisdom was
understood as a gift from *God although it could be acquired by study
and education. According to the *Book of *Proverbs*, wisdom worked
with God in the activity of *Creation and the *philosopher *Philo
equated it with the divine *logos.

WISDOM LITERATURE Books written in the cultural tradition
of *wisdom. (See *ECCLESIASTES*, *ECCLESIASTICUS*, *JOB*,
PROVERBS, *WISDOM OF SOLOMON*).

WISDOM OF SOLOMON Book of the *Apocrypha. The *Wisdom
of Solomon* is ascribed to King *Solomon, but in fact dates from the
hellenistic period. Its theme is the importance of *Wisdom.

WISSENSCHAFT DES JUDENTUMS (Ger. 'Science of Judaism').
A 19th century methodology for the study of Jewish History.

WITNESS A person who gives evidence before a court. In general
the evidence of two witnesses is necessary to prove a criminal charge
against the accused. (See also *BET DIN*).

WOMEN According to the *Bible, woman was created as
'helpmeet' to man, to bear children and to be a good wife and mother.
Although women suffer the same penalties in law as men, they have
no right to initiate a *divorce and are excused all positive time-bound
commandments. Although nowadays *Orthodox Judaism teaches that
women are 'equal, but different', Orthodox men still thank *God in

the *liturgy that they were not born as women. Nonetheless many of the *rabbis in the past seem to have loved and respected their wives. *Progressive Judaism teaches the absolute equality of women and has female as well as male *rabbis and *cantors. This idea is anathema to the Orthodox. (See also *NIDDAH).

WORLDS, THE FOUR   *Kabbalistic doctrine. The Kabbalists identified four worlds of *creation each corresponding with one of the letters of the *Tetragrammaton. The worlds are the source of all being, creation, formation and the *angelic realm.

WORLD TO COME   The new world established in the days of the *Messiah. (See also *HEAVEN).

WORSHIP   See   *BENEDICTION,   *FASTING,   *FESTIVAL, *KIDDUSH, *KIDDUSH HA-SHEM, *LITURGY, *PRAYERBOOK, *SABBATH,   *SACRIFICE,   *SYNAGOGUE,   *TABERNACLE, *TEFILLAH, *TEMPLE.

WRITINGS   See *HAGIOGRAPHA.

WRITTEN LAW   The law and commandments written down in the *Pentateuch. Written law is frequently distinguished from the *Oral law.

YAALEH   (Hebrew. 'May it arise') Hymns sung in the *synagogue at the evening service on *Yom Kippur. It is based on the *Yaaleh ve-yavo *prayer.

YAALEH VE-YAVO   (Hebrew. 'May it arise and come') Prayer said with the *Amidah and *grace at meals on the *New Year and at *festivals.

YAD   (Hebrew. 'Hand') The pointer used in reading the *Torah *scroll. (See *TORAH ORNAMENTS).

YAH   See *NAMES OF GOD.

YAHAD   (Hebrew. 'Unity') Term used by *Qumran set. Yahad means unifying spirit and the adherents of the sect were described as men of the yahad.

YAH RIBBON OLAM (Aramaic. 'God, master of the universe') Well-known Aramaic hymn. The Yah Ribbon Olam is often sung at table during the *Sabbath meal.

YAHRZEIT Anniversary of the death of parent, spouse, child or sibling. The custom of yahrzeit is widely observed although the *Sephardim call it nahalah. *Kaddish is said and a twenty-four hour memorial *candle ignited. Yahrzeit is also observed for eminent individuals.

YAHWEH God's sacred name which is never articulated. (See *NAMES OF GOD, *TETRAGRAMMATON).

YAHWIST Editor of one of the sources of the *Pentateuch. According to the *documentary hypothesis, the Pentateuch was compiled from four different sources. The Yahwist source, J, is distinctive because *God is referred to as the *Tetragrammaton. The source is thought to date from the 9th Century BCE.

YALKUT (Hebrew. 'Compilation') Title of several anthologies of *midrash. These include the Yalkut Reuveni composed by Reuben Kahana in the 17th Century to accompany the weekly *Torah reading, the Yalkut Shimoni of the 13th Century compiled by Simeon Kayyara covering all the *biblical books and the 14th Century Yalkut ha-Makhiori.

YAMAIM NORAIM (Hebrew. 'Days of Awe') *Rosh Hashanah, *Yom Kippur and the *ten days of repentance between them. The *rabbis taught that humanity stands before *God for judgment on Rosh Hashanah and judgment is finally pronounced on Yom Kippur.

YARMULKE Skull cap worn by *Orthodox men. The practice of wearing a yarmulke only goes back to c.12th Century. It is worn at all times by the *Orthodox while the less observant only cover their heads for *prayer.

YEAR, JEWISH See *CALENDAR.

YEAR OF RELEASE See *SABBATICAL YEAR.

YEKUM PURKAN   (Aramaic. 'May Redemption Come') *Aramaic *prayers recited after the reading of the *Torah *Scroll. They date from the *gaonic period.

YELAMMEDENU   (Aramaic. 'Let him pronounce') An alternative title for the *Tanhuma.

YESHIVAH   *Talmudic academy. The term yeshivah was used for the *amoraic academies in Babylon and *Israel, for the academies in *Sura and *Pumbedita and also for local academies. The institution spread to Spain, North Africa, Italy, France, Germany, Bohemia, Austria, Poland, Russia, Lithuania, the British Commonwealth and the United States. Originally they were organised by well-known scholars and were supported by the community. The curriculum was based on talmudic study, but also, as time went on, included *minhagim, *posekim, *responsa and *musar. A yeshivah education became a necessary preparation for *semikhah and the title *'rabbi' was awarded on graduation from the 14th Century. The *yeshivot of Eastern Europe were destroyed in the *holocaust, but famous yeshivot still flourish in Israel, the United States and the British Commonwealth. (See also *RABBINICAL SEMINARIES).

YETZER HA-RA   (Hebrew. 'The evil inclination') The tendency of human beings to choose evil rather than good. (See also *YETZER HA-TOV).

YETZER HA-TOV   (Hebrew. 'The good inclination') The promptings to do good rather than evil. The *rabbis taught that every human being had both a *yetzer ha-ra and a yetzer ha-tov which were in constant conflict.

YETZIRAH, SEFER   See *SEFER YETZIRAH.

YHWH   See *TETRAGRAMMATON.

YIDDISH   Language of the *Ashkenazic community. Yiddish is written in Hebrew letters. Although it died out in Western Europe, it continued to be used in Russia, Lithuania, Hungary, Poland and the Ukraine. Before the *holocaust, there were thought to be approximately eleven million native Yiddish speakers. Immigrants to the

United States often spoke Yiddish, but were anxious that their children should be assimilated into the English-speaking culture so Yiddish was often forgotten.

YIDDISHKEIT (Yiddish. 'Yiddish culture') Yiddish culture or the Yiddish milieu.

YIGDAL (Hebrew. 'May he be magnified') Hymn based on *Maimonides' *thirteen principles of the Jewish faith. It is printed in the *Siddur at the beginning of the *morning daily service. The *Sephardim recite it at the end of their *Sabbath and *festival *evening services.

YIHUS (Yiddish. 'Descent') Distinguished ancestral descent.

YISHTABBAH (Hebrew. 'Praised') A *benediction. The Yishtabbah consists of thirteen praises which are said to correspond with the *thirteen attributes of mercy. It ends one section of the daily *morning service.

YIKZOR (Hebrew. 'He will remember') A memorial *prayer. The Yikzor is said for members of one's family on the final day of *Pesah, on the second day of *Shavuot, on *Shemini Atzeret and on *Yom Kippur.

YOM HAATZMAUT (Hebrew. 'Independence Day') *Israel Independence Day. Yom Haatzmaut celebrates the State of Israel's declaration of independence. It takes place on Iyyar 5.

YOM KIPPUR (Hebrew. 'Day of Atonement') Most holy day of the Jewish year. Yom Kippur takes place on Tishri 10 after the ten days of *penitence. It is a *fast day. No work may be undertaken and no food or drink may be touched from sunset of *Kol Nidrei until twenty-five hours later. Services take place throughout the day in the *synagogue. In the days of the *Temple, Yom Kippur was the one day of the year when the *High Priest would enter the *Holy of Holies to *pray on behalf of the people. The *rabbis taught that the book of Judgment (see *BOOK OF LIFE) was finally closed on Yom Kippur so the day is spent praying for *forgiveness.

YOM KIPPUR KATAN (Hebrew. 'Minor Day of Atonement') *Fast observed the day before the *new moon. *Psalms and *selihot are added to the usual daily *afternoon service.

YOM TOV (Hebrew. 'A good day') A *festival.

YOTZER (Hebrew. 'He creates') *Benedictions said either side of the *Shema. The term Yotzer can refer to the whole daily *morning service, to the immediate *hymn sung before the Shema or to all the special hymns sung round the Shema on *Sabbaths and *festivals.

YOTZEROT (Hebrew. *Yotzers) All the *hymns chanted in the daily *morning service.

YONTIF (Yiddish. 'Good day') A *festival.

YOREH DEAH The laws of *kashrut as laid down in Jacob ben Asher's *Code, the *Arbaah Turim.

ZADDIK (Hebrew. 'Righteous Man') A *righteous man. The zaddik was much praised in *Biblical and *rabbinic literature and, according to legend, as long as there are fifty righteous men in the world, *God will not destroy it. The *Hasidim give the title of Zaddik to their leaders. The Hasidic Zaddik is thought to have attained *mystical union with God. He is greatly revered as the ladder between *Heaven and earth and members of his sect make *pilgrimage to visit his court, listen to his words and share in his meals.

ZADOK (11th Century BCE) *Biblical *Priest at the time of King *David. Zadok was descended from *Aaron. He *anointed *Solomon to succeed David and Solomon appointed his son as the next *High Priest. From then, until the time of the *Maccabees the High Priesthood remained in Zadok's family.

ZADOKITE FRAGMENTS Two manuscripts found in the Cairo *Genizah. Another copy was found at *Qumran. The Zadokite fragments include a history of the world and the rules of an ascetic Jewish sect.

ZADOKITES The self-designation of the members of the *Qumran sect. The *High Priesthood was no longer held by members of the Zadokite family when the *Dead Sea Scrolls were written. The members of the Qumran sect believed themselves to be the remaining faithful of *Israel and in the *Manual of Discipline, it is recorded how new initiates placed themselves 'under the authority of the sons of *Zadok'.

ZAKKAI, JOHANAN BEN   See *JOHANAN BEN ZAKKAI.

ZAYDE   (Yiddish. 'Grandfather') Old man, grandfather.

ZEALOTS   Jewish rebels in the War against Rome 66–73 CE. The activities of the Zealots in the siege of *Jerusalem and at *Masada are described by *Josephus in The Jewish War.

ZECHARIAH, BOOK OF   One of the twelve *minor *prophets. The prophecies are dated between 520 and 518 BCE and are concerned with the restoration of *Jerusalem after the Babylonian *exile. It is possible that Chs 9–14 were composed by a different author from that of Chs 1–8. According to the *aggadah, Zechariah was one of three prophets who returned with the exiles to the *promised land and, after their death, prophecy departed from *Israel.

ZEDAKAH   (Hebrew. 'Charity') Charity, philanthropy. The *rabbis greatly encouraged zedakah and particularly praised the kind of charity which was done secretly.

ZEDAKAH BOX   (Hebrew. 'Charity Box') Charity Box. A charity box is part of the furniture of every Jewish home to encourage philanthropy within the family.

ZEKHUT AVOT   (Hebrew. 'Merits of the Fathers') See *MERITS OF THE FATHERS.

ZEKHOR BERIT   (Hebrew. 'Remember the Covenant') *Penitential hymn recited on the eve of *Rosh Hashanah and at the concluding service of *Yom Kippur.

ZELOPHEHAD'S DAUGHTERS   Biblical characters appearing in *Numbers 26. Because of the legal precedent of their case, *women

197

could inherit their father's property provided they were married to a man of the same *tribe.

ZEMIROT (Hebrew. 'Songs') *Psalms and *hymns. The *Sephardim call the psalms recited before the main part of the *Morning Service zemirot, while the *Ashkenazim use the term for the hymns sung during and after the *Sabbath meal.

ZEPHANIAH One of the *Biblical *minor *prophets. The *Book of Zephaniah* was probably composed in the 7th Century BCE and is a vivid prediction of the *Day of Judgment.

ZERA'IM (Hebrew. 'Seeds') One of the six orders of the *Mishnah*. Zera'im primarily deals with the agricultural laws of the land of *Israel.

ZERUBBABEL (6th/5th Century BCE) Leader of the returned *exiles from Babylon. Zerubbabel's exploits are described in the books of *Ezra*, *Nehemiah*, *Haggai* and *Zechariah*. The *rabbis taught that with the *Prophet *Elijah, he would teach the *Torah in the *World to Come.

ZIKHRONO LI-VERAKHAH (Hebrew. 'May his memory be for a blessing') Expression used when mentioning someone who has died.

ZIKHRONOT (Hebrew. 'Remembrances') A *benediction in the *Musaf service of *Rosh Hashanah. The Zikhronot remembers *Noah, slavery in Egypt, the *covenant and the *Akeda. The custom of reciting it is mentioned in the *Mishnah*.

ZIMZUM (Hebrew. 'Contraction') Kabbalistic theory of *Creation. The kabbalists taught that there had to be zimzum, before *God could make space for the creation.

ZION A hill in the city of *Jerusalem. Zion can also refer to the whole city. According to the *prophets, the whole world would turn to Zion to learn about *God at the end of time.

ZIONISM Movement dedicated to restoring the land of *Israel to the Jewish people. Since the destruction of the *Jerusalem *Temple in 70CE, the desire to return has been preserved in folklore and the *liturgy. The modern Zionist movement was launched in 1897 at the first Zionist Congress under the leadership of Theodor *Herzl with the stated aim of 'establishing a home for the Jewish people in Palestine. Although Zionism was seen as a solution to the problem of *Anti-Semitism, many *Orthodox Jews felt *Zion would only be restored in the *messianic era and many *Progressive Jews believed Zionist aspirations would call into question their future in the *diaspora. British support to the Zionist hope was nominally given in the *Balfour Declaration, but it was the *holocaust which finally persuaded the great powers that a Jewish homeland was necessary. After the foundation of the State of Israel, Zionist organisations have concentrated on raising money for Israeli projects and encouraging *Jews of the diaspora to make *aliyah.

ZITZIT (Hebrew. 'Fringes') Fringes attached to the four corners of a garment to fulfil the *Biblical injunction of *Numbers 15:37–41 and *Deuteronomy 22:12. *Women are not obliged to wear fringes because it is a positive time-bound commandment. The *sages taught that the commandment reminded every male *Jew of his identity and duties. (See also *TALLIT, *TALLIT KATAN).

ZOGERIN (Yiddish. 'Sayer') A woman who recites the *prayers in the vernacular for the benefit of *women in the *synagogue who cannot read *Hebrew.

ZOHAR (Hebrew. 'Splendour') A *Kabbalistic work. The Zohar is a collection of several works supposedly dating back to the 2nd Century. It contains a mystical commentary on the *Pentateuch and on much of the *Hagiographa. It was probably composed by Moses b. Shem Tov in the 13th Century and was enormously influential in kabbalistic circles. Many commentaries have been written on it.

ZUGOT (Hebrew. 'Pairs') Pairs of *sages through whom the *Oral Law developed. Traditionally the zugot form the link between the last of the *prophets and the first of the *tannaim. The earliest pair was Yose b. Joezer and Yose b. Johanan and the final pair was *Hillel and *Shammai.